# MANAGEMENT BY
## OBJECTIVES
## AND RESULTS
# IN THE PUBLIC SECTOR

# MANAGEMENT BY OBJECTIVES AND RESULTS IN THE PUBLIC SECTOR

**GEORGE L. MORRISEY**

President, MOR Associates
*Buena Park, California*

**ADDISON-WESLEY PUBLISHING COMPANY**
Reading, Massachusetts • Menlo Park, California
London • Amsterdam • Don Mills, Ontario • Sydney

# FOREWORD

When the talk in MBO circles comes to finding new frontiers, it is the public sector which most often comes to the fore. George Morrisey is especially well qualified to write about that. Not only does he know MOR, which is his distinctive brand of Management By Objectives, but he also knows the federal government and other parts of the public sector at the grass roots level. Many articles I read about MBO in the public sector are written by jargon-laden staff people who work at bureau or agency head levels, whipping out lofty studies, often cluttered with mathematical nonsense. Morrisey knows how things work where the middle managers and supervisors operate. His materials on life in the bureaucracy are shockingly lifelike. Finding the ownership of the turf, dealing with elected officials who often have hidden agenda other than results and effectiveness and also with the bureaucracy, where it is nearly impossible to fire somebody, are not treated as reasons MOR won't work, but as realities of administration which any management system must cope with.

This book should be read, not just by administrators, but also by professors of public administration, potential public servants, every legislator, and just plain interested citizens who want to learn how their government actually works, and how it could be improved without miracles.

George S. Odiorne

# PREFACE

## Why Was this Book Written?

The original version of this book, *Management by Objectives and Results* (Addison-Wesley, 1970), has been adopted by many governmental training organizations as the official text for their MBO training programs, in spite of its industrial orientation. Feedback I have received from those organizations adopting it is that its operational "how-to" approach made it relatively easy for most managers to understand and apply the process. However, there was still the inevitable resistance from some who said, "That may be fine for a profit-making organization, but it really doesn't apply to us." There are some significant differences in making the MOR (MBO) process work in public-sector organizations, although in most cases these differences are more in degree than in kind. Therefore, at the urging of many managers and trainers in government who found the first book useful, I have responded with a "how-to" book that addresses these differences in a positive way and that provides "real world" illustrations drawn from public-sector applications. Furthermore, to add credibility to the process, I invited representatives from four different levels of government, with whom I have worked, to share with you candidly their experiences in implementing MOR, including problems as well as successes.

A second reason for writing this book is that it has been six years since the original version was completed. I have learned quite a bit more about making the process work during that period, both from my own experience as a manager (including two years with the federal government) and from my subsequent role as a consultant. Through data gathered from the many seminars I have conducted during that time, the wide diversity of organizations — public and private — with which I have worked, and professional colleagues with whom I have been associated, as well as personal application, I have modified the process to the point that it is now both simpler and more comprehensive than the earlier one. It is still conceptually consistent with the original, so that those who are familiar with that one should not have difficulty in making the transition. In addition, I have incorporated into this version several new optional working tools (Decision Matrix, Alternative Evaluation Chart, Action Plan Format, for example) that have been developed and validated since then.

## Who Is Responsible for Implementing MOR?

All members of management and, to a certain degree, all employees have a responsibility in the implementation of MOR. In fact, without reasonable cooperation at all levels, the likelihood of substantial success is quite limited. For our purposes, we will concentrate on this process as it applies to members of management (although many individual employees will be able to apply the same principles and methods to their own jobs). For identification, we will divide members of management into three categories.

1.   *Top management* usually includes the executive officers, the heads of major functional units who report to the senior executive, and in some cases an elected or appointed governing body (commission, city council, school board, for example). The role of this group, normally, is to establish policy and determine broad, total-organization objectives, beginning with a clear determination of the organization's roles and missions — its reasons for existence. Top management will also specify, where appropriate, objectives related to such things as major

program thrusts, major areas or clientele to be served, key economic issues, research and development, etc. This group is concerned primarily with the large-scale "what-to-do's" and relatively little with the "how-to-do's."

2. *Middle management* generally comprises those managers who have other members of management reporting to them and who are accountable for the efforts of several organizational units. Their starting point is also a clear determination of their own roles and missions, which encompass those of their subordinate managers and directly support those of their superiors. From that base, they determine their own objectives, which will be most concerned with such key results areas as production output, operational innovations, cost effectiveness, managerial effectiveness, etc. This level of management is about equally concerned with the "what-to-do's" and the "how-to-do's."

3. *First-line management* represents supervisors over individual employees who carry out the tasks required to meet the objectives of the organization. As with the managers in the other two categories, their objectives begin with a clear determination of their own roles and missions. However, these roles and missions may have been defined largely by their superiors, in keeping with those of the larger organizational unit represented. Subsequent objectives will, in general, be short-term (semiannual, quarterly) in nature and directed toward such key results areas as unit output, individual productivity, employee development, quality control, etc. First-line managers generally have a heavy concern for the "how-to-do's" and a relatively modest one for the "what-to-do's," many of which are likely to have been identified by their superiors.

## For Whom Is this Book Written?

This book is designed as a guide for individual members of management at all levels, from the top on down. Although it deals with the establishment of total organizational roles, missions, and objectives, it addresses itself primarily to those of individual managers, regardless of level, and the operations for which they are accountable. Most of the illustrations used will apply to middle and first-line management. However, members of top management as well as individual line and staff specialists will be able to apply the same principles and techniques to the development of their own approach to managing their operations.

What if the top-management decision makers have not established clearcut objectives that are consistent with the principles covered in this book, or what if they do not manage in a manner that encourages this form of managerial activity? Is the MOR process impossible to implement without an impetus from that top group? No! Needless to say, the process would be much less complicated and its implementation would be much smoother and faster if there were clear direction from above and consistent understanding at all levels of management. In the "real world," however, such a situation may not exist. This does not relieve the individual manager of the responsibility for managing as effectively as possible.

The truly professional manager, regardless of position in the chain of command, can and in fact must continually work toward improving his or her managerial effectiveness within the environment. This may well include a systematic education of the boss. Actually, realistic and significant inputs from subordinate managers frequently will lead to a clearer definition of objectives and understanding of the management process at higher levels.

## A Word about Sex

Although presumably sex can and, I suspect, frequently is, managed by objectives and results, my reference here is related to *gender*. Recognizing the fact that the word *manager* is neither male nor female in its derivation, I have been converted by my feminist colleagues (notably Mary Fuller, Dru Scott, Doris Seward, and Theo Wells) to a writing style that eliminates male-dominant language. Furthermore, I must confess, once I conditioned my mind to thinking in that vein, it was not nearly as difficult to make the change as I thought it was going to be. A manager, man or woman, should be able to follow the language in this book without having to make a mental translation.

## How Can this Book Be Used?

This book will serve ideally as a *text for an organizational training program* on Management by Objectives and Results. Several effective approaches to conducting such a program are described in the *Instructor's Guide,* which is available separately from the publisher.

It will also function effectively as an *MOR manual,* supplemented by specific organizational illustrations, for someone wishing to institute a uniform organization-wide approach.

It will work hand-in-hand *with the self-teaching audiocassette program* on MOR, which is available separately from the publisher or from MOR Associates (P.O. Box 5879, Buena Park, CA 90622). Together, they provide an effective learning experience for the individual manager, a small informal group (such as a manager and his or her immediate subordinates), or as a part of a formal training program. *The workbook that accompanies this program is also available separately for seminar use.* (As of this writing, tailored versions of the audiocassette program are in preparation for use by municipal governments and by school systems. Contact MOR Associates for further information.)

For use as an *individual study guide* for the working manager or student of management, we make these recommendations:

1. Read the Preface, Chapters 1 and 2, plus Chapter 12 for an overview of the MOR philosophy and process. You also may wish to look at Chapter 11, which deals with special public-sector concerns.

2.   Determine which of the following alternatives best serves your individual needs:

a) Selective learning of specific techniques to supplement your existing knowledge.

b) Concentrating on learning the objective-setting and action-planning steps for use in your individual or unit efforts.

c) Learning and applying the entire process to your job.

3.   If you have selected 2(a) as most appropriate for you, the recommendation is easy. Study and practice those steps which will satisfy this need. A word of caution, however: you should be aware that some of the techniques described may not work as effectively outside the total MOR context.

4.   If 2(b) seems best for you at the moment, Chapters 6 and 7 will be of most value to you. We recommend that you identify one major work effort that would be suitable for initial application of this approach. Then, following the guidelines given, write out the objective(s) and action plan(s) required to accomplish it. Concentrating on only one major effort will give you an opportunity to learn from the experience, after which the application of MOR can be further expanded as desired.

5.   If you are ready to commit yourself to 2(c), you may wish to begin with one or more objectives (as in item 4 above), or you can start right off with defining your roles and missions or key results areas. (The first part of Chapter 10 may prove helpful in making the actual determination of where to start.) The physical act of writing out the various steps described and having them reviewed by others, as appropriate, is critical to the effective learning of the MOR process. In this respect, we strongly recommend that you concentrate initially on developing the skills in a few key areas of work effort, gradually working the approach into the total job.

6.   Use the book as a continual reference, particularly Chapter 12 and the various working tools and checklists, as you continue your application of the MOR process.

7.   Don't get discouraged when you hit the inevitable periods of setback and frustration in application of the MOR approach. Stay with it, and both your satisfaction and effectiveness will increase as you continue to develop your skill.

## Acknowledgments

Thanks go to the many managers, in both the public and private sectors, who have participated in my seminars, as well as those who have given me direct feedback on my writings, for forcing me to refine the MOR process to the point that it is now, more than ever, a truly practical approach that any dedicated manager can use. I am particularly grateful to:

1.   *Donn Coffee,* with whom I worked for 2½ years in conducting the Managing By Objectives seminars for AMR International, for a stimulating growth relationship that not only made a major contribution to the improvement of the MOR process itself, but also helped provide the vehicle for me to establish myself firmly in the world of management consulting;

2.   *George Odiorne,* for his much-appreciated Foreword to this book, but even more for being the individual who, more than any other, is responsible for establishing Management By Objectives as one of the most widely recognized managerial approaches throughout the world;

3.   *Jim Bussard, Dennis Butler, Doug Rabel, Doris Seward,* and the top management of their respective organizations, for sharing their experiences in the "real world" of working with and implementing Management by Objectives and Results;

4.   *Addison-Wesley,* finally and belatedly, for taking a chance nearly ten years ago on an unknown trainer who thought he could be a writer, without whose help I would not be achieving the objectives I have today.

*Buena Park, California*                                            G. L. M.
*January, 1976*

# CONTENTS

1  **Introduction: The MOR Concept as Applied in the Public Sector** ................................................. 1

What MOR is! What it is not! ............................................ 2
Management work versus operating work ......................... 5
What functions and activities are included in management work? .................................................................... 8
Cost-benefit analysis ...................................................... 12
In summary ..................................................................... 15

2  **The MOR Process** ............................................................. 17

The MOR funnel ............................................................. 17
Steps in the MOR process ................................................ 18
In summary ..................................................................... 23

3  **Defining Roles and Missions** .......................................... 25

What are roles and missions? .......................................... 25
Why do we need to define roles and missions? ................. 25
Where does the statement come from? ............................. 26
Where do organizational unit roles-and-missions statements come in? ......................................................... 28
What factors should be included? .................................... 29
How should statements be prepared? .............................. 32
In summary ..................................................................... 33
*Clarifying Corporate Roles and Missions* ......................... 34
*Clarifying Organizational Unit Roles and Missions* .............. 35

*Key Questions for Evaluating a Statement of Roles
and Missions*................................................................... 36
*Sample Statements of Roles and Missions*............................ 36

**4  Determining Key Results Areas** ......................................... 43

What are key results areas? .............................................. 43
The principle of "the critical few" ..................................... 44
Guidelines for determining key results areas ...................... 46
Sample key results areas................................................... 48
Setting priorities on your key results areas ........................ 49
Applying key results areas to a group............................... 51
In summary .................................................................... 52
*Guidelines for Determining Key Results Areas* ..................... 52

**5  Identifying and Specifying Indicators
of Effectiveness** ................................................................ 54

What are indicators? ....................................................... 54
Why use indicators?......................................................... 55
Guidelines for identifying and specifying indicators............. 56
Sample indicators ........................................................... 60
How to identify and specify your indicators ....................... 61
The MOR agreement......................................................... 61
In summary .................................................................... 63
*Guidelines for Identifying and Specifying Indicators* ............ 63

**6  Selecting and Setting Objectives** ....................................... 65

Identifying objectives....................................................... 66
    What is an objective? ................................................ 66
    What should be objectivized?...................................... 67
    Must we objectivize everything? ................................. 67
    How do we determine our objectives — using the
    MOR funnel? ............................................................ 68
    How do we determine our objectives — without
    using the MOR funnel?............................................... 70
    What about "subjectives"?........................................... 75
    How do we set priorities on objectives? ....................... 76
    What do we do with a priority list of objectives?........... 82

Writing objectives.............................................................. 83
    How do we write meaningful objectives? .................... 83
    Guidelines for writing objectives............................... 84
In summary ....................................................................... 96
*Guidelines for Writing Objectives* ...................................... 97
*Key Questions for Evaluating Objectives* ........................... 98
*Sample Objectives* ........................................................... 98

7   **Preparing Action Plans** ...................................................... 105

Programming .................................................................... 106
    Why should we program an objective?....................... 106
    The alternative evaluation chart ............................... 107
    What other approaches to programming can be used? ... 112
    How do we program an objective? ............................ 114
    Programming breakdown........................................... 116
    Action plan format................................................... 118
Scheduling, budgeting, fixing accountability, and
reviewing and reconciling................................................. 122
    What is scheduling?................................................. 122
    What is budgeting? .................................................. 128
    What is fixing accountability? ................................... 134
    What is "reviewing and reconciling"? ......................... 135
In summary ....................................................................... 137
*Guidelines for Programming an Objective* .......................... 138
*Key Questions for Evaluating Action Steps* ......................... 139
*Key Questions for Review and Reconciliation
in Planning* ...................................................................... 140
*Sample Programmed Objectives* ....................................... 140

8   **Establishing Controls**...................................................... 144

What are the economic considerations of control? .............. 145
What should be controlled? ............................................... 146
How do we control?........................................................... 148
    Establishing standards — what is likely to
    go wrong? ............................................................... 149
    Measuring performance — how and when will
    you know?............................................................... 158
    Taking corrective action — what will you do?.............. 165
In summary ....................................................................... 168
*Key Questions for Evaluating Control Measures* ................. 168

**9  Communications — the MOR Catalyst** .............................. 170

Communications benefits and applications ......................... 170
Methods for effective MOR communications ...................... 176
    1. Individual (one to one) .......................................... 176
    2. Intraunit (team applications) ................................... 178
    3. Intergroup (both internal and external to the
       total organization) ................................................. 181
    4. Organization-wide (particularly
       top-management role) ............................................ 182
    5. Support or staff units (special concerns) ................... 184
In summary ................................................................. 186

**10  Implementing MOR in Public-Sector Organizations** ............ 188

From the individual manager's perspective ......................... 189
From the perspective of the total organization ................... 195
    Critical factors .......................................................... 195
    How to get MOR started ............................................ 203
    Program emphasis based on management level ............. 207
In summary ................................................................. 211
*Individual Manager's Worksheet for
Implementing MOR* ...................................................... 211

**11  Special Public-Sector Concerns and
How to Deal with Them** .................................................. 213

Leadership — elected officials, political appointees,
military turnover, etc ...................................................... 215
Relation to legislative bodies ........................................... 216
Jurisdictional problems — whose "turf" is it? ...................... 217
Headquarters versus region/area —
who's running the show? ................................................ 218
Communication within the hierarchy —
what's going on? ........................................................... 219
Relation to PPB and other management systems
— the "paper mill" ........................................................ 220
Relation of special projects to normal work
— what do "they" really want? ......................................... 221
Setting priorities under austerity conditions
— asking for the impossible ............................................. 222

Impact of civil service, automatic progression,
and other personnel systems............................................. 223
In summary .................................................................... 224

12  **Summary: The MOR Process in Brief**................................ 226

In summary .................................................................... 232

**Bibliography** ................................................................ 233

**Appendix: "Experience" Articles**..................................... 242

Management by Objectives and Results in the
Bureau of Indian Affairs   *Douglas E. Rabel* ......................... 244

The Evolution of MBO in a State Governmental Agency
*Dennis E. Butler* .............................................................. 249

MBO in Alberta Highways and Transport
*D. J. Bussard*.................................................................. 261

MOR in Local Government — A Case History
*Doris K. Seward*.............................................................. 270

# 1

# INTRODUCTION: THE MOR CONCEPT AS APPLIED IN THE PUBLIC SECTOR

When Management By Objectives (MBO) came into vogue in the early 1960s (it's been around much longer, but not necessarily under that label), it was seen as applicable primarily in the private sector, the so-called profit-making organizations. Its potential contribution to the improvement of "bottom line" results was obvious. However, many managers discovered that the more they got into it, the wider they found its application. It became increasingly evident that MBO was really a philosophy of management, one that could be applied to virtually anything, including many vital contributions that never show up directly on the "bottom line."

As this approach to management became increasingly popular in the private sector, it was inevitable that it would find its way into various governmental operations as well. This was due to: (1) the alertness of a significant number of forward-thinking managers already in the public sector, who recognized a good thing when they saw it; and (2) an unusually heavy influx of experienced managers from the private sector in the late 1960s and early 1970s who carried with them the managerial tools and techniques that had worked for them previously. These internal factors, coupled with a dramatic increase in external pressure to "show us what we get for our tax dollar," resulted in more and more public-sector organizations adopting MBO as their *modus operandi*.

The original version of this book, *Management by Objectives and Results* (Addison-Wesley, 1970), was written from the private-sector point of view. Since that time, I have personally served as a manager and internal consultant with the federal government and, more recently, as an external consultant and trainer on MOR (MBO) to managers from a wide variety of federal, state, county, and municipal organizations. These experiences have clearly identified the fact that there are some significant differences in application of the process in the public sector (not the least of which is the political scene and the relationship to elected and politically appointed officials). However, my experiences also indicate that most of the differences from the private sector are more in degree than in kind. These differences will be identified, illustrated, and dealt with openly throughout this version, with Chapter 11 devoted to those problems or differences that are most often raised by managers in the public sector.

## What MOR IS! What it is NOT!

*Management by Objectives and Results* (MOR) is a further refinement of the MBO process, incorporating a closed-loop approach to ensure that the *results* achieved do in fact resemble the objectives that were set. I see this as considerably more than a semantic difference, as will become evident.

MOR is a commonsense, systematic approach to getting things done and is based on principles and techniques that many good managers have been practicing for decades. In spite of the new jargon that has come into vogue (this book will be kept as jargon-free as is humanly possible), there is nothing mysterious about MOR. It does not require a manager to stop what he or she has been doing successfully for years and learn a whole new approach. That would be idiotic. MOR does require the manager to focus on *results* rather than on activities, building on the strengths that he or she has developed over the years, with modifications and additions as good judgment dictates.

Management methodology today can be placed on a continuum between two theoretical extremes.

MAR _____ MOR

At one end of the continuum is Management by Activity or Reaction (MAR). In this approach, planning is accomplished immediately prior to or in concert with action, and there are frequent changes in plan due either to lack of time in which to consider alternatives or to lack of a predetermined objective. Thus we have what is sometimes called seat-of-the-pants management. This extreme is illustrated by the manager who comes to work in the morning without any real idea of what will happen that day. The first crisis that comes along — an upper-management demand for a COB (close of business) report on an action item, a group of visiting dignitaries, or a call from an influential member of a key legislative committee — sets the stage for the day. Effectiveness is measured by the flurry of activity that goes on and the effort that is put forth rather than by the results produced.

At the other end of the continuum is Management by Objectives and Results (MOR). Here, management defines in advance the results to be achieved and the action plans required for the achievement of these results. Implicit in this management approach is a plan for overcoming obstacles and for establishing priorities when crises do occur (as they will). A style of management at this extreme does not even require the presence of the manager at any given time.

In practice, neither extreme is likely to exist in its purest form. It is unrealistic to hope that any manager will be so gifted with foresight that there will never be a requirement to manage by reaction in response to unexpected conditions. On the other hand, very few managers will continue to survive in today's competitive world by managing strictly on a day-to-day basis. This is why we began by speaking of a continuum between two extremes. A given manager's location on the continuum will vary substantially from day to day and even from hour to hour. We could probably reach almost unanimous agreement, however, that management is more effective when the preponderance of effort is directed toward the right-hand end of the continuum — toward objectives and results.

The MAR extreme might be equated with "fire fighting," whereas MOR is analagous to "fire prevention." Again, we could probably agree that "fire prevention" represents a far more professional approach to management than "fire fighting" does. Therein, of course, lies a major paradox. Most of our experience in organizations indicates that far more recognition and reward go to those individuals who are able to extinguish those "fires" than to those who prevented them from ever starting in the first place. Consequently, if we hope to engineer any kind of a lasting "shift to the right" in terms of management approaches, there must also be a shift in our approach to recognizing effective performance.

The MOR process is simple — deceptively simple. Most managers and students of management do not have great difficulty in comprehending it intellectually. After all, it is perfectly logical. The difficulty comes in application, since MOR does require systematic planning, an uncomfortable activity for many of us. MOR can be illustrated graphically as a horizontal funnel, as shown in Fig. 1.1. As a process, MOR moves from the general to the specific. Its purpose is to subdivide a large, complex effort, e.g., combatting unemployment among the disadvantaged, until it reaches a manageable unit size, e.g., providing subsidized training in saleable skills in a given community. Conceptually, this is consistent with many of the management systems that have been introduced in various governmental organizations over the past several years, such as PPBS (Planning-Programming-Budgeting System), WBS (Work Breakdown Structure), PERT (Program Evaluation Review Technique), WPM (Work Package Management), PMS (Perfor-

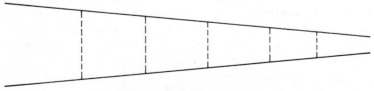

**Fig. 1.1** The MOR funnel.

mance Management System), PARA (Policy Analysis and Resource Allocation), and OPS (Operational Planning System), to name a few. My admittedly biased point of view suggests that although MOR is compatible with all of these, it is nonetheless more encompassing and less administratively demanding than most other management systems. Furthermore, MOR can be designed to facilitate, rather than duplicate, existing budgeting and reporting requirements, e.g., PPBS.

In Chapter 2, we will examine the six separate steps in the MOR funnel: defining roles and missions, determining key results areas, identifying and specifying indicators of effectiveness, selecting and setting objectives, preparing an action plan, and establishing controls. First, however, let's take a look at the dual role of any manager and some of the conflicts it creates.

## Management Work versus Operating Work

In order to put the job of a manager into proper perspective, we need to examine the nature of the work performed there. A manager is concerned with two general types of work — management work and operating work. The ratio between the two will vary substantially from manager to manager, depending on the individual, the management level, the type of effort being supervised, and the organizational environment.

Management is defined here, and is interpreted throughout this book, as "the effective use of limited resources to achieve desired results." Consequently, this definition can be applied to the head of a major organization of several thousand people or to a specialized one-person operation. In most situations, however, management includes supervising the work of others, with the time and effort expended by these "others" as part of the "limited resources" at the manager's disposal.

Management work, in this context, represents the work a manager does that directly affects, but is not an actual part of, the output of a given organization or organizational unit. It includes the functions of planning, organizing, staffing, directing (leading), and controlling the manager's own work and that of subordinates. Operating work is all other work the manager does, including direct contributions to unit output and any collateral duties the manager performs as an individual (such as staff assistance to a superior or serving as an organizational representative).

There is a legitimate place for both kinds of work in every manager's portfolio. An agency director is performing *management* work when conducting a priority-setting meeting with his or her bureau chiefs. The personal presentation of the results of that meeting to a legislative committee would be legitimate *operating* work for an agency director to perform. However, the personal investigation by the director of factors leading to a given bureau chief's priority decisions would be operating work that is questionable at best and meddling or duplicating at worst.

The problem with this dual role, of course, is that the manager may not recognize the difference between the management and operating parts of the job. Our purpose in mentioning them here is to draw attention to what is, in most situations, the primary part of a manager's job — the *management* work. It's essential that a manager realize that time and effort spent in performing operating work are done at the expense of the primary job, and the consequences must be carefully evaluated.

The point made above may seem so obvious that it is superfluous to mention. But is it? Let's take a look at a couple of examples.

A deputy secretary of a major department receives a call from an influential legislator inquiring about a specific decision affecting one of the legislator's constituents. The deputy secretary, in turn, calls the regional director in whose jurisdiction it took place. Without considering other qualifying factors, which of the following answers would be more likely to indicate a regional director who is on top of his or her management job?

- "We made that decision because . . ."
- "I don't know the specific reasons, but I will have the answer back to you within 30 minutes."

A specially appointed panel of citizens looking into administrative practices has requested a detailed briefing on the methods used in an experimental project being conducted in a specific department. In view of the importance of the briefing, which of the following decisions should the department head make in order to do justice to his or her management job?

- Make the presentation personally to demonstrate full knowledge and capability at all levels.
- Have the individual in charge of the project make the presentation (accompanied by the department head, if necessary).

Although there will be many valid exceptions to this observation, we believe that as a general rule, the second answer in each of the above examples would be more likely to indicate the more effective *manager*. In the first example, for instance, a regional director who is so familiar with the details of all local decisions has probably gained that familiarity at the expense of the management work for which s/he is primarily employed.

Nevertheless, it will be a strong temptation for the manager to take the line of least resistance and to get involved in operating work. This is what Louis Allen calls the *Principle of Operating Priority:* "When called upon to perform both management work and operating work during the same time period, a manager will tend to give first priority to operating work."\* Such behavior is, of course, justified in an out-and-out emergency, but not in the normal course of work. Why, then, does a manager give priority to operating work? Here are three major reasons:

1. In general, operating work involves a technology with which the manager is more familiar. After all, substantially more time and effort, both educationally and on the job, have probably been spent in the technical field than in management. In fact, the individual's technical competence was no doubt a major consideration in the management-selection process.

---

\* Louis A. Allen, *The Management Profession,* New York: McGraw-Hill, 1964, p. 77. Quoted by permission of the publisher.

2.    Operating work is likely to provide more immediate personal satisfaction than does management work. To illustrate this point, Ed Green has stated that planning (management work) involves three things we don't like to do: (a) we have to think, (b) we have to do paper work, and (c) we have to use orderly procedures.*

3.    Ability to solve difficult operating or technical problems has traditionally been considered, in many organizations, to be the trademark of the successful manager. Compare the number of high-level managers you know who arrived there chiefly on their fire-fighting capabilities with those who have made it on the basis of skill in fire *prevention*. This is not to detract from the fire fighters, because few organizations could survive without people who have that capability. However, the old maxim about an ounce of prevention cannot be ignored in today's world. Yet a manager must be much more astute to recognize in a subordinate the ability to *prevent* serious operating problems from arising than to recognize the ability to solve them after they have arisen.

Generally speaking, the truly professional manager is much less spectacular in approach than the seat-of-the-pants manager. However, the results produced usually are far superior, and this, after all, should be the true measure of managerial effectiveness. Knowing the difference between management work and operating work and keeping them in proper perspective so that the total job gets done are essential characteristics of the professional manager.

## What Functions and Activities Are Included in Management Work?

We have talked about the difference between management work and operating work, but what, precisely, is management work? Most of the accepted authorities in management litera-

---

* Excerpted from a filmed address by Edward J. Green, *How to Manage Change Through More Effective Planning*, American Management Association, New York.

ture have developed very similar listings of the functions and activities of management. With no pretense at originality, then, let's identify what we consider to be the five functions and their related activities that make up what we call management work.

*Function I. Planning.*    Determining what work must be done.

1. *Defining roles and missions.* Determining the nature and scope of the work to be performed.
2. *Determining key results areas.* Determining where to invest time, energy, and talent.
3. *Identifying and specifying indicators of effectiveness.* Determining measurable factors on which objectives may be set.
4. *Selecting and setting objectives.* Determining results to be achieved.
5. *Preparing action plans.* Determining how to achieve specific objectives.
    a) *Programming.* Establishing a sequence of actions to follow in reaching objectives.
    b) *Scheduling.* Establishing time requirements for objectives and action steps.
    c) *Budgeting.* Determining and assigning the resources required to reach objectives.
    d) *Fixing accountability.* Determining who will see to the accomplishment of objectives and action steps.
    e) *Reviewing and reconciling.* Testing and revising a tentative plan, as needed, prior to commitment to action.
6. *Policy making.* Establishing rules, regulations, or predetermined decisions.
7. *Establishing procedures.* Determining consistent and systematic methods of handling work.

*Function II. Organizing.*    Classifying and dividing the work into manageable units.

1. *Structuring.* Grouping the work for effective and efficient production.

2. *Integrating.* Establishing conditions for effective teamwork among organizational units.

*Function III. Staffing.*   Determining the requirements for and ensuring the availability of personnel to perform the work.

1. *Determining personnel needs.* Analyzing the work for personnel capabilities required.
2. *Selecting personnel.* Identifying and appointing people to organizational positions.
3. *Developing personnel.* Providing opportunities for people to increase their capabilities in line with organizational needs.

*Function IV. Directing (leading).*   Bringing about the human activity required to accomplish objectives.

1. *Assigning.* Charging individual employees with job responsibilities or specific tasks to be performed.
2. *Motivating.* Influencing people to perform in a desired manner.
3. *Communicating.* Achieving effective flow of ideas and information in all desired directions.
4. *Coordinating.* Achieving harmony of group effort toward the accomplishment of individual and group objectives.

*Function V. Controlling.*   Ensuring the effective accomplishment of objectives.

1. *Establishing standards.* Devising a gauge of successful performance in achieving objectives.
2. *Measuring performance.* Assessing actual versus planned performance
3. *Taking corrective action.* Bringing about performance improvement toward objectives.

Each of the functions and activities identified here is performed by every supervisor/manager at every level. The differences are ones of magnitude and frequency. Figure 1.2 shows the variation in the percentage of effort devoted to each of the five functions at three levels of management.

As is readily apparent from the illustration, the biggest variation in proportionate effort is in the directing function. The closer the manager is to production activity, the larger is the proportion of effort likely to be devoted to the directing function. Conversely, the further away from production, the less time and effort should be devoted to directing and more attention given to the other functions. Obviously, the actual mix of the various functions will not be as smooth as in Fig. 1.2 and will be influenced by other factors as well. Nevertheless, the marked change in the mix as a manager proceeds up the management ladder is inescapable. Therefore, a highly successful first-line supervisor will not necessarily make a good middle manager. Nor, on the other hand, will a middle manager who possesses the necessary skills to perform effectively at that level be a guaranteed success as a first-line supervisor. They are different jobs.

Although it is important to recognize all of the management functions and activities and their relationships with one another, we will not explore each of them in detail. Instead, we will concentrate our attention on the functions that play the key roles in Management by Objectives and Results — that is,

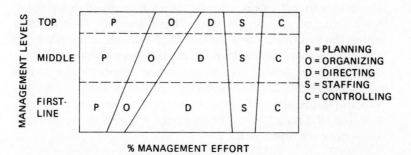

**Fig. 1.2** Proportion of management effort devoted to planning, organizing, directing, staffing, and controlling.

on planning and controlling, together with the communicating that is essential to making them work.

## Cost-Benefit Analysis

Before getting into the details of the MOR process, we should reach a general understanding of the managerial exercise we refer to as cost-benefit analysis. In a sense, cost-benefit analysis is a process closely akin to decision making. It relates directly to the risk-taking aspects of a manager's job. Taking risks is a basic and inescapable part of any manager's responsibilities. The truly effective professional manager will, in essence, put his or her job on the line every day of the week.

In examining cost-benefit analysis from this perspective, we must recognize that every managerial decision we make *costs* us something. As any modern economist will proclaim, "There is no free lunch." Presumably, also, any managerial decision we make results in some *benefit*. The skill of the successful manager comes in making a careful *analysis* to ensure that in the vast majority of situations, the benefit derived from a decision will outweigh the cost. This sounds simple enough, but is it?

The benefits to be gained from a particular decision are in general not very difficult to identify. The costs, on the other hand, are not so readily apparent — primarily because we have a tendency to think only of out-of-pocket costs. In this regard, Peter Drucker points out that "there are no profit centers within the business; there are only cost centers. The only thing one can say with certainty about any business activity, whether engineering or selling, manufacturing or accounting, is that it consumes efforts and thereby incurs costs. Whether it contributes to results remains to be seen."* (Although private-sector oriented, the parallels to public-sector effort in these Drucker references are obvious.)

---

* Peter F. Drucker, *Managing For Results,* New York: Harper & Row, 1964, p. 5. Quoted by permission of the publisher.

Drucker also has identified four main cost categories, as follows:*

1. *Productive costs.* "The costs of efforts intended to provide the value the customer wants and is willing to pay for."
2. *Support costs.* Necessary costs of doing business (personnel, accounting, for example) that provide no direct value to the customer by themselves.
3. *Policing costs.* "The costs of activities which do not aim at getting something done but at preventing the wrong things from happening." (See Chapter 8.)
4. *Waste.* This includes the cost of "not-doing" something, as well as the more obvious costs of scrap and ineffective effort.

The problem of failing to identify costs was vividly brought home in an incident that took place in a seminar I was conducting for a moderate-size organization. As a part of the program, each participant was expected to develop an objective leading to a significant improvement in operations. Since it was a period of expansion for this organization, availability of floor space was a particularly critical problem. Therefore, one of the unit managers was understandably elated as he described his objective to the group:

M: My objective will result in the release of 1000 square feet of floor space within one month — and, furthermore, it won't cost us a dime!

GM: Great! And you say it won't cost anything?

M: That's right!

GM: Tell me — how much time have you put into the development of this idea already?

M: About ten hours. But that isn't a cost — I'm getting paid anyway.

---

* *Ibid.,* pp. 83–84; abridged and adapted by permission of the publisher.

GM: Oh! Then you wouldn't have been doing anything else productive during that ten hours.

M: Well, I did have to put some projects aside while I was working on it, but this was a lot more important.

GM: I'm sure you're right — but it's still a cost. Will there be any production down time as a result of this action?

M: Probably about three to five days while we move some of the equipment over to another building. And that's a cost, I'll have to agree.

GM: Will there be any problems with staff morale as a result of these equipment moves?

M: I hadn't even thought of that. I imagine that might present some problems.

GM: From what you have said, I would guess that this is still a valid objective in that the benefits will substantially outweigh the costs. But let's not kid ourselves that there is no cost involved when we approach what appears to be a worthwhile objective.

As it turned out, the estimated cost of implementing this objective, when translated into dollars, was about $20,000. This was determined to be a modest enough investment in view of the benefit, so the organization proceeded with the move. However, it was a long way from "not costing us a dime!"

What are some of the costs that should be considered before making a positive decision on implementing an objective? Here are just a few of the factors that might be overlooked. There are many more. The development of such a list directed to your specific operation might be a valuable reference document.

| *Tangibles* | | *Intangibles* |
|---|---|---|
| Management or staff time | Floor space | Constituent dissatisfaction |
| Timing of appropriations | Safety | Poor public image |

| Tangibles | | Intangibles |
|---|---|---|
| Data-processing requirements | Flow time | Interunit disputes |
| Equipment required | Inspection | Individual resistance |
| Maintenance and repair | Training | Job dissatisfaction |
| Material costs | Clerical effort | Individual rivalries |
| Material handling | Waste, errors | Rumors |

In doing a cost-benefit analysis, you could merely draw a mental picture of the related benefits and costs, making a perfectly valid decision in a matter of moments. Or, if the determination is critical enough, you could devote many hours to a detailed analysis of all factors making the final decision. In either case, the time and effort invested *before* you commit yourself to a course of action will provide a valuable return. It is far more economical to make a decision not to proceed with the implementation of an objective, on the basis of such analysis, than it is to discover when the job is already half-completed that you made a mistake. For this reason, cost-benefit analysis is a practice that should be applied throughout the MOR process.

## In Summary

The role of the manager today is becoming recognized more and more as a complex one requiring a separate and distinct set of knowledges and skills. Seat-of-the-pants management, generally speaking, will not satisfy the managerial needs of today's (and tomorrow's) environment. In recognizing these facts, more and more public-sector managers are adopting an approach that has been in use for a longer period in the private sector, known as MBO (Management By Objectives) or MOR (Management by Objectives and Results). In essence, this approach breaks down the job of a manager into its basic functions and activities, selects those that are most important to effective management, and lays them out in a logical train which, if followed realistically, will almost inevitably lead to greater productivity and job satisfaction. It places the total job of a manager into proper perspective, drawing particular attention to the costs involved in whatever effort is expended, so that wise decisions may be made.

The balance of this book will be devoted to a detailed analysis of the MOR process and how it can be applied effectively in the "real world" of the manager in a public-sector organization.

# 2

# THE MOR PROCESS

In Chapter 1, we described all of the functions and activities of management as part of our introduction to the subject of Management by Objectives and Results, yet we indicated that there are just six principal steps in the MOR process. These fall within the management functions of planning and controlling. To suggest that the organizing, staffing, and directing functions do not play vital roles in the MOR process would be foolhardy indeed. Obviously, the best plans in the world are of little value in accomplishing objectives unless we also have an effective organization, properly selected and assigned people, and well-balanced direction. Our intent here, however, is to zero in on those specific functions and activities which appear to be most critical to the establishment of the MOR approach. Planning and controlling, in our view, are the management functions around which this concept revolves. There will be regular references, however, to the impact of people and organizational actions required.

## The MOR Funnel

As we suggested in Chapter 1, the basic process is simple, but *deceptively* simple. The MOR process is like a horizontal funnel; it takes something that is large and unmanageable and reduces it until it reaches the point where it *is* manageable. The funnel concept is further amplified through the six steps themselves, in that MOR starts with a position that is broad and general (roles and missions), but with each succeeding step becomes more specific. The process is then integrated through a human dimension that promotes understanding, involvement, and commitment. (Although a modest departure from the flow diagram that appeared in the original version of this book, as in Fig. 2.1, this funnel is conceptually consistent with it.) Figure 2.2 represents the funnel which we will be referring to throughout this book. We will briefly describe each of the steps here, with a detailed analysis included in later chapters.

## Steps in the MOR Process

1.  *Roles and Missions* describe the nature and scope of the work to be performed. They establish the reason for the organization's or unit's existence. (Throughout this book, the term "organization" will be used to describe the total body; the term "unit," any smaller part of it, regardless of size. This is in order to avoid semantic confusion over words such as "department," "section," "branch," etc., which mean vastly different things in different organizations.) Thus "organization" can be the entire body, e.g., Veterans Administration, Bureau of Indian Affairs, Pennsylvania Department of Environmental Resources, Alberta Department of Highways and Transport, Los Angeles County Assessor's Office, Whittier Union High School District, City of Buena Park, or the specific organizational unit(s) for which a particular manager is accountable, whether that be a region or area with several hundred employees or a small operation with three technical specialists and a secretary. The treatment of roles and missions for the total organization is somewhat different from that for a unit within it. We will deal with both in Chapter 3, but the primary emphasis will be on the unit level. A description of the economic, functional, and other commitments involved, plus a determination of the philosophical basis for conducting the unit's affairs, are an integral part of this step in the MOR process. Once established, it is not likely to change unless there is a significant change in what the unit will be doing.

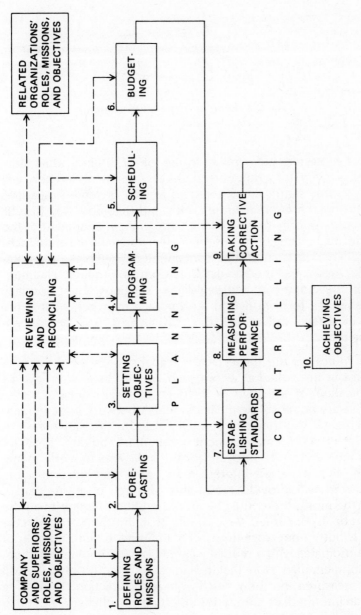

**Fig. 2.1** The MOR process.

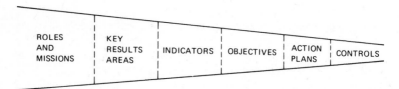

**Fig. 2.2** Six steps in the MOR funnel.

2.    *Key Results Areas* relate to the job of the individual manager. Unless it is a one-person unit, factors identified here will have some significant differences as well as some similarities with those identified under roles and missions. Key Results Areas fix priority on where the time, energy, and talent of the individual manager or, in some cases, a specific group of technical specialists should be concentrated. Examples of Key Results Areas are Productivity, Cost Control, Strategic Planning, Staff Development, and Legislative Relations. They normally are limited to from five to ten for each manager, so that the "critical few" rather than the "trivial many" can be concentrated on.

3.    *Indicators* are those factors, capable of being measured, that can be looked at within each key results area to give an indication of effective or ineffective performance. Clearly, these are not absolute measurements (there are none in management), and they can be manipulated with relative ease. (I have yet to see a management system that I couldn't "beat" if I set my mind to it.) In order for the indicators to work, managers with a vested interest must agree that the indicators selected will provide reasonable visibility of performance. Furthermore, there must be an assumption of integrity on the part of all concerned. An example of an indicator of Productivity is output per work-hour; of Staff Development, number of subordinates with a mutually agreed on and implemented development plan. Note that the indicators identify only *what* will be measured, not how much or in what direction. They serve as an intermediate step, prior to setting objectives, designed to

increase the probability that we are directing the use of our resources to where they will get the best payoff.

4. *Objectives* are statements of measurable results to be achieved. Generally, they will relate to one or more of the manager's key results areas and indicators. They can be clearly expressed according to this model: To (action or accomplishment verb) (single key result) by (target date) at (cost). For example, "To increase output per work-hour by 10%, without loss of quality, effective January 1, 1976, at an implementation cost not to exceed $5000 and 100 work-hours"; "to reach agreement on and begin implementation of an individual development plan with not less than four of my immediate subordinates within First Quarter at a cost not to exceed current budget and 40 hours of my time."

5. *Action Plans* are the sequence of actions to be carried out in order to achieve the objective. An action plan incorporates the substeps of programming, scheduling, budgeting, and fixing accountability, plus reviewing and reconciling, which will be described in detail later. It's the part of the MOR process that describes how the objective will be achieved, by when, at what cost, and it also fixes accountability for completion of each piece of action. This helps establish a hierarchy of objectives in that many action steps, in turn, will become objectives for subordinates. Action plans are broken down only to that amount of detail required for the accountable manager to make his or her contribution to the objective. The responsibility for determining further detail should rest on the shoulders of the individual performing the action.

Each of the five steps covered thus far falls within the management function of planning. MOR is, essentially, a planning effort, and consequently that is where most of the instruction in this book is directed. However, plans by themselves have no value. Many organizations go through elaborate planning exercises once or twice a year, reproduce the results of those exercises, and distribute them to members of management, who promptly shove them in the bottom drawer and get back to work. Perhaps, by sheer coincidence, what is actually accomplished may bear some resemblance to some of what was planned, but it was not achieved through any conscious attention to those plans. That is why I consider the phrase "Management By Objectives (MBO)" to be incomplete and have added the words "and Results" to make the total concept of MOR. There must be a means of closing the loop, and this is incorporated in the sixth step in the MOR process.

6.    *Controls* are designed to keep the accountable manager informed of progress toward objectives. They have one purpose only — to alert us when we are about to get into trouble, in sufficient time to take the necessary corrective action. If we never needed to take corrective action, we would not need controlling as a function of management. However, since in most cases we need some mechanism for ensuring the accomplishment of our objectives or in making a rational shift in direction, if necessary, Controls are an essential step in the MOR process. To the extent possible, control mechanisms should be visual (I favor simple charts, where practical) and should provide for "adequate visibility in a timely fashion (sufficient to take corrective action if required) with the least expenditure of time and effort."

We have briefly identified the six principal steps in the MOR process, but it is still not complete. It would be possible to follow the steps mechanically in a one-way, top-down manner. A senior manager could tell each subordinate exactly what his or her roles and missions, key results areas, indicators, objectives, action plans, and controls should be. Furthermore, if this were the first time the senior manager's expectations had been clearly spelled out, it is entirely conceivable that subordinate performance would improve. However, that is not where the real payoff comes. MOR must be seen as a *human* process, not a mechanical one. Therefore, *Communication* can be identified as the catalyst that ties the whole process together (see Fig. 2.3). The process must serve as a communication vehicle among the people affected. As people become *involved* in the

COMMUNICATION

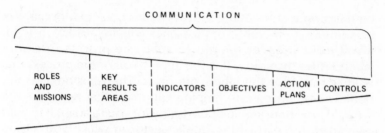

**Fig. 2.3** The completed MOR funnel.

decisions that affect them, they become *committed* to carrying them out. Real management power comes through performance, not mere obedience. Therefore, paradoxically, to get real power, we must give it away. MOR can and should be a tool for tapping further the potential of people within an organization to contribute more effectively to that organization's efforts. The days of "the organization man" are fast disappearing. If we hope to realize maximum payoff from use of the MOR process, we must clearly recognize that what goes on a piece of paper is not important. It is the thinking, dialogue, inputs, sharing, negotiation, agreement, reviewing, revising, and evaluating among concerned *people — communication —* that produces the results. The pieces of paper that may be generated serve only to document that process and to provide a tangible focus for further *communication.* MOR need not and should not become another "paper mill." Only when it is clearly seen as a human rather than a mechanical process can MOR begin to produce the kind of real results of which it is capable.

## In Summary

Management by Objectives and Results (MOR) is a relatively simple process — deceptively simple. It is based on a commonsense, logical approach to the use of familiar and proven principles and techniques of management. The labels we place on the various steps of the process in this book may or may not be somewhat different from the ones you are already using. If it will make it easier for you to apply the process, use your labels rather than ours. It is the application of the process that is important, not the labels put on it. The remainder of this book will be devoted to helping you make that process work for you, providing ample opportunity for you to adapt it to your own style, the part of the public sector in which you are involved, and the circumstances that affect the way you manage.

# 3

# DEFINING ROLES
# AND MISSIONS

## What are Roles and Missions?

A statement of roles and missions — that is, a statement describing "the nature and scope of the work to be performed" — in effect describes the organization's or unit's reason for existence. The differences, as applied to the total organization or a smaller unit within it, are primarily ones of degree and derivation. For the total organization, the statement should include the broad identification of the type of operation for which it is responsible, its major areas of service, clientele or user groups, organizational approach, plus the philosophical basis for its operation. For the unit within the total organization, the roles-and-missions statement should include the unique or distinctive contribution to be made to the overall organizational objectives, the economic, functional, and other commitments to be made, and the major types of work that should be undertaken by the unit, as well as any philosophical considerations that need to be spelled out at that level. This statement provides a logical starting point for determining objectives and a means of testing their validity and establishing accountability for results.

## Why Do We Need to Define Roles and Missions?

Have you ever observed an organization in which:

1. Two or more units performed essentially the same work, with obviously wasteful duplication?

2. Critical work was not performed, because accountability for results was not specifically fixed and everyone assumed that "somebody else" was doing it?

3. Individual employees (including some managers) saw little or no relationship between what they were doing and the apparent reasons for the existence of the total organization?

4. Substantial effort was being expended on work that contributed little or nothing to, or in some cases actually had a significant negative effect on, the economic welfare of the total organization?

5. There were marked disagreements among units as to who was supporting whom in production (with the result that little was accomplished)?

Anyone who has worked in organizations, in either the public or the private sector, for a reasonable period of time has at least observed, if not been involved in, situations in which any or all of the above existed. Although there is no cure-all for such problems, a clear statement of what piece of the action a specific organizational unit has will go a long way toward reducing them.

Aside from reducing or eliminating problems such as those described, a valid statement of roles and missions is the baseline from which all unit objectives should be drawn. In other words, any objective accepted by a manager should be in direct support of the unit's statement of roles and missions; otherwise, serious questions should be raised as to whether any significant effort should be devoted to that objective.

## Where Does the Statement Come From?

Ideally, a clear, concise, and comprehensive statement of roles and missions for the total organization provides the basis for roles-and-missions statements of smaller units within it. In fact, if no organization-wide statement exists, each manager must create one, at least conceptually, before the unit's roles and missions can be defined. The process of preparing such a statement at the top-management level can be a difficult, time-consuming, and exacting kind of an exercise, if done correctly. In this step, perhaps more than in any other in the process, the discussion and analysis that take place among key members of management are far more critical than the statement that comes out on a piece of paper. All too often, what was perfectly obvious to one member of top management may take on a substantially different appearance when interpreted by another member of the same group. Management must examine, and reexamine on a regular basis, "what business we are in and what should be the scope of our operation." The lack of clear agreement at the top level is an open invitation to the dissipation of efforts at lower levels.

The list of "think questions" entitled "Clarifying Corporate Roles and Missions" on p. 34 identifies the key issues that need to be discussed periodically at the top-management level. Obviously, there will be varying degrees of importance associated with each of these questions, depending on the circumstances and people involved. Although all of the conclusions reached as a result of that discussion will not necessarily be included in an organizational roles-and-missions statement, they will help to clarify those factors that need to be emphasized.

For any top-management group considering undertaking such an effort, let me urge that you:

1. Make arrangements for the services of a competent consultant or "disinterested third party" who can serve as a facilitator for the group.

2. Set yourselves an objective, including the amount of time to be devoted to it, for the completion of a first draft. Endless fine tuning or debating over the choice of words serves little useful purpose. You are far better off coming out with an imperfect statement relatively quickly so that you can circulate it among those who have to relate to it — with a commitment to review and possible modification after a reasonable trial run.

3. Share the results of your efforts down through the organization as quickly as possible so that others can be guided accordingly. A well-thought-out statement of organizational roles and missions is a powerful tool for effective management communications. Use it!

## Where Do Organizational Unit Roles-and-Missions Statements Come In?

The rationale for establishing and periodically reexamining unit roles and missions is threefold: (1) it provides a basis for determining where unit resources should be invested and what kinds of objectives should be set; (2) it serves as a communications vehicle up, down, and across organizational lines to help ensure a clear understanding of who should be doing what; and (3) it is a means whereby the unit manager and others concerned can periodically reevaluate the unit's efforts in terms of current relevancy. Consider the following examples.

An Accounts Payable supervisor changed the unit's mission from one of processing paperwork to one of "ensuring timely and accurate meeting of outside financial commitments." The results? A first-year saving of more than $20,000 in net terms discounts and a marked reduction in turnover of suppliers and internal friction with Purchasing and the using organizational units.

A County Assessor's unit head added a requirement to "educate the taxpayer in effective compliance with legal requirements" to its traditional appraising, assessing, and auditing functions. The result? A marked reduction in the number of appeals and complaints.

A Congressional Relations unit for a major federal service bureau adopted a posture of *"anticipating* and responding promptly to inquiries from individual members of Congress" rather than waiting for problems to arise and then trying to deal with them. The result? Within three months the unit was able to standardize its procedures and reduce a 45-day backlog to less than 10 in spite of a 10% reduction in work force.

If clear, concise statements of roles and missions exist at all higher levels of management, the job of the individual manager in defining one at the unit level is relatively easy. The manager simply identifies that portion of the superior's statement for which s/he is to be held accountable and, in consultation with the superior, key subordinates, and perhaps some peer managers, defines it more precisely as an operational base for the unit. In turn, as appropriate, key subordinates may define their own statements, consistent with that of the unit manager.

If clear, concise statements do *not* exist at all higher levels of management, the process may be a bit more difficult and time-consuming, but it still can and should be performed if the unit's objectives are to be relevant. It may require some research and considerable creative thinking to accomplish this, however. The set of "think questions" entitled "Clarifying Organizational Unit Roles and Missions" on p. 35 is designed to help get at some of the critical issues. Select those questions that are particularly relevant for your unit and, in consultation with other concerned people, answer them as best you can to form a data base from which your unit's statement of roles and missions can emerge.

## What Factors Should Be Included?

Each statement of roles and missions by a manager will be different from that of any other manager. However, some of the factors identified here should be included in every such statement, whereas others should be used only as appropriate. The following is a brief description of each of these factors, beginning with the universal factors, i.e., those that apply to all unit statements of roles and missions.

### Universal Factors

1. *Broadness of scope; continuity of application.* The statement should be broad enough to cover all significant areas of performance expected of the organizational unit and should not indicate a specific termination period. As such, it is an ongoing statement of the nature of work performed. (The only

exception to this would be a specific project-oriented unit whose functions would cease upon completion of the project.) The statement should not have to be changed unless something of major importance (such as a principal function, product, service, or area) is added or removed.

2. *Economic commitment.* The statement should include a commitment to the economic motives of the organization which, in the case of most governmental operations, could be stated as "cost-effective use of available resources." This may appear academic, but when a manager makes a commitment, in writing, to ensure that all elements of his or her unit will contribute toward the achievement of the organization's economic motives, the unit's efforts will carry a much more pertinent meaning than mere identification of functional activities.

3. *Production (line) or support (staff) determination.* The purpose of this factor is to clarify the relationship with the unit's principal customers, clients, or users. The words "line" and "staff" are frequently misunderstood and in many cases present some emotional barriers. Here, we will use the word "production" (in place of "line") to designate those units or individuals whose services are used primarily by an *external* customer — in other words, those who are directly accountable for the delivery of all or a portion of the total organization's mission. We will use the word "support" (in place of "staff") to refer to those units or individuals whose principal efforts are directed toward meeting the needs of an *internal* customer — either production units or other support units within the total organization. With some operations — personnel and accounting, for instance — this relationship is quite clearcut. In others, however, it will depend on the nature of the total organization's roles and missions. For example, if the mission of an information systems unit in a federal agency is to provide essential data to state and local government organizations, it would be a production unit; if the primary function of that unit is to provide data to other parts of the same agency, however, it would be a support effort.

Our purpose in determining the production or support relationship in the statement of roles and missions is not to subordinate one function to the other. Each has a critical role to play. However, it is vital that each statement of roles and missions define clearly the unit's relationship to the *total* organization's roles and missions. In the case of support operations, it is also imperative to recognize the necessity of providing *understood and accepted* advice and service, not merely advice and service. This means that the support unit should not only make its services available, but also see that those services are understood and used properly.

4. *Functional commitment.* The nature of the work performed within the unit must be described in terms that will clearly determine the validity of the unit's subsequent objectives.

5. *Unique or distinctive nature of work.* Every unit (and most workers) in an organization should make some unique or at least distinctive contribution. If two or more peer units in an organization have identical statements of roles and missions, the risk of duplicated effort or, worse still, effort gap is obvious. Assignment to different shifts or different geographical locations may, of course, lend uniqueness to otherwise identical statements. In most cases, however, the uniqueness of the statement will relate to those particular activities in which the unit is involved.

**Optional Factors (to be used if and when appropriate)**

1. *Product.* This factor should be included in the statement if the unit is directly related to one or more specific deliverable products for those organizations in which production or distribution of products is a part of its total mission — for example, safety education materials produced by a Department of Public Safety.

2. *Service.* A more frequent delineation would be related to specific services provided under a broad umbrella of ser-

vices — for example, immunizations as a part of a County Health Department's services.

3. *Market.* When a particular unit is focusing on a specific part of a larger market or group of customers, clients, or users, that market should be identified. Examples of this might be philatelic sales (sales to stamp collectors) by the Postal Service or clerical placement by a State Department of Employment Development.

4. *Geographic area.* If the work performed within the unit is limited primarily to one geographical area, that delineation should be a part of the unit's roles-and-missions statement.

5. *Philosophical or legal issues.* If the nature of the unit's work is such that specific philosophical or legal issues (such as affirmative action, environment, state-of-the-art, leadership in the profession, etc.) are major influencing factors, these should be spelled out.

## How Should Statements Be Prepared?

The following step-by-step process is recommended as a logical method by which you can define your statement of roles and missions. Whether or not you follow each step precisely will depend on your particular situation.

1. Identify the total organization's roles and missions (either from its formal statement or by your own analysis).

2. Identify the roles and missions of the major functional unit of which you are a part.

3. Identify your superior's roles and missions in relation to those of his or her superiors.

4. Determine that portion of your superior's roles and missions for which you should reasonably be held accountable.

5. Determine appropriate answers to the "think questions" entitled "Clarifying Organizational Unit Roles and Mis-

sions" (p. 35) that are relevant for you. (If possible, involve your key subordinates in this discussion and analysis.)

6. Prepare a rough draft of your roles-and-missions statement, including the economic, functional, and other commitments you should make for your unit, together with the major elements of the work to be performed.

7. Review this draft in depth with your superior, your key subordinates, and any peer managers to whom this would be relevant. Modify it as appropriate.

8. Check your modified draft statement against the "Key Questions for Evaluating A Statement of Roles and Missions" (p. 36). Force yourself to analyze it objectively. Invite others to assist you in the process.

9. Prepare a final draft and submit it to your superior for approval. (That approval is essential, since this statement will in effect be your charter for future work to be performed in your unit.)

10. When the final draft has been approved, duplicate it and distribute copies to those directly concerned.

11. Review this statement at least once a year or whenever major changes in your roles and missions take place. Update the statement as appropriate.

## In Summary

A clear, well-thought-out statement of roles and missions that is agreed to by a manager and his or her superior and subordinates is a major step in the process of managing by objectives and results. With it, the manager can properly evaluate the activities in which the unit is engaged and determine what objectives should be pursued. Without it, the manager may remain unaware that many activities being performed within the unit make relatively little contribution to the overall objectives of the company. The first real attempt at writing a meaningful statement of roles and missions may be difficult and time-consuming. The effort, however, will pay off in much more significant results, and subsequent efforts by the manager and those others who are affected will become easier.

## CLARIFYING CORPORATE ROLES AND MISSIONS

(The following "think questions" are designed to assist members of a top-management group in the development of a statement of roles and missions for the total organization.)

1. What business are we in? Why do we exist?
2. Who are our primary and secondary customers/clients/ users?
3. What are our principal products/services?
4. What are our principal markets/outlets/distribution channels?
5. What is different about our business from what it was 5–10 years ago?
6. What will/should be different about our business 5–10 years in the future?
7. What are our principal economic concerns/interests?
8. What are our principal sources of funding (revenue, appropriations, grants, etc.)?
9. What philosophical issues are important to our organization (related to organizational image, leadership in profession/community, environment, political factors, affirmative action, innovation/risk-taking, state-of-the-art, quality, timeliness, organization structure, management approach, administrative practices, etc.)?
10. What special considerations do we have in regard to:
    a) Legislative bodies/constituents?
    b) Parent organization?
    c) Employees?
    d) Customers/clients/users?
    e) Suppliers?
    f) General public?
    g) Others (specify)?

## CLARIFYING ORGANIZATIONAL UNIT ROLES AND MISSIONS

(The following "think questions" are designed to assist individual unit managers, together with others having a vital interest, in developing a statement of roles and missions for their specific organizational units.)

1. What business is the total organization in? Why does it exist?

2. What business is our organizational unit in? Why do we exist?

3. Who are our unit's primary and secondary customers/clients/users? Are we principally a production or a support operation?

4. What are our unit's principal products/services/functions?

5. How do these products/services/functions contribute to the total organization's roles and missions?

6. What is different about our unit's business from what it was 5–10 years ago?

7. What will/should be different about our unit's business 5–10 years in the future?

8. What is our unit's principal economic base (income generator/self-sustaining, cost center, separately funded and how, part of a larger cost center, assigned budget, etc.)?

9. What should be the nature of our economic commitment to the total organization?

10. What is unique or distinctive about our unit's work as compared with that of other units in the organization?

11. What philosophical issues are important to our organizational unit (related to organizational image, leadership in profession/community, environment, political factors, affirmative action, operational strategies, innovation/risk-taking, state-of-the-art, quality, timeliness, organization structure, management approach, administrative practices, etc.)?

12. What special considerations do we have in regard to:
    a) Legislative bodies/constituents?
    b) Upper management?
    c) Employees?
    d) Customers/clients/users?
    e) Suppliers?
    f) Peer organizations or units?
    g) General public?
    h) Others (specify)?

## KEY QUESTIONS FOR EVALUATING A STATEMENT OF ROLES AND MISSIONS

1. Does it include all *pertinent* (e.g., economic, functional, product, service, market, geographic) commitments?

2. Is there a clear determination of production or support relationship?

3. Is it unique or distinct in some way?

4. Is it consistent with, without duplicating, peer statements of roles and missions?

5. Is it understandable, brief, and concise?

6. Is it continuing in nature?

7. Is the complete function stated and self-contained?

8. Does it provide a clear linkage to superior and subordinate roles-and-missions statements?

## SAMPLE STATEMENTS OF ROLES AND MISSIONS

In the following pages are several sample statements of roles and missions for total organizations and organizational units in the public sector. Although these are either direct copies or adaptations from actual statements, the sources have not been identified. The circumstances that prompted some of the entries may be quite different from those facing managers of similar operations. These statements are intended only as illustrations, not as prescriptions. You need to develop your own statement, one that is related to your unique situation.

## County Assessor's Office

To serve the public in the performance of our legal functions in equally appraising and assessing property in MOR County by:

1. Observing moral, ethical, and professional standards.
2. Ensuring cost-effective use of available resources.
3. Rendering service pertinent to property assessments to promote harmonious relations.
4. Pursuing standards of performance that meet organizational needs and enhance job satisfaction and growth needs of individuals.
5. Providing leadership in assessment administration.

## Hospital Center

The mission of the MOR Hospital Center is to:

1. Provide superior health services to eligible beneficiaries.
2. Participate in the training and education of medical and allied health personnel.
3. Expand medical knowledge through the advancement of research.

## Area Office — Federal Agency

To carry out the mission of the MOR Federal Agency in our assigned geographical area by:

1. Continually assessing and responding to the related needs of the people and communities being served.
2. Effectively interpreting the Agency's mission to those being served and to the general public.

3. Providing constructive feedback to the Agency on local acceptance of Agency programs and the need for new or modified services.

4. Ensuring cost-effective use of available resources.

5. Providing opportunities for meaningful and satisfying service and personal and career growth for all Area employees.

6. Interpreting and practicing the Agency's commitment to Affirmative Action.

## Fire Department

To provide high-quality, cost-effective emergency and preventive services to the MOR community, related to the protection of life and property from fire and allied causes, including:

1. Rapid response to emergency situations.

2. Continuous education on fire prevention for the people of the community.

3. Regular inspections for potential fire hazards and the taking or recommending of appropriate corrective action.

4. Investigation into fire causes for corrective or preventive purposes.

5. Maintenance of all emergency equipment in optimum service condition.

6. Continuous new and refresher training for all personnel.

## Chief, State Division of Highways

To contribute to the State Department of Transportation's efforts to provide safe, efficient transportation for the people and communities of this state by planning, building, maintaining, and operating a state highway system and cost-effectively managing the following program categories:

- *Maintenance and Operations.* Provides highway and toll bridge maintenance and operations, bridge and roadway reconstruction and restoration, resurfacing, protective betterments, and toll revenue operations.
- *Improvements.* Provides special safety improvements, new highway and toll bridge construction, roadside services and enhancement, and traffic operational improvements.
- *Local Assistance.* Administers federal and state assistance to city and county road, street, and highway programs.
- *General Support.* Ensures the provision of all necessary support services plus related statewide planning and research.

Overall, this division exists in order to:

1. Ensure the continuous maintenance and improvement of the state highway system in serving all people and communities throughout the state.
2. Ensure cost-effective use of available resources in pursuit of its mission.
3. Cooperate, to the fullest extent possible, with all related federal, state, county, and city organizations in effectively meeting the state's transportation needs.
4. Provide opportunities for career and personal satisfaction and growth for all division personnel.
5. Be alert and responsive to useful new developments in highway systems management.

## Principal, MOR High School

To contribute to the MOR Union High School District's efforts to ensure the provision of quality education and a meaningful growth experience for all people served in our geographical area by cost-effectively managing the following units:

- *Curriculum and Instruction.* Ensures the availability, proper preparation of, and instruction in a balanced program of required and elective subjects in line with legal requirements, assessed needs of our students, and current state-of-the-art in education.

- *Guidance.* Provides assistance to students in identifying and creatively planning for development of current and potential skills, talents, and interests, with a view to providing educational and vocational direction along lines that will result in selection of a personally satisfying life's work.

- *Activities.* Provides cocurricular opportunities for participation in student government, student publications, sports programs, and other student activities designed to develop student awareness of and skill in the qualities of good citizenship and self-fulfillment.

- *Administration.* Ensures the provision of all necessary support services plus effective communications with the community at large.

Overall, this school administration exists in order to:

1. Help prepare all students in our area to assume a productive and satisfying role in life.
2. Ensure cost-effective use of available resources in pursuit of our mission.
3. Create and maintain a working environment that will enhance job satisfaction and growth needs of both certificated and noncertificated personnel.
4. Build and maintain a healthy relationship with the community at large.
5. Develop and maintain pride in our school and community.
6. Contribute to, as well as learn from, the current state-of-the-art in education.

### Supervisor, Management Training — MOR Federal Agency

To contribute to the cost-effective use of the MOR Federal Agency's available resources by providing understood and accepted advice and service in the areas of management and administrative training through managing the following activities:

- Conducting training-needs analyses.
- Designing, developing, promoting, conducting, and administering training programs and services.
- Evaluating training effectiveness.
- Coordinating intraagency training activities.
- Establishing and maintaining effective working relationships with appropriate local educational institutions.
- Identifying, evaluating, and securing outside training expertise as needed.
- Building and maintaining a knowledge of current developments in training technology and theory.
- Advising management on effective and efficient use of training resources.

Overall, this group exists in order to:

1. Assist agency managers in meeting their short- and long-term commitments to the agency, to their subordinates, and to themselves through provision of services designed to increase individual and organizational effectiveness.

2. Establish and maintain an awareness throughout the organization of the importance of building a creative balance between meeting organizational and individual needs and desires.

3. Significantly influence the total organization's commitment

to Affirmative Action by example as well as through teaching and consulting.

4. Create a receptive audience for our services.

5. Contribute to, as well as learn from, the current state-of-the-art in training and development.

# DETERMINING KEY RESULTS AREAS

## What Are Key Results Areas?

Key results areas help determine where the individual manager should be investing his or her time, energy, and talents. The same principle can also be applied to a group, as we shall see a bit later. Initially, however, we will concentrate on your job as an individual manager. Your statement of roles and missions covers the entire scope of work for which you are accountable. Unless yours is a one-person operation, there undoubtedly are some functions within your roles and missions that will be carried out primarily by others, requiring very little attention on your part. On the other hand, some things—staff development, for example—should represent a key results area for every manager with subordinates, whether or not they are identified as such in the unit's roles and missions.

*Key* results areas are just that. They do not cover everything a manager does; such a list would be unmanageable. They identify those areas where *results,* not activities, are significant enough to warrant specific attention by the manager. There are many other things a manager does in the course of the daily routine that will happen regardless of whether or not objectives are established for them. There are others which, in all probability, could be reduced in intensity, delegated, or eliminated altogether.

## The Principle of "The Critical Few"

The point about selective determination of key results areas might best be illustrated by a basic principle of economics, as shown in Fig. 4.1. It is sometimes referred to as Pareto's Law or, as I prefer to call it, the Principle of "The Critical Few." A variation on the concept of Cost-Benefit Analysis as presented in Chapter 1, this is designed to show the relationship between the cost of the input and the value of the output as we set priorities on where our efforts should be directed.

In Fig. 4.1, the specific numbers are not important, but they do serve as a symbol of the relationship. These relationships can be divided, roughly, into three groupings. The first has an input cost of 15 and an output value of 65. We refer to this relationship as "the critical few." The second has an approximately equal balance between input and output (20 and 20), representing efforts that are important, but not necessarily "critical"; "maintenance" is the label we have put on these efforts. The third, and much more insidious, grouping indicates an input cost of 65 and an output value of only 15. This, the op-

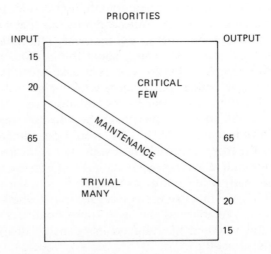

**Fig. 4.1** The principle of "The Critical Few."

posite of "the critical few," logically becomes "the trivial many."

Dealing with these groupings in reverse order, think of the many activities in which you get involved for which the value received is limited at best. Such things as routine meetings, telephone calls, paperwork, etc., seem to eat up an inordinate amount of time and effort with little, if any, significant payoff. Some of this is beyond your control, to be sure. However, most managers can exert far more influence over these than they might like to admit. By the way, the fact that something may fall into "the trivial many" for a given manager doesn't necessarily mean that it is not important. The question is more a matter of its priority among the other demands on the manager. For those activities that seem to fall into "the trivial many" category, the manager's first choice of corrective action should be to determine which ones could be eliminated entirely and which ones could be delegated to subordinates. For those activities in this category which are unavoidable — certain routine meetings and phone calls, for example — one technique for controlling them is to mentally, verbally, or in writing set objectives at the outset as to what is to be accomplished through the activity, including when the activity should be concluded. These objectives can, and in many cases, should, be negotiated with other people involved in the activity. In all probability, they are feeling a similar sense of frustration and would welcome an opportunity to limit the investment in time and effort they will be making.

The middle, or "maintenance," grouping could include important ongoing productive efforts that are largely self-sustaining and other kinds of repetitive functions whose output is valuable but for which the input can be standardized or, possibly, reduced without adversely affecting the output.

"The critical few" represents a concentration of effort where the payoff is greatest. We will talk more about this later on when we get into controls. Here, we are concerned about those areas where a significant investment of the manager's time, energy, and talents can make the greatest contribution to the unit's roles and missions. Depending on the circumstances, this might fall in such key results areas as: staff development and training, strategic or operational planning, quality control, or legislative relations.

## Guidelines for Determining Key Results Areas

There are nine basic guidelines that under normal circumstances will help a manager determine his or her key results areas. These are summarized on pp. 52–53.

1.   *They will identify all major areas within which the accountable manager will be expected to invest time, energy, talent, and other resources during the projected period of commitment (usually six months to one year).*   The key here is the degree to which the manager is personally involved. All of the elements of normal production, which could represent 80% of the unit's total effort, might be incorporated under one key results area, such as "operating results," unless the manager is more involved than what might be considered normal supervision. The closer the manager is to first-line supervision, the shorter the usual projected time span.

2.   *They will include both managerial and operational responsibilities of the accountable manager.*   In Chapter 1, we differentiated between management work and operating work. Management work represents effort that (a) directly affects, but is not an actual part of, unit output, and (b) for which the resultant activities will be carried out largely by others — for example, strategic or operational planning. Operating work, by contrast, covers areas (a) that are a part of unit output or that represent collateral duties and (b) the activities which will be performed primarily by the manager personally, such as product or service design, contract negotiations, or personal staff assistance to higher management. Every manager, regardless of level in the organization, will perform a certain amount of both kinds of work. This helps to put them both into perspective whereby the total job of the manager can be projected.

3.   *They will cover both normal work output expectations and innovations or improvement efforts.*   Even though "normal

work output" may require a relatively small proportion of managerial effort, it still needs to be identified as a key results area so that it is not ignored in favor of exclusive attention to innovative efforts.

4.   *They will include "soft" or difficult-to-measure areas, such as Staff Development, Organizational Relationships, and Public Relations, as well as "hard," tangible areas that are easier to measure, such as Operating Results, Cost Control, and Productivity.* It is still possible to come up with measurable objectives in the "soft" areas, but only if we call attention to them at this stage.

5.   *They will not necessarily cover the entire job, but will instead identify "the critical few" areas in which priority effort should be directed.* Once again, we are talking about *key* results areas, not the routine everyday tasks that will get done anyway. The only time we might wish to identify the latter as key results areas would be if we were planning to do something about changing them.

6.   *Each will be limited, generally, to one, two, or three words.* More than that usually gets into more detail than is appropriate at this stage.

7.   *They will not represent activities as such, but rather areas within which activities and, more importantly,* results *will occur.* This, again, is why the number of words should be limited. These are discreet categories of effort leading to results.

8.   *Each will not be measurable as stated, but will contain elements that are capable of being made measurable.* The next step, Identifying and Specifying Indicators of Effectiveness, will suggest what those elements might be; the fourth step, Selecting and Setting Objectives, will help establish how much. It is possible for a single key results area to produce several objectives.

9.   *Collectively, they will form a basis for effective communication up, down, and across organizational lines.* Even before getting into the reaching of agreements on objectives, a

sharing of perspectives on identifying the areas of effort that require the manager's personal attention can be a revealing and highly productive form of communication. In fact, the dialogue that can take place around these perspectives can go a long way toward bringing about cooperative effort, even if the manager goes no farther with the MOR process than this step.

## Sample Key Results Areas

This is a list of frequently used key results areas for managers in the public sector. Many of these would not be appropriate for a given manager's job, and there are others, not identified here, that would be more pertinent. Use this list as a guide, not a prescription.

*Common to all managers*

| | |
|---|---|
| Staff Development | Personal Output |
| Staff Morale | Personal Staff Assist- |
| Organizational Rela- | ance to Management |
| tionships | Self Development |
| Social Responsibilities | ANTICIPATION/INNOVATION |

*Common to many managers*

| | |
|---|---|
| Strategic Planning | Legislative Relations |
| Operational Planning | Public Relations |
| Operating Results | Management Communications |
| Productivity | Organizational Image |
| Quality Control | Client/User Contacts |
| Cost Control | Product or Service Design |
| Funding Management | Legal Responsibilities |
| Unit Administration | Contract Negotiations |

Check this list against the nine guidelines described above. Then look it over and mark those that truly represent *key* results areas for you. (I have highlighted "ANTICIPATION/ INNOVATION" in that list to draw attention to the fact that most managers need to be alert to new opportunities and changing circumstances that will affect their operations. Establishing this area as a key results area may stimulate a manager to look ahead rather than wait for something to happen.) Finally, use the guidelines to identify any areas not covered here, but in which you either are or should be investing a significant amount of your time, energy, and talents.

A list of from five to ten key results areas is about normal for most managers. Although there will be exceptions, a list of more than ten key results areas is likely to be either too detailed or representative of a manager who is spread too thin. By the same token, a list of less than five key results areas generally will be too broad to be useful or may indicate a managerial level that could be eliminated or that could assume more responsibility.

## Setting Priorities on Your Key Results Areas

Determining what are or should be key results areas provides its greatest value, of course, to the individual manager in sorting out his or her own priorities. An additional benefit comes from being able to either negotiate or communicate with others in terms of these priorities. Even if a manager and his or her superior can agree on what the key results areas ought to be, there may well be substantial differences in point of view as to the relative importance of these areas. Also, it is not at all unusual to have subordinates and peer managers gain a much greater appreciation of the manager's responsibilities through the use of this tool — to the point that they are able to play a more supportive role in working with that manager.

One way to approach the setting of priorities on key results areas is to list them and then calculate the percentage of your total time and effort you have actually spent on each over the past six months. (To aid in your objectivity, you might wish to ask your secretary or some other co-worker to make a similar analysis of how you have spent your time — *before that person has seen your figures*.) I recall a seminar I was conducting for a large state government department and the reaction I received from the chief of one of its major bureaus (well over 1000 employees).

c: I just realized I have been spending about 25% of my time running errands for the Deputy. Am I supposed to list that?

GM: Is the Deputy aware of the time and effort that it's taking?

c: Of course not.

GM: Would you like him to be?

c: Well — yes, I suppose I would. But I can't call it "running errands."

GM: Call it "Staff Assistance to the Deputy" if you prefer. At any rate, this is a way in which you can communicate the impact of his demands in a relatively nonthreatening way. Although it is conceivable that his reaction might be that that is the way it should be, it is more likely that he will suggest that you work together to reduce that impact so you can spend more time and effort elsewhere.

An additional dimension can be added by listing your key results areas, analyzing what is happening "now", then projecting what "should be" your proportionate investment over the next six months to a year. For example, the following might be the way a field manager for a Washington-based service bureau could look at the situation:

| Key Results Areas | Now (%) | Should be (%) |
|---|---|---|
| Operating Results | 40 | 15 |
| Operational Planning | 5 | 20 |
| Public/Community Relations | 5 | 10 |
| Unit Administration | 40 | 15 |
| Management Communications | 5 | 5 |
| Staff Development | 5 | 20 |
| Anticipation/Innovation | 0 | 5 |
| Organizational Relationships | 0 | 5 |
| Self-Development | 0 | 5 |

It is quite clear that this manager feels that too much time and effort are being devoted to Operating Results (representative of effort that, more properly, is the responsibility of subordinates) and Unit Administration (where a more efficient approach seems needed). On the other hand, this manager feels that more time and effort should be spent on Operational Planning, Staff Development, and to a lesser degree on Public/Community Relations, with three previously ignored areas — Anticipation/Innovation, Organizational Relationships, and Self-Development — needing some attention. We are not necessarily suggesting that this is an appropriate list or priority balance for such a field manager. However, it does provide a basis for that manager to sit down with superiors, subordinates, or peer managers to discuss it in a rational manner, making some modifications if needed.

## Applying Key Results Areas to a Group

Up to this point, we have been looking at key results areas as a means for determining where a *manager's* time, energy, and talents should be invested. The process can be applied equally well to a group of technical specialists performing similar kinds of work, particularly where the unit manager is also a working member of the group. In this situation, however, the key results will tend to be somewhat more technical and specific and will more closely resemble some of the content in the unit's statement of roles and missions. For example, in our illustration of the management training group whose roles and missions are described on p. 41, the group's key results areas might look like this:

Training Needs Analysis
Program Design and Development
Program Presentation
Program Administration/Coordination
Program Promotion/Evaluation
Special Projects
Staff Development

The real value in this application, of course, comes from the group members sitting down together, discussing and reaching a consensus on where the group's resources should be invested. A commitment from each of the group members to make it work then becomes a much higher probability than if the manager makes the decision and merely informs the group.

## In Summary

Determining Key Results Areas is the second step down the MOR funnel. It further breaks down the unit's roles and missions into categories requiring a significant investment of the unit manager's time, energy, and talents or, in some cases, that of the entire group for a specific period of time, usually six months to a year. These will not be objectives in themselves, but will represent areas within which objectives can and should be set. Key results areas also serve as a valuable communications tool in discussing with, negotiating with, or — if necessary — simply informing other concerned people about where time, energy, and talent should be invested. The next step, Identifying and Specifying Indicators of Effectiveness, will provide a more tangible way to determine specifically what should be done in each of the key results areas.

## GUIDELINES FOR DETERMINING KEY RESULTS AREAS

Under normal circumstances, a manager's key results areas will meet the following criteria:

1. They will identify all major areas within which the accountable manager will be expected to invest time, energy, talent, and other resources during the projected period of commitment (usually six months to one year).
2. They will include both managerial and operational responsibilities of the accountable manager.
3. They will cover both normal work output expectations and innovations or improvement efforts.
4. They will include "soft" or difficult-to-measure areas, such as Staff Development, Organizational Relationships, and Public Relations, as well as "hard," tangible areas that are

easier to measure, such as Operating Results, Cost Control, and Productivity.

5. They will not necessarily cover the entire job, but will identify "the critical few" areas where priority effort should be directed.

6. Each key results area will be limited, generally, to one, two, or three words.

7. They will not represent activities as such, but rather areas within which activities and, more importantly, results will occur.

8. Each key results area will not be measurable as stated, but will contain elements that can be made measurable.

9. Collectively, key results areas will form a basis for effective communication up, down, and across organizational lines.

# 5

# IDENTIFYING AND SPECIFYING INDICATORS OF EFFECTIVENESS

## What Are Indicators?

Indicators are those measurable factors within a given key results area on which it is worthwhile to set objectives. They identify only *what* will be measured, not how much or by when (that comes in the objective). They may represent "hard" numbers, such as units of production per work-hour or number of clients served. They could be problems that need to be overcome, e.g., interpreting changes in the law to constituents or eliminating a backlog of work. Or they could be "soft" numbers indicating effectiveness in *subjective* key results areas, such as turnover of personnel or absenteeism as indicators of Staff Morale or number of complaints or requests for service as indicators of Client/User Satisfaction.

Several years ago, while I was serving as a management training specialist at North American Aviation (now Rockwell International), the number of student-hours achieved (number of participants attending multiplied by the total number of hours in training) was established as one of the standards for measuring the effectiveness of training programs. Considering myself to be a professional who was more concerned with quality than with volume of effort, I and several others in the department raised a strong protest to this method of measurement. "Are we supposed to crank out bodies or provide a worthwhile training experience? How can we do justice to our identified training requirements if we have to play the numbers game?" Once the hue and cry had subsided and we discovered that we were going to have to live with this as one of our methods of measurement, an interesting thing happened. We found that there was a distinct correlation between the number of student-hours produced in a given training program and the quality of instruction provided. The records of student enrollment and attendance were better in those programs which provided training that participants and their superiors felt satisfied their training needs. Furthermore, the emphasis on production of student-hours strengthened the individual training specialists' feeling of responsibility to promote optimum enrollment and to follow up on absentees. It helped us realize that developing and presenting an effective training program was only part of our job. The best-developed program in the world is worthless if no people or if the wrong people participate in it. Consequently, I used student-hours as one of my indicators of effectiveness in subsequent training management positions I held in the public as well as the private sectors.

The key in this step lies in the meaning of the word "indicator." It is not an absolute measure; there are none in management that I am aware of. It is something that suggests "effectiveness" to those who must look at it. Since in most cases several factors could be observed, the secret is in the *agreement* reached among those concerned that one of these factors represents something that is worth tracking or doing something about.

## Why Use Indicators?

After identifying key results areas, most of us naturally tend to leap immediately into the setting of objectives. It is possible to do that. In fact, we might be able to set up a comprehensive list of objectives that relate to our key results areas, but they might be on the wrong things. For example, under Staff Development we might select as an indicator "number of subordinates enrolled in training classes." This could lead to several misapplications: a small number of employees enrolling in a large

number of classes (with remaining employees not participating
at all); people enrolling (to get the "brownie points" for doing
that) but not fully participating; people enrolling in training
classes that make little or no direct contribution to their job
performance. Perhaps a more appropriate indicator might be
"number of subordinates with mutually agreed-on and implemented development plans. This is a good example of a
"soft" indicator, and it is also one that could be manipulated
fairly easily. (I have yet to see a management system I couldn't
beat if I set my mind to it.) The value in this kind of an indicator
lies in its implied individualized action. For monitoring purposes, the numbers are easy to track. However, if the number
is to have significance, the manager must sit down, on a one-
to-one basis, with each of the subordinates concerned to discuss and reach the necessary agreement; furthermore, the development plan probably will require some active participation
on the part of the manager as well as the subordinate, involving
on-the-job as well as off-the-job development efforts.

The principal benefit of applying the Indicator step comes
from both the individual mind-stretching and the mental stimu-
lation that take place through dialogue with others who are
also concerned about results. For some key results areas, particularly those that are project-oriented, the specific outcomes
or objectives are so obvious that spending any significant
amount of time or effort on this step would accomplish very
little. In most areas, however, there is a fairly wide variety of
indicators that might be selected. Perhaps the indicator that
appeared most obvious at the outset is not the most useful one
in setting objectives. By taking a look at a larger set of potential
indicators than is likely to be used, the manager, with the help
of other concerned people, has the opportunity to examine
several alternatives and then select those that will provide the
greatest meaning in terms of objectives that should be set.

## Guidelines for Identifying and Specifying Indicators (summarized on pp. 63–64)

Under normal circumstances, a manager's indicators will meet
the following criteria.

1. *They are measurable factors, falling logically within a given key results area, on which objectives may be set.* That last phrase is a key here. There are many measurable factors — such as flow time, budget adherence, accuracy standards, etc. — that may prove extremely useful during the Controls step, but are of little value at this stage. *Most indicators will be equally useful as control measures, but not all control measures will function as indicators.* One of the problems that many managers have with the Indicator step is a natural tendency to identify indicators *after* objectives have been set. Although there is no denying their value as control measures, their use as factors in determining the result content of objectives can provide a major breakthrough in realistic planning.

As an added consideration under this guideline, there will be some indicators that may provide visibility under two or more key results areas. For example, units of production per work-hour could relate to Operating Results, Productivity, or Cost Control. It is perfectly legitimate to use a single indicator and, subsequently, a single objective to establish anticipated results in more than one key results area, provided, of course, that it carries a significant meaning and is not just a "numbers game." In most situations, however, an indicator will relate logically to only one area.

2. *They may represent:*

a) *"Hard" numbers,* e.g., units of production per work-hour or number of clients served. These are usually the easiest kinds of indicators to identify, but are not always the most useful in setting objectives other than for ongoing production efforts. Also, there is a risk of becoming too "number happy" and looking for so many different ways to measure the same thing that the numbers lose all meaning as a tool for effective management. I recall visiting a production unit of a public utility and seeing a whole series of index charts on the wall. I asked the supervisor what his objective was in connection with one of the charts. He said, "98." When I asked how much he had achieved that month, he said, "67." He also indicated that his objective for the following month was "98" and that his plan for achieving it was to "work harder." Good luck!

b) *Problems* to be overcome, e.g., interpreting changes in the law to constituents or eliminating a backlog of work. Indicators do not necessarily have to have numbers in order to be measurable. The identification of certain things that need to be changed or completed is equally appropriate as a measurable factor to be included in the objective statement of results to be achieved.

c) *"Soft" numbers,* or indicators of effectiveness in subjective areas, e.g., turnover of personnel or absenteeism related to Staff Morale, or number of complaints or requests for service related to Client/User Satisfaction. In many key results areas, the actual results either are so subjective that it is almost impossible to get a firm fix on them, or they will show up so far in the future — for example, Career Development or Research and Development — that it is impractical to set objectives in terms of those results. Consequently, we must look for "soft" number indicators that might represent signs that we are heading in the right direction or for measurable activities, the performance of which should logically lead to the improvements we are seeking. Although this may appear to violate the principle that we should be measuring results and not activities, it is legitimate if the activities are the only tangible things we can look at during the life of the objective. This also assumes that our analysis leads us to the conclusion that the activities will bring about the results we want and will not be just activities for activity's sake.

3. *They usually identify only* what *will be measured, not how much or in what direction,* e.g., rework as a percentage of total effort, not 10% reduction in rework (the latter is almost an objective). Indicators only identify where effort should be focused. In some cases, it may be necessary to go through some additional analysis after the indicator is identified in order to establish a realistic target. In other cases, the indicator may stay

constant over several measurement periods, but the amounts to be achieved may change, depending on the circumstances of the moment. In order to get as objective a perspective as possible, it is important to decide analytically on *what* will give us the best visibility *before* we get into the more emotionally laden dimension of how much is "good."

4. *They will fall, principally, into one of the following time dimensions, in descending order of usefulness:*

a) *Concurrent* indicators, or factors that can be identified in advance and tracked during performance against objectives — for example, output per work-hour, cost per unit output, document release time. Concurrent indicators, whose value will become even more evident later when we get into controls, are the most versatile kinds of indicators.

b) *Pre*indicators, or factors identified *before* the fact that will point toward a course of action — for example, economic trends, pending legislation, election year impact. These can help us reduce the amount of "reactive" management we must go through. Any field manager for a governmental service organization who has continued with "business as usual" during the waning months of an election year has probably learned "the hard way" the importance of keeping up to date on election issues that affect his or her operation.

c) *Terminal* indicators, or factors that can be measured only after the fact — for example, project completion, specific problem solution, number of promotions. The difficulty with this category is that all we can do is ask, "How come?" if we don't make it. It's usually too late to do anything about it. Most of us tend to look first for terminal indicators, the least useful of the three categories. Although we may have no choice, we should try to identify some legitimate *concurrent* indicators before settling on one that is terminal or after-the-fact in nature.

5. *The cost of identifying and monitoring them will not exceed the value of the information.* Although this has more impact when we get into the Controls step, if we don't keep this guideline in mind prior to setting our objective, we may end up with a millstone around our necks. For example, specific cost breakdown per client served might be a desirable place for improvement to take place. However, in some cases, the cost of acquiring that data could make it prohibitive. To the extent possible, indicators should be tied in to data that are both easy and inexpensive to get.

## Sample Indicators

The following is a list of frequently used indicators related to typical key results areas for managers in the public sector. These indicators are designed only to stimulate your own thinking, since there are many others that might serve as well or better for you in your situation.

| *Productivity* | *Organizational Image* | *Staff Development* |
|---|---|---|
| Output per work-hour | Favorable mentions in media | Training participation |
| Output per individual | Public information programs | Number of promotions |
| Schedule maintenance | Publications by personnel | MOR use by staff |
| Down time | Involvement in local community | Cross-training plan |
| Turnaround time | Interorganizational cooperative efforts | Number of subordinates with development plan |
| Problems overcome | | |

| *Operational Planning* | *Legislative Relations* | *Staff Morale* |
|---|---|---|
| MOR application | Response time to legislators | Personnel turnover |
| Staff loading | Inquiries handled favorably | Absenteeism |

| Operational Planning | Legislative Relations | Staff Morale |
|---|---|---|
| Work flow plan | Funding approved | Number of grievances |
| Resource determination | Major programs approved | Number of new ideas |
| Control checks | Plan for informing legislators | Voluntary participation |

## How to Identify and Specify Your Indicators

Start by selecting one of your key results areas in which the outcome is not perfectly obvious and clearcut. Then, individually or, preferably, together with others who are concerned, brainstorm as many different potential indicators related to that area that you can think of, regardless of whether or not they are appropriate to use right now. (Some might be useful in the future.) Review your list, evaluating the items against the guidelines, and select those that seem most useful in identifying the desired results you wish to achieve during the projected period you will be using for your objectives. Some of your key results areas may require more than one indicator and consequently more than one objective during this time period, whereas one indicator and objective might be sufficient for others. Conceivably, there could be one key results area — Self-Development, for example — for which you may not wish to identify an indicator or an objective at the moment, but might want to keep it in front of you as an area that does need attention.

## The MOR Agreement

At this stage in your planning efforts, you might wish to start pulling the pieces together into one location. Figure 5.1, a suggested format for an MOR Agreement, incorporates key results areas, indicators, and objectives. Here, on a single sheet of paper, it is possible to establish your principal commitments for a period of time, possibly six months to a year, for your own use and for sharing with your boss, subordinates, and peers, as

_____ 's MOR Agreement from _____ to _____

KEY RESULTS AREAS
Indicators                                                     Objectives

Example:

PRODUCTIVITY                              To reduce turnaround time on requests for ser-

  Turnaround time                        vice to max. two working days, effective 6/1/76,

_____        at implementation cost of 60 work-hours.
_____        _____
_____        _____
_____        _____
_____        _____
_____        _____
_____        _____
_____        _____
_____        _____
_____        _____
_____        _____
_____        _____
_____        _____
_____        _____
_____        _____
_____        _____
_____        _____
_____        _____
_____        _____
_____        _____

PROGRESS REVIEW SCHEDULE _____

**Fig. 5.1** The MOR Agreement.

appropriate. There is also a space for a "Progress Review
Schedule" at the bottom, which we will refer to later on, under
controls. As shown in the example, key results areas are entered on the broad line with indicators shown directly under-
neath. Objectives that are related to the indicators will be written on the lines to the right. Some completed sample MOR

Agreements are given in Figs. 6.6 and 6.7, starting on p. 103, which you can refer to if you wish.

## In Summary

Often, people find Identifying and Specifying Indicators of Effectiveness to be the most difficult step in the MOR process to relate to. This is because our normal inclination is to write the objective first and then try to identify indicators. That is understandable, since many of the factors identified here will be equally useful as standards for control, particularly those that are concurrent in nature. Although the MOR process can work if the Indicator step is omitted, many managers who have disciplined themselves to identify indicators *before* setting objectives have found it to be one of the most useful tools in the process for opening up practical new ideas for increasing their effectiveness. The investment in time and energy is small, and the potential payoff is tremendous.

## GUIDELINES FOR IDENTIFYING AND SPECIFYING INDICATORS

Under normal circumstances, a manager's indicators will meet the following criteria:

1. They are measurable factors, falling logically within a given key results area, on which objectives may be set.
2. They may represent:
   a) *"Hard"* numbers, e.g., units of production per work-hour or number of clients served;
   b) *Problems* to be overcome, e.g., interpreting changes in the law to constituents or eliminating a backlog of work; or
   c) *"Soft"* numbers, or indicators of effectiveness in subjective areas, e.g., turnover of personnel or absenteeism related to Staff Morale.

3. They usually identify only *what* will be measured, not how much or in what direction, e.g., rework as a percentage of total effort, not 10% reduction in rework. Indicators only identify where effort should be focused.

4. They will fall, principally, into one of the following time dimensions, in descending order of usefulness:

   a) *Concurrent* indicators — factors that can be identified in advance and tracked during performance against objectives, e.g., output per work-hour.

   b) *Pre*indicators — factors identified *before* the fact that will point toward a course of action, e.g., economic trends, election year impact.

   c) *Terminal* indicators — factors that can be measured only after the fact, e.g., project completion, number of promotions.

5. The cost of identifying and monitoring them will not exceed the value of the informatiion.

# 6

# SELECTING AND SETTING OBJECTIVES

The setting of objectives is the most obvious step in the process we call Management by Objectives and Results. In fact, this step can be used independently of the rest of the process when it is desirable to do so. It is particularly useful in planning special projects, meetings, business trips, personal pursuits — anything for which it is important to focus on the results to be achieved. Without objectives, most activity that is performed has little meaning. Suppose you start out on an automobile vacation trip without a clear destination, heading from Los Angeles to San Francisco, changing your mind en route and going toward the Grand Canyon, deciding at the Arizona border that San Diego would be nicer at this time of year, and, finally, determining that you really didn't want to take the trip after all, so you head back home. Now, if the primary purpose of such a trip were to enjoy the traveling without concern for getting anywhere, the activity would be fine. However, how many organizations do you know in either the public or private sector that can afford the luxury of performing activity for its own sake, without concern for what is accomplished? Objectives form the basis for determining what activities should be performed and also help establish criteria for evaluating how well they are being performed. Therefore, the setting of objectives is one of the keys to effective management.

Although it would be possible to come up with a beautiful set of organizational unit objectives that meet all of the construction criteria (spelled out later in this chapter) without going through the other steps in the MOR process, it is equally possible that such objectives might be on the wrong things. The first three steps in the MOR process — Roles and Missions, Key Results Areas, and Indicators — are specifically designed to identify those critical factors on which objectives should be set. If we have worked our way logically through these steps, the process of writing meaningful objectives is not difficult. Therefore, obviously, our first recommendation is to let your objectives emerge from the analysis you have gone through in the earlier steps. As an alternative, we will identify an analytical approach you can use to identify your objectives if you have elected to *start* with the objective-setting step.

In this chapter, we will deal with two aspects of the objective-setting process: (1) identifying the objectives (which includes assignment of priorities) and (2) writing the objectives in a form that will make them effective management tools.

## Identifying Objectives

### What Is an Objective?

An objective is simply a statement of results to be achieved. For the first time in the process, we are identifying the specific measurable accomplishment we hope to achieve within specific time and cost constraints. Such a statement contains four major elements: (1) an action or accomplishment verb, (2) a single measurable key result, (3) a date or time period within which the result is to be accomplished, and (4) the maximum investment, in terms of money, work-hours, or both, we are willing to make toward its accomplishment. An objective follows the model: To (action or accomplishment verb) (single key result) by (target date) at (cost). For example, "To reduce by 10% the cost of Operation A by January 1 at an implementation cost not to exceed 50 work-hours"; "To develop and implement a new work flow plan for the unit effective March 1 at a cost not to exceed 60 work-hours"; "To achieve a minimum of 95% on-time filing of Homeowner Exemptions in our community by legal deadline at a cost not to exceed $5000 out-of-pocket and 200 work-hours."

Note that these statements of objectives do not include a justification for their existence nor a description of how they should be accomplished. An objective identifies only the *what, when,* and *how much.* The "why" comes before, and the "how" comes afterward.

## What Should Be Objectivized?

Anything can be objectivized, from eliminating the national debt to washing a pane of window glass. In this regard, the accountable manager must decide what work efforts should be put into objective form. To be truly effective, the list of objectives which a manager prepares at the beginning of a forecast period (quarter, half-year, year, etc.) should reflect all of the key results expected. Much of today's emphasis on objectives is concentrated primarily on new or innovative efforts. But to be meaningful, objectives must include the *normal work output* of the unit as well. Far too many of today's "objectives" take on the aspect of special projects, which tend to fall by the wayside when the going gets rough. Or, what may be worse, so much emphasis is put on these special objectives that normal work output suffers. This is not to say that innovative objectives should be discouraged. On the contrary, innovations or improvements to normal work output are absolutely essential to maintaining an effective operation. However, they must be approached realistically, and normal work output must not be allowed to suffer as a consequence of the attention they receive.

## Must We Objectivize Everything?

Ideally, as indicated above, a manager's list of objectives will reflect *all of the key results* expected. Realistically, however, particularly during the initial attempts at instituting the MOR approach, it may be either impractical or too formidable a job. Therefore, it may be desirable to introduce the approach gradually, particularly if subordinates are likely to resist "newfangled ideas." (Actually, if introduced properly, with active participation by subordinates, MOR can be one of the most effective *motivational* tools the manager has.) Starting out with a relatively small number of objectives, which may reflect only part of the manager's total operation, can be an effective method of gaining familiarity with the approach without abruptly turning the current system completely upside down. As the manager and others who are affected gain increased confidence in using the MOR approach, it can be expanded in digestible doses until it finally covers the entire operation.

Even after gaining confidence in the MOR approach, the serious-minded, professional-acting manager will examine the operation very carefully to determine what work activities should be placed into objective form. If there were a different objective for every task, the manager's job would be interminable, with nearly all of his or her time and effort being spent in writing and tracking objectives. The manager, therefore, must gather similar tasks into workable groupings, analyze these groupings, and concentrate attention on those work activities for which the writing of objectives yields the most promise of benefit — because they will provide better visibility, lead to more effective and efficient production, or make the jobs of all concerned (manager, subordinates, superiors, and peers) easier and more satisfying. There is no formula that can define precisely where that point is. It is up to each individual manager to make his or her own determination — recognizing that *the primary purpose of an objective is to serve as a working tool, not as a publicity instrument to impress others.*

### How Do We Determine Our Objectives — Using the MOR Funnel?

Assuming that the first step in the MOR funnel, Roles and Missions, will stay fairly constant once it has been established, the next two steps — Key Results Areas and Indicators — are designed to lead logically to the establishment of objectives. Following are a few hypothetical examples of objectives that might come as a result of that flow.

## Key Results Areas

| Indicators | Objectives |
|---|---|
| 1. Productivity (turnaround time) | • To reduce turnaround time on requests for service to a maximum of two working days, effective 6/1/76, at an implementation cost of 60 work-hours. |
| 2. Operational Planning (work flow plan) | • To develop and implement a new work flow plan for the unit, effective March 1, at a cost not to exceed 60 work-hours. |
| 3. Organizational Image (publications by personnel) | • To have a minimum of four articles, presenting a positive image of the organization, written by unit personnel and published in professional journals during the current fiscal year at a cost not to exceed 80 work-hours. |
| 4. Quality Control (rework as a percentage of total effort) | • To reduce the amount of rework to an average level not to exceed 5% of total effort, effective April 15, at an implementation cost not to exceed $2000 and 50 work-hours. |

Your own objectives, flowing out of your key results areas and indicators, will be quite different from these, naturally. However, the example just presented does illustrate how one step leads into the next. These three steps, which are included in our suggested MOR Agreement format, represent the only parts that under normal circumstances are negotiated between the manager and his or her superior. The Action Plan may be negotiated with subordinates and peer managers who are involved, but in most cases it should not be a concern of the superior unless it appears that the objective will not be reached. This is one way of helping the boss to resist the temptation to "retreat to the familiar."

If you wish, take one or more of your key results areas and indicators now and try writing some objectives that are appropriate for your operation. If you prefer, you can wait until we have covered the section on Writing Objectives, later in this chapter.

## How Do We Determine Our Objectives — Without Using the MOR Funnel?

If, for any reason, you have chosen not to work through the Key Results Areas and Indicators steps in the MOR process, there are still many ways in which objectives can be established. Here is one relatively simple and logical way to approach it.

This method suggests that there are two types of analysis and three general routes of analysis, as illustrated in Fig. 6.1. Let us emphasize here these are not categories of objectives, but rather a means of determining what the objectives should be. As the figure shows, the first type of analysis, *Production Analysis,* leads to examination of (1) *normal work output.* The second type, *Improvement Analysis,* leads to examination of (2) *normal work output improvements* and (3) *personal or organizational capability improvements,* i.e., ways of making the unit more effective.

In order to make a realistic start down any of these routes of analysis, a manager must go back to the unit's statement of roles and missions, job description, charter, or whatever documents may exist that spell out what work the unit should be performing. These will provide the basis for determining the areas in which efforts should be applied and the means of validating objectives and establishing accountability for results.

In addition, any objectives adopted must relate to and support the roles, missions, and objectives of the manager's immediate superior and, ultimately, the entire organization. In other words, the manager should have a clear understanding of what higher-level objectives have been established. However, as pointed out in our discussion of roles and missions, the lack of clearly defined higher-level objectives neither prevents nor excuses the manager from determining his or her own. It merely makes the job more difficult.

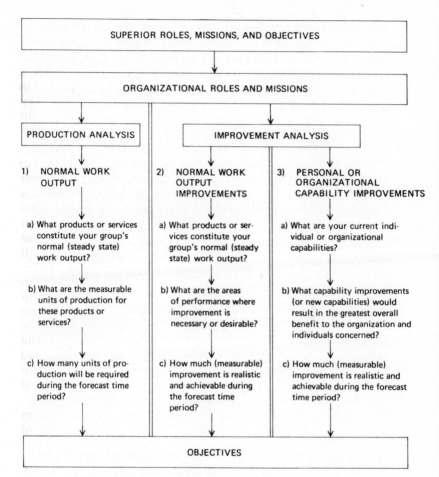

**Fig. 6.1** Analysis routes for determining objectives.

Now let us examine Fig. 6.1 in greater detail, beginning with "Production Analysis." Much of the work that is being done in many organizations is reasonably well standardized and follows a production pattern. It well may represent the largest portion of the unit's effort. However, any possible improvement within this effort would probably be limited to a "learning curve" improvement, based on added experience in doing the job. If objectives are going to reflect *all of the key results* expected, however, and are to be used as the basis for determining the unit's budget, this work must be more closely analyzed. This leads us to our first route of analysis.

1. *Normal work output* encompasses the steady-state units of production (products or services) provided by the manager and his or her organizational unit. In many cases, there is a reasonably standard procedure or specification for normal output, and since the terms of that procedure or specification are probably already spelled out in writing, they need not be included in the objective statement except in generalities. (If no such procedure or specification exists, it might be advantageous to set an "improvement" objective to prepare and implement one.) The objective statement will usually be introduced by the phrases "to produce" or "to provide" and should represent a realistic statement of the organization's needs or expectations during the time period covered in the plan. The time period for accomplishing the objective may be stated specifically, established as a daily, weekly, or monthly standard, or may be assumed to cover the total forecast span (fiscal year, quarter, etc.).

Here are some typical public-sector examples of objectives that might be determined by the normal work output route of analysis:

- To provide resurfacing for X lane miles of state highway during FY 1977 at a cost not to exceed $Y.

- To provide X units of outpatient care during FY 1977 at a cost not to exceed $Y.

- To produce minimum sales of $X in Series E bonds in Region IV during FY 1977 at a cost not to exceed $Y and Z work-hours.

- To provide direct service to a monthly average of X different eligible recipients at a personnel cost not to exceed Y professional and Z clerical employees.

- To produce X student-hours in management training during First Quarter at a direct cost not to exceed $Y and Z work-hours.

Now, what about "Improvement Analysis?" This kind of analysis is designed to determine what new or innovative types of effort should be followed. It is absolutely essential in today's world of work that we continually look for ways to improve our operations. Without such improvement, we will find ourselves falling more and more under the scrutiny of the critical public eye, to the point that we may have unwelcome change forced upon us. Objectives negotiated at the highest level (between an agency or department head and the chief executive or administrative officer, for example) usually will come about through this kind of analysis. As a general rule, objectives arrived at through one of the two routes of Improvement Analysis will have more of a project orientation than those covered in Production Analysis. Also, particularly at lower levels in the organization, they will frequently be of relatively short duration in terms of actual completion. The choice of which of the two routes under Improvement Analysis to take depends on whether the manager's primary concern is for output improvement or capability improvement.

2.    The analysis of *normal work output improvements* focuses on significant innovations, breakthroughs, or new developments that may raise the rate of production or provide new or expanded services. Here are some typical objectives that might be arrived at through this route:

- To increase the number of nonmandatory audits by X% in FY 1977 at a cost not to exceed $Y and Z work-hours.
- To decrease the average turnaround time on claims filed from A to B, effective 10/1/76, at an implementation cost of $X and Y work-hours and a maintenance cost not to exceed Z work-hours per month.
- To reduce hospital admissions by X% during FY 1977 at a cost not to exceed Y units of outpatient care.

- To reduce school property loss and damage due to vandalism by a minimum of $X in FY 1977 at a cost not to exceed $Y and Z work-hours.

- To expand coverage to include A, B, and C, effective 1/1/77, at an implementation cost of $X and Y work-hours and a maintenance cost not to exceed Z work-hours per month.

3. *Personal or organizational capability improvements* include objectives that may not relate specifically to production units, but should result in increased efficiency and effectiveness, ability to take on new and different assignments, improved working environment, and greater versatility. The following are some objectives that might be established by this route:

- To develop and implement by 9/1/76 a self-monitoring system for service employees at a cost not to exceed $X and Y work-hours.

- To have a minimum of three people fully qualified to perform each unit operation by 12/1/76 at a cost not to exceed X work-hours.

- To have a voice-actuated dictation system operational by 11/1/76 at a cost not to exceed $X and Y work-hours.

- To implement MOR with four of my key subordinates by 10/1/76 within the current training budget at a cost of 40 work-hours each plus 40 hours of my time.

These three routes of analysis are not intended to provide rigid prescriptions for determining objectives. If using them will aid you in more effectively determining what your objectives should be, they will have served their purpose. The end result of this analysis should be a list of objectives covering your planned accomplishments, regardless of which of the three routes of analysis may have been followed. A list of valid objectives is what is important, not the means by which they were determined. For instance, an objective "to produce X units by (date) at a cost not to exceed $Y and Z work-hours" could, conceivably, result from following all three routes. It could represent the products or services that make up the organization's normal work output plus a significant improvement requiring a change in method and a substantially broadened organizational capability. These could be spelled out more specifically in the action steps, which, in turn, could be formed into objectives themselves, should it prove desirable. (This process will be discussed more fully in the next chapter.)

## What about "Subjectives"?

A particularly gnawing question usually occurs to the forward-thinking manager about this time, especially as related to the third analysis route — personal or organizational capability improvements. "What if I can identify certain intangible, but nonetheless critical, capability improvements that I want to bring about, such as improving communication with my employees or developing better teamwork? How can I come up with measurable objectives that will show I achieved them?"

The answer to this is, "You can't!" or, if you can, the actual results are likely to be too far in the future to be of much immediate value. These "subjectives" usually cannot by themselves be stated in measurable terms as we have described them. If, however, you have determined that such improvement should be placed in objective form, you need to identify "soft" indicators (see Chapter 5) or specific measurable activities which, if accomplished, should logically lead to such improvement. Although there is, of course, no guarantee of success, the measurable activities identified below each of the following "subjectives" should result in some progress in the desired direction. One way to improve the likelihood of their working, of course, is to get the agreement, in advance of those that will be affected.

*To Improve Communication with My Employees:*

- Conduct a weekly staff meeting with a planned agenda; review and evaluate employee participation and reaction following each meeting as a guide to future sessions.

- Conduct individual discussions related to job outlook and personal development on a planned schedule of no less than two employees per week.
- Make an informal visit at least once a week to the work areas of each of my subordinate supervisors, giving praise and encouragement whenever possible to the supervisor, his or her group, and individual employees.

*To Develop Better Teamwork in My Unit:*

- Identify major barriers to effective teamwork (through individual interview and personal analysis) by (date); develop a plan for the systematic removal or modification of these barriers by (date); implement plan.
- Conduct biweekly orientation meetings for all employees to provide them with information on new developments plus up-to-date reports on what each employee unit within the organization is doing.
- Temporarily assign key employees, on a specified schedule, to other than their own work units for the purpose of having them understand the activities and systems as well as the work flow among related units.
- Conduct tours, for individuals or small groups of employees, of the entire organizational operation, at least twice each week until all employees have been included.

## How Do We Set Priorities on Objectives?

Regardless of how the objectives are determined, most managers will be able to identify more objectives than can reasonably be accomplished within the resources available. Here is where subjective judgment must be exercised. No computer and no formula (at least none that I am aware of) will provide the manager with a meaningful evaluation of such factors as apparent urgency, external and internal pressures, availability of resources, and long-term versus short-term payoff. However, there are some tools that can be used to increase the *objectivity* of those *subjective* judgments.

Our earlier discussions of Cost-Benefit Analysis and the Principle of the Critical Few pointed out the need to determine the value of the output of a given course of action in relation to the cost of the input. Obviously, this is one of the strongest determinants in the setting of priorities, but it is not the only one. Here are a couple of techniques for placing objectives into priority order.

*Priority Groupings*

In the first of these techniques, we recommend separating objectives into three groupings, as illustrated in Fig. 6.2. *Got-to-do's* are those objectives by which success or failure in assigned roles and missions can be judged. They are basic to the survival of the organization or unit. Ideally, they are dictated strictly by their critical relationship to the effective accomplishment of the total organization's roles, missions, and objectives. Realistically, they may also be strongly influenced by such things as special demands by higher-level management or key clients/users or legislators, availability of restricted resources, personal preferences, and need for experimentation. In short, these are the objectives which, in the manager's best judgment at the time of examination, *must* be accomplished if the unit's existence is to be justified.

*Ought-to-do's* are those objectives which are necessary for *improved* performance, but which are not necessarily survival-oriented. Any successful manager will have several objectives in this category, as well as in the first one. They can be considered vital to the effective growth of the organization or unit, but their curtailment, postponement, or elimination cannot be considered catastrophic.

*Nice-to-do's* are those objectives which are highly desirable for improved performance, but which could, if necessary,

| GOT-TO-DO'S | OUGHT-TO-DO'S | NICE-TO-DO'S |
|---|---|---|
| | | |

**Fig. 6.2** Priority groupings for objectives.

be eliminated, postponed, or scheduled as "down time" effort. These items put "polish" on a unit, provide an opportunity for trying out new and unproven approaches, recognize and accede to political interests (both internal and external), and fill the voids when more critical work is slow. Objectives in this category should be pursued whenever possible, but recognized for what they are and, thus, held in perspective.

A single objective conceivably could appear in all three of these groupings. It might be absolutely essential to produce 100 units (of production) in order for the organization or unit to survive, thus making it a "got-to-do." Or, 125 units might be necessary to achieve what is really expected, even though you could get by with 100, putting it into the "ought-to-do" column. However, 150 units would be well beyond what is expected and would be highly desirable, provided its achievement was not at the expense of another, more important, objective. This would be considered a "nice-to-do."

*The Decision Matrix*

The second tool or technique recommended for use in setting priorities, called a *Decision Matrix,* is particularly useful when there is a relatively large list of objectives or projects that need to be put in priority order (see Fig. 6.3). You may enlarge and reproduce Fig. 6.3 for your own use, provided full credit, as worded in the caption, is included. (The shaded boxes prevent the comparison of the same two items more than once.) The Decision Matrix space provides for comparing up to 14 items. However, the form can be extended to accommodate any number. All that is needed is a larger piece of paper and a few more lines. I have used this tool successfully with as many as 38 different projects. As a working tool, the Decision Matrix has many uses in both personal and work-related activities. Consider using it any time you are faced with comparing several similar factors, e.g., choosing optional equipment for a new car (or choosing from among several new car models), deciding on home furniture additions, buying stocks or bonds, de-

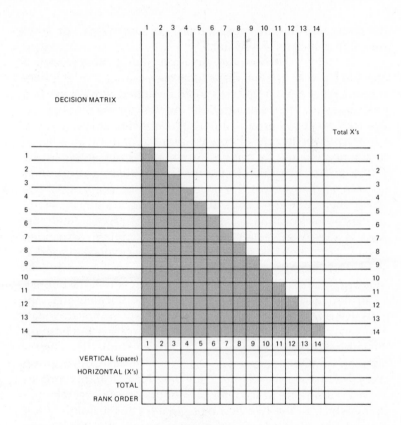

**Fig. 6.3** Decision Matrix. (Copyright 1974 by George L. Morrisey, MOR Associates, Buena Park, CA 90622)

termining on-the-job cross-training requirements, or even selecting names for a new baby.

An example of how the Decision Matrix can be used is given in Fig. 6.4. Assume that a local high school district is considering what new programs should be added or what existing programs should be expanded during the coming school year. The staff executive group (superintendent, principals, and key administrative staff) has been asked to come up with a list of recommendations, in priority order, to be presented to the School Board. In group discussion, the executive group comes up with 11 that are worth considering at the present time: a comprehensive Career Education Plan, a Work-Study program, an expanded Vocational Skills program, Student-Community Forums (to foster better mutual understanding), expanded Physical Education, expanded cocurricular activities, expanded Music and Fine Arts, concentrated remedial work in Basic Skills (reading, mathematics, and oral and written communications), a Current Issues and Events program, a Certificated Staff Appraisal and Development program, and a Noncertificated Staff Appraisal and Development program. These are listed both on the left-hand side of the Decision Matrix and under the corresponding numbers across the top. Next, the executive group takes the first item — Career Education Plan — and compares it, on a one-to-one basis, with each of the other programs, deciding which of the two deserves greater consideration at the present time. In this case, the group agrees that the Career Education Plan is more important than the Work-Study program and therefore puts an X under that column. The group also agrees that this item should rank higher than any of the next five items on the list, so X's are put under those columns as well. However, the group feels that number one has a lower priority than the eighth item — the Basic Skills remedial effort — so that column is left blank. The group considers it to be more critical than Current Issues and Events (so an X is entered) and less vital than either of the Staff Appraisal and Development programs (so those columns are left blank). The group follows the same process through each of the remaining programs

| DECISION MATRIX | 1 Career Education Plan | 2 Work-Study prog. | 3 Vocational Skills prog. | 4 Student-Commun. Forums | 5 Exp. Physical Educ. | 6 Exp. co-curr. activ. | 7 Exp. Music & Fine Arts | 8 Basic Skills (remedial) | 9 Current Issues & Events | 10 Cert. Staff A&D prog. | 11 Noncert. Staff A&D prog. | 12 | 13 | 14 | Total X's | |
|---|---|---|---|---|---|---|---|---|---|---|---|---|---|---|---|---|
| 1 Career Education Plan | | X | X | X | X | X | X | | X | | | | | | 7 | 1 |
| 2 Work-Study prog. | | | | X | X | X | X | | X | | | | | | 5 | 2 |
| 3 Vocational Skills prog. | | | | X | X | X | X | | X | | | | | | 5 | 3 |
| 4 Student-Commun. Forums | | | | | | | | | X | | | | | | 1 | 4 |
| 5 Exp. Physical Educ. | | | | | | | X | | X | | | | | | 2 | 5 |
| 6 Exp. co-curr. activ. | | | | | | | X | | X | | | | | | 2 | 6 |
| 7 Exp. Music & Fine Arts | | | | | | | | | X | | | | | | 1 | 7 |
| 8 Basic Skills (remedial) | | | | | | | | | X | X | X | | | | 3 | 8 |
| 9 Current Issues & Events | | | | | | | | | | | | | | | 0 | 9 |
| 10 Cert. Staff A&D prog. | | | | | | | | | | | X | | | | 1 | 10 |
| 11 Noncert. Staff A&D prog. | | | | | | | | | | | | | | | 0 | 11 |
| 12 | | | | | | | | | | | | | | | | 12 |
| 13 | | | | | | | | | | | | | | | | 13 |
| 14 | | | | | | | | | | | | | | | | 14 |
| | 1 | 2 | 3 | 4 | 5 | 6 | 7 | 8 | 9 | 10 | 11 | 12 | 13 | 14 | | |
| VERTICAL (spaces) | 0 | 0 | 1 | 0 | 1 | 2 | 1 | 7 | 0 | 8 | 8 | | | | | |
| HORIZONTAL (X's) | 7 | 5 | 5 | 1 | 2 | 2 | 1 | 3 | 0 | 1 | 0 | | | | | |
| TOTAL | 7 | 5 | 6 | 1 | 3 | 4 | 2 | 10 | 0 | 9 | 8 | | | | | |
| RANK ORDER | 4 | 6 | 5 | 10 | 8 | 7 | 9 | 1 | 11 | 2 | 3 | | | | | |

Program/Project Rank Order

1. Basic Skills (remedial)
2. Certificated Staff Appraisal and Development program
3. Noncertificated Staff Appraisal and Development program
4. Career Education plan
5. Vocational Skills program
6. Work-Study program
7. Expanded cocurricular activities
8. Expanded Physical Education
9. Expanded Music and Fine Arts
10. Student-Community Forums
11. Current Issues and Events

**Fig. 6.4** Decision Matrix example.

until every one has been compared directly with every other one. From that point on, it is a matter of simple arithmetic. The open spaces under each of the top columns are totaled downward and entered on the "Vertical" line. The X's by each of the side columns are totaled across and then entered on the "Horizontal" line. When the two columns are added together, the item with the highest total (in this example the Basic Skills effort) turns out to be number one on the priority list, with each of the others falling out in descending order, as shown at the bottom of Fig. 6.4. If two or more of the programs had ended up with the same "total," it would mean that there had been some inconsistency during the analysis. However, even if that were so, the items' "rank order" could be determined simply by comparing each subjectively against each of the others with the same "total." The reasons, in this illustration, for selecting one particular program as more critical than others are not important. Undoubtedly, there will be representatives of high school districts reading this who, legitimately, would end up with a substantially different rank order for similar programs. The process of using paired comparisons in the Decision Matrix, however, allows the individual(s) involved in setting such priorities to consider the pros and cons of each in reaching a rational decision. Try it, it works!

## What Do We Do with a Priority List of Objectives?

Once objectives have been put in some sort of priority order, regardless of what process may have been used to get there, partial or total tradeoffs among them can be made. When such things as available resources, urgency, personal considerations, and other relevant factors are taken into consideration, some shifts in schedule or a modest reduction in the quantity or quality of some objectives might make it possible to accomplish more.

In other words, the list of objectives resulting initially from such analysis should be set up as tentative, and modifications and rearrangements should be made until the final priorities have been established. In fact, as we shall see later, this concept of setting up a trial approach is fundamental to the initial planning efforts within Management by Objectives and Results. A single objective may have to be modified, or possibly even dropped, as the manager gets into the action-planning step or as other unanticipated factors come to light. This is one of the many advantages in this approach to managing. It enables the manager to change directions before it is economically too late, should it appear that the original estimate was inaccurate.

In this manner, it is possible for a manager to list, in descending order, more objectives than might be accomplished realistically. A line can be drawn under those to which a firm commitment will be made, on the basis of anticipated resources. Remaining objectives that have been identified should be carried "below the line," to be implemented if sufficient resources become available or if changing circumstances make later priority tradeoffs necessary or desirable.

Now, with a list of prioritized objectives, the manager is in a position to: (1) determine where to direct his or her own efforts as well as those of the unit; (2) prepare appropriate plans of action to accomplish the objectives; and (3) properly evaluate added assignments that are not covered by these objectives and, if necessary, make additional tradeoffs.

## Writing Objectives

### How Do We Write Meaningful Objectives?

Once we have determined the basic elements of the objectives we want to establish, we must write them so that they will become effective working tools. As stated earlier, the manager soon learns that it is a lot easier to talk about objectives than it is to write them. However, certain criteria can be applied to writing a meaningful objective.

First, simplicity is the key to well-stated objectives. No advantage is gained by using a tool unless it makes the particular job for which it is designed easier, more productive, and more efficient. The simpler the tool, the more likely it is to be used.

Similarly, if the process of preparing an objective requires more time and effort on the part of the manager to get essentially the same results as would have been achieved through seat-of-the-pants management, why use it? Therefore, we strongly advocate use of the KISS principle (*Keep It Simple and Short*) in preparing objectives. An objective should describe, in the simplest terminology possible, the results the manager expects to achieve and, in so describing them, should make the process of achieving these results clearer and simpler.

Second, a truly meaningful objective need not be absolutely defensible in the eyes of all who read it. To make it so would require far more verbiage than is necessary or desirable. Nor should it be written as a statement to impress others with the magnitude and importance of the operation. That is not its purpose. The objective should be designed primarily as a communications instrument for those with a *need to know:* (1) the individual manager who formulates the objective for his or her operation and hence will be held accountable for its achievement; (2) the manager's superior, who must review and approve the objective; (3) the manager's subordinates, who will be charged with attaining or contributing to the attainment of the objective; and (4) any peer managers or others whose efforts will be significantly affected by it. Generally, one can assume that those with this need to know are somewhat familiar with the factors identified in the objective as well as the reasons for its being formulated in the first place. If not, the necessary explanations should be given verbally or in a separate written statement. They should not clutter up the objective statement itself.

### Guidelines for Writing Objectives

The following ground rules will aid in the formulation of objectives. Although a given objective may not necessarily conform to all of these criteria, it should nonetheless be checked against each of them. Only when a conscious determination has been made that a specific ground rule does not apply should it be by-passed as a factor in validating a particular objective. (These Guidelines are also listed on pp. 97–98.)

1. *It starts with the word "to," followed by an action or accomplishment verb.* The achievement of an objective must come as the result of action of some sort. However, this action should not reflect mere activity. There needs to be an implicit or explicit accomplishment associated with the action. "To meet with staff . . ." is an activity; "to reach agreement with staff . . ." is an objective.

2. *It specifies a single key result to be accomplished.* We must be able to look at the one key thing that will tell us whether or not the objective has been achieved. The Indicator step is particularly helpful here in identifying what that one key thing should be. Consequently, if each step in the MOR funnel has been followed systematically, the indicator will become a part of the single key result. If "response time" is the indicator, the single key result should identify the span of time that should cover. If there is more than one result identifiable in the objective, one of them must be clearly the final measurement. The objective "to develop and implement a system of Management by Objectives and Results . . ." contains two results. However, it is clear that "implement" is the single key result, with "develop" identifying something else that must take place prior to the key result. Identifying multiple results to be achieved — for example, "to reduce cost of operation by 20% *each* in Areas 1, 4, and 7 . . ." weakens the objective, because failure to achieve in one of the areas implies failure to achieve the total objective, even though the other two areas might meet their targets satisfactorily. If these three areas need to be identified for special cost-reduction targets, each should have a separate objective. Furthermore, it is very possible that each objective will require a different action plan in order to ensure its achievement. If, however, all three areas are virtually identical and one person can be held accountable for the performance in all three, the objective should read "to reduce *total* cost of

operation in Areas 1, 4, and 7 by 20% . . ." In this way, the single key result can be identified by adding together the reductions in all three areas.

3. *It specifies a target date for its accomplishment.* It's fairly obvious that in order to be measurable, an objective must include a specific completion date or time span, either stated or implied. In fact, it is so obvious that it has been missing from more than two-thirds of the objectives I have seen. If the objective is of a continuing nature, as in normal work output, the target date could be assumed to be the end of the forecast period (month, quarter, fiscal year, etc.). However, every manager should have some objectives that will be accomplished at various points throughout that period. If all of a given manager's objectives have an implied completion date of "some time during the fiscal year," that office might be an interesting place to observe during the twelfth month.

4. *It specifies maximum cost factors.* Applying a Cost-Benefit Analysis and the Principle of the Critical Few which we discussed earlier, it should be evident that the results of an objective have value only in relation to the cost of achieving it. Yet in the thousands of objectives I have seen over the years, less than 10% of them have contained even an implied reference to cost limitations. To be sure, there will be some objectives, particularly at higher levels, for which the specific cost will be relatively meaningless, such as in long-range planning. For other objectives, the cost may be a part of the result, as in cost reduction, or may be relatively insignificant. However, particularly at the middle-management level and below, the cost factor should be considered as one of the most critical elements. If we can define management as "the effective use of *limited resources* to achieve desired results," the application of those resources becomes an essential part of the management process. Costing out one's objectives and their subsequent action plans can be one of the most practical methods available to the manager in determining how best to allocate those *limited resources.*

Many managers are reluctant to identify costs as a part of an objective. First, we tend to think that if the benefits are worthwhile, the objective will be accomplished regardless of cost. This could be a one-way ticket to disaster. Many overzealous managers have discovered the hard way that it is easy to overcommit on what can be accomplished with what is available. This leads to a second concern of some managers — that written cost projections become commitments that can come back to haunt them if those commitments are not met. A third concern of many managers in the public sector is that objectives with stated costs might be interpreted out of context by legislators or others with a particular bias. (These are the ones that seem to end up being quoted in the media in a less than flattering manner.) The fourth, and probably most frequent, reason for not entering costs is that it is usually quite difficult to accurately estimate the cost of accomplishing something, particularly that most elusive cost of all — the time of people. Most managers' initial cost estimates will tend to be low, partially because our egos lead us to believe that we can do something faster and cheaper than we really can, and partially because there will usually be some requirements that we will overlook at this stage. In spite of that tendency, a *poor* estimate is still better than *no* estimate, because a poor estimate at least provides us with something against which we can track our progress. Furthermore, carrying the process to the next step, Action Planning, we have an opportunity to validate or modify our original cost estimates by costing out the action steps as well, which are usually easier to project.

Although the cost estimates made in connection with the setting of objectives can be extremely useful in preparing a unit budget or in communicating to others the actual cost of certain work efforts, their primary value should be seen in providing the accountable manager with the visibility necessary to get the best mileage out of the *limited resources* s/he has available. If the manager is unduly concerned about how the cost information included in a statement of an objective will be interpreted "up the line," and if there is not a firm requirement for such data in the submission of objectives, an individual manager might choose to use an implied "within existing budget" cost umbrella. In such a situation, however, the manager should still make specific cost estimates for his or her own use in managing unit resources. In most cases, though, we strongly recommend the *inclusion* of projected costs in objectives that are submitted for approval, as a means of keeping others informed about what's happening as well as of demonstrating managerial competency.

For all practical purposes, costs should be identified as dollars for out-of-pocket expenses and as work-hours/days/months for human effort. Although the cost of human effort could, technically, be translated into dollars, the number of work-hours (time invested by each person added together) required is normally more useful for planning purposes.

I have devoted a fair amount of space in this chapter to the cost element (an entire chapter could easily have been devoted to this one topic) because I consider it to be the most generally neglected element in the objective-setting step. Although it may require some extra effort on your part to include it as a part of each of your objectives, the value that you will get from that added visibility, regardless of whether or not you use it for communication with others, will eventually, if not right away, make your total planning job much easier and less frustrating. You still have the option of leaving costs out when, in your judgment, they are not critical. Leaving them out inadvertently or because they are difficult to establish could be a sign of short-sighted management on your part.

*These first four guidelines* are by far the most critical and should be considered actively with every objective you have. The remaining 12 guidelines may vary from extremely critical to a minor concern, depending on the circumstances. Become familiar with them so you can use them as aids in the effective preparation of your own objectives, when it makes sense for you to do so.

5.   *It is as specific and quantitative (and hence measurable and verifiable) as possible.* The objective "to increase services to our clientele . . ." has little meaning. The objective "to in-

crease services to our clientele by 10% . . ." (assuming we can measure these services) gives us something specific to shoot for. Although many types of objectives lend themselves easily to quantification through the use of numbers or percentages, there are just as many that do not. The management skill then comes in determining what *measurable* factors can be identified that will serve as reasonably reliable indicators of successful performance. Perhaps the biggest problem here is in overcoming the manager's emotional resistance to "putting numbers on quality." The response, generally, is something like, "There's no way you can come up with an accurate, foolproof method of quantifying creative effort." That answer is absolutely correct, and that is where the Indicator step can be particularly helpful in providing the necessary tangibility. (You may wish to review Chapter 5 if you need some help in this.) Some objectives, particularly project-oriented ones, are more easily measured by the completion of certain events or milestones. These are still quantifiable, even though they may not contain numbers.

6. *It specifies only the "what" and "when"; it avoids venturing into the "why" and "how."* Once again, an objective is a statement of "results to be achieved." It is not a justification for its own existence. The "why" bridge should have been crossed before the actual writing of the objective was begun. The use of the first three steps in the MOR process or of the analytical process illustrated in Fig. 6.1 on p. 71 should have helped establish the "why." Although no one would deny that it is important that those people affected by an objective understand the reasons why it was written, this is better handled through a verbal explanation or, if necessary, a separate statement of rationale. "To increase personal counseling services by 10% . . ." identifies the result desired. "To increase personal counseling services by 10% in order to accommodate the anticipated upsurge in unemployment . . ." gets into justification, which does not belong in the actual statement of objective.

Similarly, the *means* of accomplishing an objective is not normally included in the objective statement. The "how" relates to Action Planning (discussed in the next chapter). The objective "to increase personal counseling by 10% through the addition of two new social workers . . ." suggests that there is only one way to achieve it and thus automatically rules out other alternatives. Most objectives may be achieved by several acceptable approaches, the relative values of which might vary under changing circumstances. On the other hand, if it is critical that the objective be accomplished by only one method, it is acceptable to include the "how" in the objective — for example, "to increase services by 10% through the use of workers employed with revenue-sharing funds."

The important thing to bear in mind in relation to this particular guideline is to strive toward keeping the objective statement down to its bare essentials, stressing once more the "simplicity" aspect of preparing an objective.

7. *It relates directly to the accountable manager's roles and missions and to higher-level roles, missions, and objectives.* Although this guideline is so obvious that it hardly needs stating, it can be one of the most critical in testing the validity of the objective. It is easy to get side-tracked into pursuing objectives that have only a remote relationship, at best, to the primary job of the concerned manager. Think about some of the "special assignments" you have worked on. This side-tracking comes about for many reasons — personal interests of the particular manager, lack of availability of anyone else, pet projects of key clients or members of higher management, traditional activities, to mention a few. This is not to say that a manager should.never pursue such objectives. (If nothing else, the political realities of life must be considered.) It does mean that in considering them, the manager and his or her superiors should be fully aware of this lack of relationship and of the potential impact on other objectives which *are* directly related to the primary job.

8. *It is readily understandable by those who will be contributing to its attainment.* We are concerned here with making certain that the terminology used in the objective has a similar clear meaning to all those directly concerned (the manager, superior, subordinates, and related peer managers). Whether

or not it makes sense to anyone else is not important unless it will affect them in some significant way. Adding words to clarify the objective's meaning for others may serve only to confuse it for those who have to relate to it.

9.  *It is realistic and attainable, but still represents a significant challenge.* Since an objective can and should serve as a strong motivational tool for the individual manager, it must be one that is within reach, yet not too easy to accomplish. An objective that is well beyond reach can soon create a defeatist attitude on the part of the manager; paradoxically, an objective that can be accomplished with very little effort can create the same kind of a defeatist attitude. Therefore, the objective should strike a balance, requiring a "stretch" effort on the part of the manager and his or her subordinates while still ensuring the probability of success with such an effort. Incidentally, any manager who consistently meets or exceeds all objectives that have been set probably doesn't have very challenging objectives. If you see that happening among your subordinates, you may want to take stock and see if you have placed such a premium on 100% completion that your subordinates are afraid to take a risk. The manager who wants subordinates to set challenging objectives will make certain that the individual who falls a bit short of making a really tough one gets as much or more recognition than the one who goes way over an easy objective.

10.  *It provides maximum payoff on the required investment in time and resources, as compared with other objectives being considered.* We discussed this point earlier, in the area of setting priorities, but it is a point that bears reinforcement. Since the conscientious manager normally can identify more worthwhile objectives to pursue than there are resources available, a realistic cost-benefit analysis must be applied to each objective. Taking into consideration all currently relevant factors, including political sensitivity, the manager must then determine whether the objective being examined will provide a better return on investment than those objectives it will displace.

11. *It is consistent with the resources available or anticipated.* Although related to guideline #10, this requires separate consideration. A potentially outstanding objective could be a complete waste of time and effort if, for example, it required a significant outlay of capital funds or a substantial increase in personnel during a period in which top management had already called for severe curtailment of expenses. Occasionally, one hears of a manager who gambled during such a period and, because of spectacular success, was able to get the needed backing after the project was under way. Although we certainly don't want to discourage a manager from taking prudent risks, the pursuit of an objective in full knowledge that sufficient resources to complete it are not available is anything but prudent. For every manager who has succeeded with such a gamble, there are dozens who have not. Unfortunately, what happens is that not only is the objective not achieved, but the effort expended on it (effort that might have been used productively elsewhere) is wasted. Almost inevitably, too, the morale of the manager and the subordinates who have been working on it suffers in the process. A modest delay in implementing such an objective, until adequate resources are available, could well be the mark of a truly effective professional manager.

12. *It avoids or minimizes dual accountability for achievement when joint effort is required.* There are occasions when pursuing a given objective may require the efforts of more than one individual or organizational unit. If the objective does not lend itself to subdivision into separate objectives for each participating manager, one manager should be given primary accountability, with the others identified as being in a supporting role. Generally, this kind of conflict will not arise in connection with objectives related to normal work output. However, as an example, a special task force to reorganize an agency's reporting system might be made up of several managers of organizational unit representatives. Accountability for the accomplishment of each objective being pursued by such a task force should be vested in a single manager, even though others may

be heavily involved in carrying it out. Without such accountability, there are very real dangers of redundant effort or effort gap.

13. *It is consistent with basic organizational policies and practices.* Innovation may well be a vital part of an objective. However, if it should be in direct conflict with an accepted policy or practice (methods of negotiating with vendors might be an example), something's got to give. Perhaps the policy or practice needs changing; if so, take the appropriate steps. Perhaps it is more practical to modify the objective or seek a specific exception to the policy. Perhaps the conflict is so crucial that the objective has to be abandoned, at least temporarily. Such things as labor union agreements, legislative restraints, ethical considerations, and community relations, to mention a few, are a vital part of organizational policies and practices and cannot be ignored in the objective-setting process. Otherwise, we are negating or at least diluting the effectiveness of other policies and practices that do serve a useful purpose.

14. *It is willingly agreed to by both superior and subordinate, without undue pressure or coercion.* This guideline has usually evoked several somewhat derisive chuckles from managers participating in seminars on this subject. Yet on closer examination, it is fundamental to the participative concept of Management by Objectives and Results. *Basically, the only difference between an objective and an assignment is in the degree of acceptance.* The potential for chaos is just as great when a manager hands a list to a subordinate and says, "Here are your objectives," as when that subordinate hands a list to the boss and says, "This is all I'm going to do." An objective is the projected result of work that the accountable manager has analyzed and agreed to, whereas an assignment is work that is directed, regardless of the degree of acceptance. (It is perfectly legitimate for a superior to give an assignment to a subordinate, but it is not an "objective" in the context we are describing it here.) This is not to say that a superior's ideas will not strongly influence the content of a subordinate's objective.

The "real world" makes that almost inevitable. It does say, however, that the actual content of an objective can and should be the subject of discussion and negotiation between the accountable manager and his or her superior. Since it is possible for either or both to be unrealistic in setting initial targets, such a discussion should result in a mutually agreed-on objective that reflects the best thinking of each. The motivation of the accountable manager to effectively carry out the objective normally will be greater as a result of having reached such agreement. Furthermore, it is a reasonable expectation that the final objective will be better than either would have come up with independently, since it should represent the best thinking of both.

15. *It is recorded in writing, with a copy kept and periodically referred to by both superior and subordinate.* Each of us, whether consciously or subconsciously, has a convenient "forgettery." We tend to remember the things that turn out the way we want them to and either forget or modify those things that are less than what we wish. If objectives were not put in writing, it would be relatively easy to look back on what we accomplished and, coincidentally, find that that was what our objectives were. On the other side of the coin, one of the sharpest areas of conflict between subordinate and superior is illustrated by such phrases as, "I thought you were working on something else" or "That's not what we agreed to" or "You didn't tell me that's what you expected." Having objectives in writing will not eliminate all of these problems, but it will provide something more tangible for comparison. Furthermore, it serves as a constant reminder and an effective tracking device for the individual manager to measure the progress of his or her own organizational unit. If we have a well-prepared list of written objectives, we don't have to be told how we stand. We know!

Written objectives also serve as effective communications tools during periodic progress reviews and at such times as we are faced with a requirement to add, modify, or delete certain objectives. Some managers tend to resist writing objectives down because they feel that the objectives are then "cast in concrete" and will be expected to be achieved regardless of changing circumstances. Since none of us is so clairvoyant that we can anticipate everything that will have an impact on our objectives, any such list must be flexible enough so that the objectives can be renegotiated when priorities or uncontrollable circumstances have changed sufficiently to require a reevaluation. At the same time, objectives should not be changed easily just because it looks as if we are not going to accomplish them. To do so resembles the guy who convinced everyone he was a super marksman by painting the target on the fence *after* he had fired the pistol. The suggested MOR Agreement format shown in Fig. 6.5 (p. 102) is a simple, yet practical, tool for recording objectives. Samples of completed MOR Agreements are given in Figs. 6.6 and 6.7 at the end of this chapter.

16. *It is communicated not only in writing, but also in face-to-face discussions between the accountable manager and those subordinates who will be contributing to its attainment.* The manager should never lose sight of the fact that his or her performance toward the achievement of objectives is no better than the performance of the people who will be working on them. In many cases, it is highly likely that these same subordinates will have to contribute some ideas to the establishment of the objective in the first place. One of the best ways to build an effective working team is to get the active involvement of subordinates in both the establishment and the implementation of objectives. Face-to-face discussions in addition to the written word, will help to dispel any misunderstandings that may exist about the objective as well as to clarify the role that each subordinate will play in helping to carry it out.

As was pointed out earlier, this list of guidelines is not designed as a foolproof pattern. It is designed to provide the manager with some realistic and consistent criteria by which to prepare an effective and meaningful written objective. Individual circumstances may dictate the need for exception to one or more of these criteria. When an exception is made, however, it should be with conscious awareness on the part of the accountable manager that the specific ground rule being overlooked does not apply in this particular case. A separate listing (without elaboration) of these guidelines is included at the end of this chapter, together with a set of Key Questions For Evaluating Objectives which can be used as a check on objectives that have been drafted, plus a series of sample objectives that have been modified in line with these guidelines and some sample MOR agreements.

## In Summary

Setting objectives is perhaps the most critical step in this management process we call Management by Objectives and Results. Without valid, clearcut objectives, the remaining functions and activities of management are relatively meaningless. The first three steps in the MOR funnel, Roles and Missions, Key Results Areas, and Indicators, are designed to lead to the establishment of worthwhile objectives. Also, although there are many similarities between setting objectives and defining roles and missions (Chapter 3), they serve a different purpose. Roles-and-missions statements are, in general, continuing and nonspecific in nature. Objectives, on the other hand, are quite specific and have an identified point of completion. The first establishes what kinds of work are to be performed; the second adds substance, direction, and measurability.

The exercise of identifying and writing objectives is deceptively simple. If approached lightly, it will become just another series of "paper exercises." However, by concentrating on proper analysis, determination, and written definition of objectives, either by following the steps in the MOR funnel or by the steps described in Fig. 6.1 (p. 71), the likelihood of achieving a well-balanced, effective, and efficient plan of operation is substantially higher. Your first attempt at doing it will probably prove frustrating and less effective than you would like. However, subsequent efforts will prove to be much easier to do and more satisfying in results. In fact, experience has shown that the manager who works diligently at preparing objectives for *three successive periods* will rarely be satisfied to return to any other approach.

## GUIDELINES FOR WRITING OBJECTIVES

Under normal circumstances, a well-formulated objective meets the following criteria:

1. It starts with the word "to," followed by an action or accomplishment verb.

2. It specifies a single key result to be accomplished.

3. It specifies a target date for its accomplishment.

4. It specifies maximum cost factors.

5. It is as specific and quantitative (and hence measurable and verifiable) as possible.

6. It specifies only the "what" and "when"; it avoids venturing into the "why" and "how."

7. It relates directly to the accountable manager's roles and missions and to higher-level roles, missions, and objectives.

8. It is readily understandable by those who will be contributing to its attainment.

9. It is realistic and attainable, but still represents a significant challenge.

10. It provides maximum payoff on the required investment in time and resources, as compared with other objectives being considered.

11. It is consistent with the resources available or anticipated.

12. It avoids or minimizes dual accountability for achievement when joint effort is required.

13. It is consistent with basic organizational policies and practices.

14. It is willingly agreed to by both superior and subordinate, without undue pressure or coercion.

15. It is recorded in writing, with a copy kept and periodically referred to by both superior and subordinate.

16. It is communicated not only in writing, but also in face-to-face discussions between the accountable manager and those subordinates who will be contributing to its attainment.

## KEY QUESTIONS FOR EVALUATING OBJECTIVES

Use the following questions for your own evaluation of your objectives or as a guide for your colleagues as they assist in that evaluation.

1. Is the objective statement constructed properly? To (action or accomplishment verb) (single key result) by (target date) at (cost).
2. Is it measurable and verifiable?
3. Does it relate directly to the accountable manager's roles and missions and to higher-level roles, missions, and objectives?
4. Can it be readily understood by those who must implement it?
5. Is the objective a realistic and attainable one that still represents a significant challenge to the accountable manager and his or her organizational unit?
6. Will the result, when achieved, justify the expenditure of time and resources required to achieve it?
7. Is the objective consistent with basic organizational policies and practices?
8. Can the accountability for final results be clearly established?

## SAMPLE OBJECTIVES

Here are several statements of objectives typical of managers from various public-sector organizations. They are shown in their original form, followed by comments on them, and then in a revised form to make them consistent with the guidelines. Comments are related primarily to construction of the objective statement, specificity, and measurability, with no attempt here to examine validity or relevance, which are dictated by individual circumstances.

*Original.*    Improve Basic Skills effectiveness in our school.

*Comments.*    What is "effectiveness"? How will you know when you get there?

*Revised.*    To improve student performance in Basic Skills by a minimum of 10%, as measured by standard tests, by May 31 at a direct cost not to exceed 150 work-hours and $1000.

*Original.*    Develop and implement more effective program measures (continuous).

*Comments.*    This comes closer to a part of a roles-and-missions statement. Set a more specific target in the most critical program areas and then set new ones once those have been implemented. What is your basis for determining "more effective"?

*Revised.*    To develop and implement, by January 1, new measurement methods, in line with national criteria, for the two most critical program areas, as determined by unit staff, at a cost not to exceed 200 work-hours.

*Original.*    Study and report on alternative methods of acquiring 30-acre parcel adjacent to MOR Freeway and funds available for future development purposes.

*Comments.*    "Study and report" are only activities. If the intention is to acquire the parcel, the objective should proceed with that in mind. The objective can still be modified or rejected if the initial data developed make the proposal unacceptable.

*Revised.*    To initiate acquisition of 30-acre parcel adjacent to MOR Freeway, using the most cost-effective method available (to be determined), by November 1, at a cost of initiation not to exceed 100 work-hours and $500.

*Original.*    Report on long-range Police and Fire space needs and the economics and feasibility of alternative site locations for either separate or joint facilities.

*Comments.*   "Report" is only one step related to an objective on long-range facility plans. Focus on the implementation of a plan.

*Revised.*   To develop and begin implementation of a long-range Police and Fire facility plan by March 1 at a development cost not to exceed 250 work-hours and $2000.

*Original.*   To improve personnel management by conversion of bureau records to microfiche.

*Comments.*   First part of statement is justification. Assume that the conversion is justified and focus instead on the specific results.

*Revised.*   To complete conversion of bureau records to microfiche by October 1977 at a contract cost of $15,100 and a coordination cost not to exceed 200 work-hours.

*Original.*   Improve the overall management of the food stamp program to ensure compliance with federal and state regulations, to increase the accuracy of eligibility and benefit determination to eliminate abuses to the program, and to ensure optimum food stamp coupon issuance service.

*Comments.*   This is more "noble intentions" than a statement of results to be achieved. Can you measure the accuracy of eligibility and benefit determination? If so, concentrate on that and avoid explaining why you are doing it in the objective statement itself.

*Revised.*   To establish, by January 1, a system of validating eligibility of food stamp applicants that will ensure a minimum 95% accuracy by June 30 at an implementation cost not to exceed 200 work-hours and no increase in current budget for maintenance.

*Original.*   To change over from direct auditing of agencies served to monitoring their internal auditing efforts by the end of next fiscal year.

*Comments.*   Although this could, technically, be measured at the point indicated, would it be more useful to set a series of more specific, shorter-term objectives, possibly starting with a pilot effort? Incidentally, I would recommend your selecting an agency in which the degree of cooperation and support is likely to be highest for your pilot effort. In that way, you can debug your changeover process in a favorable climate before you have to tackle the difficult ones.

*Revised.* To complete changeover to internal auditing in Agency A by March 31 at a planning cost of 200 work-hours and an implementation cost of 300 work-hours. To modify changeover plan and have ready for further implementation by May 1 at an additional cost not to exceed 100 work-hours.

*Original.* To accelerate hospitalized patient use of alternative care through positive patient and family counseling.

*Comments.* How do you measure this — ratio of hospitalized to alternative care, length of hospital stay, percentage of admissions returned in given period? Also, don't limit your alternatives by specifying the "how" (the counseling reference).

*Revised.* To increase the rate of return to the community within 21 days of admission from a monthly average of 65% to 80%, effective March 31 and thereafter, at no increase in current social work staff.

_____ 's MOR Agreement from _____ to _____

KEY RESULTS AREAS
Indicators                                                    Objectives

_____        _____
_____        _____
_____        _____
_____        _____
_____        _____
_____        _____
_____        _____
_____        _____
_____        _____
_____        _____
_____        _____
_____        _____
_____        _____
_____        _____
_____        _____
_____        _____
_____        _____
_____        _____
_____        _____
_____        _____
_____        _____
_____        _____
_____        _____
_____        _____

PROGRESS REVIEW SCHEDULE _____

**Fig. 6.5** MOR Agreement format.

Area Manager's MOR Agreement from 10/1 to 9/30 (Sample)

(NTE = Not to exceed)

| KEY RESULTS AREAS<br>Indicators | Objectives |
|---|---|
| OPERATING RESULTS<br>    Production plan | 1.  To produce operating results as specified in annual production plan within assigned budget. |
| OPERATIONAL PLANNING<br>    MOR application | 2.  To initiate use of MOR for operational planning in each unit reporting to me, by March 1 at a direct cost NTE 240 work-hours and $1000. |
| PUBLIC/COMMUNITY RELATIONS<br>    # public information<br>       presentations | 3.  To make a minimum of five presentations interpreting agency's mission and programs before local civic and business groups during current fiscal year at cost NTE 75 work-hours. |
| UNIT ADMINISTRATION<br>    Amount of time spent | 4.  To reduce the amount of my time spent on office administration from a monthly average of 80 hours to 30 hours by January 31 with no increase in staff. |
| MANAGEMENT COMMUNICATIONS | 5.  To maintain current level of communications with regional and headquarters offices. |
| STAFF DEVELOPMENT<br>    # subordinates with devel-<br>       opment plan | 6.  To have a mutually agreed on and implemented development plan with each of my five key subordinates, effective January 1, within existing training budget and at a monthly investment NTE 30 hours of my time. |
| ANTICIPATION/INNOVATION<br>    # new ideas | 7.  To have at least one new service or administrative idea approved and implemented each quarter, with no increase in budget. |
| ORGANIZATIONAL RELATIONSHIPS | 8.  To establish and implement, by January 1, a plan for visitation of key office personnel to major organizations served, at a monthly cost NTE 20 work-hours. |
| SELF-DEVELOPMENT<br>    Training completed and applied | 9.  To complete self-study program on time management and apply at least two new ideas to my job by December 31, within existing training budget and work-hour investment NTE 10 hours. |

PROGRESS REVIEW SCHEDULE    First Friday, even-numbered months.

**Fig. 6.6** Sample MOR Agreement.

Police Chief's MOR Agreement from 1/1 to 6/30 (Sample)

(NTE = Not to exceed)

| KEY RESULTS AREAS<br>Indicators | Objectives |
|---|---|
| OPERATING RESULTS<br>  Master plan<br>  Rate of increase in crimes<br>  # vehicular accidents | 1.  To provide police services as specified in department master operating plan within existing budget.<br><br>2.  To reduce the rate of increase of total Part One crimes by 3% before 6/30 at no increase in budget.<br><br>3.  To reduce the number of vehicular accidents on city streets by a minimum of 5% over prior year's level at no increase in budget. |
| STRATEGIC PLANNING<br>  Approved long-range plan | 4.  To prepare and secure Council approval for a long-range expansion plan by March 31 at a cost NTE 100 work-hours. |
| PUBLIC RELATIONS<br>  Public forums | 5.  To promote and conduct a minimum of one "Meet Your Police Department" public forums each month at specified locations throughout the city at a cost NTE 150 work-hours and $500. |
| ORGANIZATIONAL RELATIONSHIPS<br>  Intercommunity cooperation | 6.  To reach agreement with counterparts in all bordering communities by 2/15 on common standards for traffic enforcement at a cost NTE 100 work-hours. |
| ANTICIPATION/INNOVATION<br>  "Blue sky" meetings | 7.  To personally conduct a monthly "blue sky" meeting of randomly selected department employees, each meeting to produce a minimum of one new idea each for current and future department operations, at a monthly investment NTE 40 work-hours. |
| STAFF DEVELOPMENT<br>  # qualified replacements | 8.  To have identified at least two qualified replacement candidates for each key position reporting to me, by 5/31 within existing budget. |
| PROFESSIONAL LEADERSHIP<br>  Association participation | 9.  To serve as a member of the Educational Committee for the International Association of Police Chiefs at a cost NTE 60 work-hours and $300 direct expense. |

PROGRESS REVIEW SCHEDULE    Last working day of each month.

**Fig. 6.7** Sample MOR Agreement.

# 7

# PREPARING ACTION PLANS

Preparing action plans is what we have described as "determining how to achieve specific objectives." It incorporates five substeps, as follows:

1. *Programming* — establishing a sequence of actions to follow in reaching objectives.
2. *Scheduling* — establishing time requirements for objectives and action steps.
3. *Budgeting* — determining and assigning the resources required to reach objectives.
4. *Fixing Accountability* — determining who will see to the accomplishment of objectives and action steps.
5. *Reviewing and Reconciling* — testing and revising a tentative plan, as needed, prior to commitment to action.

Once we have determined where we want to go, by setting our objectives, the next step is planning how to get there. That's where the action plan comes in. This is the "how" that we suggested you avoid when writing an objective. Since there normally are several different ways to get to a given location, the action plan allows us to examine different alternatives and determine what approach makes the best sense under existing circumstances. Consequently, even though some objectives may be largely prescribed from "on high," the accountable manager can still exercise substantial judgment on how it will be accomplished. *Every objective must have an action plan.* It may be very simple, or it may be very complex. It may be spelled out in writing, or it may be carried around in the accountable manager's head. Regardless of what form it takes, an objective cannot be achieved without some sort of an action plan. Since the primary purpose of an action plan is to serve as a tool for the accountable manager's use and not as an approval document, it should be prepared in as simple a manner as possible, with a view toward making the manager's job easier, not more complicated.

In the first section of this chapter, we focus primarily on the *programming* substep, which provides a data base for each of the other substeps. Next, we will cover *scheduling, budgeting, fixing accountability,* and *reviewing and reconciling,* in greater detail. For many situations, the information provided in the first section will meet the average manager's requirements in preparing an action plan. The information in the rest of the chapter can be used, at the manager's option, for further analysis when it makes sense to do so.

## Programming

### Why Should We Program an Objective?

Have you ever started out on a trip somewhere and, after having gone part way, stopped to look at a map or ask directions, only to discover — when it was too late to change course — that you could have taken a shorter or easier route? On a trip that you make often, you are probably already familiar with the various shortcuts. However, even then, have you ever discovered, on the one hand, that a new expressway has been opened up or, on the other, that some rather formidable roadblocks or detours have been established along your usual route? It won't come as any great surprise to discover that this is a fairly common occurrence among travelers. The same principle applies in pursuing a particular objective.

Programming an objective is, in effect, laying out the route you are going to follow in order to ensure its accomplishment.

This procedure allows you to evaluate the various methods by which you might work toward an objective, *before* you commit yourself to action. Although programming will not guarantee that the best means will be selected, your batting average will, in general, be substantially higher than if you went ahead without thinking about the available alternatives. Furthermore, the very act of programming may reveal that your original estimate of what would be required to accomplish the objective was inaccurate, and if so, it will still be possible to reconsider the objective before committing your resources. A decision not to pursue an objective at this stage can be just as productive as a decision to go ahead with it. It may be too late to reconsider if this discovery is made after the action is well under way. Proper programming can also aid substantially in making the best use of your resources, principally your human resources, and in providing the kind of visibility necessary to ensure that you remain "on target."

### The Alternative Evaluation Chart

Since in most situations there are several ways in which a given objective might be accomplished, let's take a look at an analytical tool called an Alternative Evaluation Chart, which can help in the selection process, as applied to a typical objective. For example, let's assume that a major federal agency has approximately 2500 managers, all but 100 of whom are situated in 9 regional and 180 local offices throughout the United States. A new Affirmative Action policy and set of implementing regulations have just been issued that will require several significant changes on the part of managers at all levels in all offices. My unit has been charged with the responsibility for seeing that these regulations are implemented effectively in all offices within three months at the lowest possible cost consistent with effective results. In my unit are five professional staff members, two clerical staff, and myself. Our starting objective is: "To initiate the effective implementation of the new Affirmative Action policy and regulations in all offices within three months at a maximum cost to be determined."

Using a facsimile of the Alternative Evaluation Chart (see Fig. 7.1) on a blank easel pad, the other professional staff members and I meet to brainstorm various alternatives for achieving this objective, and we come up with the following list. (There undoubtedly are other alternatives worth considering, but we will limit our analysis to the 11 alternatives identified here.)

1. Issue a directive from the Agency Director.
2. Train all Agency managers at series of meetings in Washington.
3. Train all Agency managers at series of meetings in each region.
4. Send staff members from our unit to all local offices to train managers.
5. Regional EEO (Equal Employment Opportunity) administrators train local managers following train-the-trainer effort by our staff.
6. Train one representative from each local office to train all remaining managers in their respective offices.
7. Filmed or videotaped training program to be distributed to all offices.
8. Audiocassette training program to be distributed to all offices.
9. Train all managers via a telephone conference call to all offices.
10. Training manual to be distributed to all offices.
11. Contract consultants to train managers in all local offices.

Having completed our brainstorming, we go back over the list and determine that three of the alternatives (2, 7, and 9) are clearly impractical because of cost, time limitations, or logistics problems. Therefore, we eliminate them from consideration. That leaves the remaining eight as having at least a possibility for potential use. We then decide to evaluate them according

ALTERNATIVE EVALUATION CHART

OBJECTIVE: _____

| ALTERNATIVES | CONTRIBUTION TO OBJECTIVE | COST | FEASI-BILITY | OTHER* | NOTES |
|---|---|---|---|---|---|
|  |  |  |  |  |  |

*Other possible criteria: impact on other objectives, impact on other organizations, absence of negative consequences, availability of resources, personal preference.

First: Brainstorm alternatives, then eliminate those that are impractical.
Then: Evaluate the remaining alternatives vertically against each of the criteria.
Alternative evaluation methods: High-Medium-Low; rank order; scale of 1–5; assigned weights related to importance of criteria; add up total "score" for each.

**Fig. 7.1** Alternative Evaluation Chart. (Copyright 1974 by George L. Morrisey, MOR Associates, Buena Park, CA 90622)

to the three basic criteria of *contribution to the objective, cost,*
and *feasibility,* using a scale of 1–5 in making our judgments.
We look first at *contribution to the objective,* which is
evaluated on the assumption that the alternative under consideration can be accomplished. Here, we judge the first alternative, "Issue directive," to be a necessary element, but one that
by itself is unlikely to make a major contribution; therefore we
rank it "2" on the scale. The next two possible alternatives,
"Train managers at region" and "Send our staff to train locally," we judge to have a high potential contribution, so we
rank each as "5." Each of the remaining options is evaluated at
a lesser amount, as shown in the first column in Fig. 7.2. (Our
reasons for the various ratings are not important for our purposes of illustrating the process, although you can probably
deduce what they are.)

Next, we look at the *cost* column. Here, to make our num-
bering system consistent, a high cost (negative factor) is identified as "1" and a low cost (positive factor) as "5," with varying
costs estimated at the other levels. Thus we find that #1, "Issue
directive," is our least expensive alternative and that #11,
"Contract consultants," will carry the largest direct cost, with
each of the others at varying degrees in between.

*Feasibility,* the third column, asks, "All things considered,
including time available, capability, support required, etc.,
what is the likelihood that this alternative will work?" Again
assigning a high number as favorable, we discover that the
directive, the audiocassette program, and the training manual
appear the most feasible, with the others somewhat less so.

In this case, we have decided that each of the criteria has
equal value, so we simply add the totals across. Had we determined that there were differing values, we could have assigned
weights to each of the criteria and multiplied the ratings accordingly. (The totals we have arrived at appear in the last
column in Fig. 7.2. We make no attempt to justify these totals
here, since your evaluation in your circumstances could, quite
legitimately, result in different totals.)

As a result of the analysis we have gone through here, we
conclude that a combination of some of these alternatives will

ALTERNATIVE EVALUATION CHART

OBJECTIVE: To initiate the effective implementation of the new Affirmative Action policy and regulations in all offices within 3 months at maximum cost to be determined.

| ALTERNATIVES | CONTRIBUTION TO OBJECTIVE | COST | FEASI-BILITY | OTHER* | NOTES |
|---|---|---|---|---|---|
| 1. Issue directive | 2 | 5 | 5 | | 12 |
| 2. ~~Train managers---Washington~~ | | | | | |
| 3. Train managers - region | 5 | 2 | 2 | | 9 |
| 4. Our staff - local offices | 5 | 2 | 3 | | 10 |
| 5. EEO administrators train | 4 | 3 | 4 | | 11 |
| 6. Local office reps train | 3 | 2 | 2 | | 7 |
| 7. ~~Film or videotape~~ | | | | | |
| 8. Audiocassette program | 3 | 4 | 5 | | 12 |
| 9. ~~Telephone conference call~~ | | | | | |
| 10. Training manual | 2 | 4 | 5 | | 11 |
| 11. Contract consultants | 4 | 1 | 3 | | 8 |

*Other possible criteria: impact on other objectives, impact on other organizations, absence of negative consequences, availability of resources, personal preference.

First: Brainstorm alternatives, then eliminate those that are impractical.
Then: Evaluate the remaining alternatives vertically against each of the criteria.
Alternative evaluation methods: High-Medium-Low; rank order; scale of 1–5; assigned weights related to importance of criteria; add up total "score" for each.

**Fig. 7.2** Example of Alternative Evaluation Chart.

give us the most effective overall approach. We regard the directive from the agency director as both essential and inevitable. For the major part of the effort, we are proposing the development of an audiocassette training program combined with a limited training manual, with supplementary instruction and guidance to be provided by the regional EEO administrators. We believe that our staff should develop the materials, train each of the EEO administrators, and be available as backup trainers if they cannot meet all of the requirements.

Once again, this illustration is only an example of how this particular tool can be used. The many variations to its use are limited only by your own imagination. The Alternative Evaluation Chart can be used individually or in a small group, such as a manager and his or her immediate subordinates. Some of its advantages are:

1. It is relatively easy to do and can be completed fairly quickly.

2. Most people enjoy brainstorming as an activity which is both mentally stimulating and fun.

3. Some ideas almost certainly will be generated that might not have been readily apparent as a result of some other approaches.

4. Alternatives can be evaluated somewhat more objectively when several criteria are used to the degree that the most practical course of action may be different from what might have been the most obvious choice at the outset.

5. Finally, when this is done as a group effort, those participating in the discussion are far more likely to support the ultimate decision, since they will have had a part in making it.

## What Other Approaches to Programming Can Be Used?

Not all objectives will require the use of a tool like the Alternative Evaluation Chart to choose from among several alternatives. However, there is still a place for some rational thinking in determining what factors should influence the approach to be taken. We will identify here several other programming approaches or influencing factors which have been suggested by members of management. Undoubtedly other approaches as good or better for your purposes will come to mind as you review this listing.

1. *Sequential.* Certain activities automatically fall in line sequentially, so that each step is dependent on the successful completion of the one immediately preceding it — for example, design of an interpretive document, preparation, distribution, etc.

2. *Like effort.* Two or more steps that require similar types of effort, such as fact-finding visits to field locations, can be grouped together to conserve resources.

3. *Individual-oriented.* Steps that relate to the particular capability of an individual worker may have to be programmed out of sequence to fit the time periods when that person is available.

4. *Key equipment loading.* Certain steps may have to be planned to coincide with availability of critical equipment, such as computers or equipment with long lead time or expensive start-up requirements.

5. *End event.* Some program steps may relate to specific end events connected with other objectives.

6. *Program schedule.* Legislative- or executive-directed programs and their related schedules may dictate the means of programming certain objectives.

7. *Decision tree.* An objective may have to be programmed one step at a time, with the understanding that decisions on subsequent steps will be based on data accumulated at the conclusion of each intermediate step.

8. *Environmental conditions.* Weather is an example of an environmental condition with a potentially strong influence on certain program steps, usually those that have to be performed out of doors.

9.  *Political sensitivities.* The influence of key legislators, other administrative agencies, public opinion, etc., obviously must be reckoned with by the realistic public-sector manager with a job to do.

10. *Personnel loading.* Availability of critical skill groups, in relation to other assignments (internally) or the labor market (externally), may well determine how an objective is to be programmed.

11. *Specific events.* Monthly reports, legislative committee hearings, open houses, visiting dignitaries, are only a sampling of special events that might dictate the way a particular objective should be programmed.

These represent just a few of the programming approaches being used successfully by managers. Individual circumstances will determine what specific approach should be followed, whether it be one or more of these or one totally different.

## How Do We Program an Objective?

As we mentioned at the beginning of this chapter, the steps to be followed in laying out a program for any objective are relatively simple and familiar. In fact, identifying them will become so obvious that we are listing them with some misgiving. The steps bear a strong resemblance to the traditional steps in problem solving. Don't let their simplicity lull you into a false sense of security, however. They still must be translated into specific actions if the objective is to be accomplished.

This method of programming includes six steps, but they may not all apply to a given objective. In many situations, two or more steps may be combined. Also, the specific sequence may vary, and some steps may be repeated several times (such as step 2 below). But virtually any objective can be programmed by use of a version of this approach. These six steps are:

1.  *Study the situation and select the method.* This step may require a substantial amount of fact-finding and analysis leading up to a decision, or it may involve simply looking at the situation briefly and deciding what method should be followed

in pursuing the objective. The use of the Alternative Evaluation Chart is one technique that can be applied here as well as in the next step.

2. *Gain agreement and support.* This may require conferring with subordinates, superiors, higher management, support units, client/user representatives, legislators, other affected agencies, or anyone else whose support is vital. It may be an extremely critical step or one of relatively little importance, depending on the nature of the objective and the degree of support necessary. The key is in remembering to give attention to this step *before* the plan is completely laid out, for two reasons: (a) there may be legitimate factors to be considered that may not be readily apparent to the manager preparing the plan, and this could save much unnecessary effort; and (b) others are much more likely to support the plan if they have been involved during its formative stages.

3. *Develop the plan.* This involves breaking down the method decided on into a sequence of events to be followed in reaching the objective. Usually, but not necessarily, it is the most complex step in programming an objective. The three questions under "Programming Breakdown" will help lend substance to this step.

4. *Test and review the plan.* This step could include a pilot run of the plan to see whether it works, or it could involve just a brief review with a few key individuals to see if what looks good on paper will really work. It could be a part of the approval cycle and might be incorporated into steps 2 or 3. It usually will include a provision for modification of the plan on the basis of test results.

5. *Implement.* At some point the plan must be translated into action. This may be merely the end point of the objective, or it may be the largest single step in the plan, with a heavy production tracking requirement.

6. *Follow up.* In any objective of reasonable complexity, there must be a provision for review and assessment of progress, followed by modification of the plan as necessary. This

aspect will be covered in much more depth in Chapter 8. It should be identified in the action plan, however.

There it is! Simple, isn't it? It's so simple that it can trap us. The problem with most simple, logical, commonsense approaches is that we tend to take them for granted and don't give them the attention they deserve. Although it is not necessary to take specific action under every step, we must discipline ourselves to consciously consider each of them in the planning process. At the same time, if we approach the process of programming an objective in a mechanical manner without careful examination of the nature and importance of each action step, we are not much better off than if we had proceeded without a clearly defined plan of action. This approach identifies a logical sequence that can be applied to most objectives.

## Programming Breakdown

In order to make the programming of a specific objective more workable, we should ask ourselves the following questions:

1.   *What major steps are necessary to achieve the results identified in the objective?* "Major" is what is vital to the accomplishment of the objective and/or involves a large block of effort. Such a step will be clearly distinguishable from others in the plan and may be affected by one or more of the factors identified earlier under programming approaches. This question should point up broad areas of accomplishment and avoid details, particularly when other people will be involved in implementing the objective. *A major action step can and, in many cases will, become a lower-level objective for a subordinate to accomplish.* "Coordinate with and gain concurrence of field units and other related organizations" could be a major action step in an objective that would make a significant change in a service that is being projected.

2.   *What priorities should be assigned to each major step?* Which steps are more important than others and should therefore get more attention? Which steps must precede which other ones? An obvious illustration is the requirement to train

people in the use of a new system before it can be implemented. Priorities are also related to scheduling factors, which are discussed later in this chapter.

3. *What are the detail steps necessary to support the major steps which have been identified?* Once the overall picture of how an objective is to be accomplished has been determined, these major steps can be broken down into workable units. This programming pattern is a derivative of the process introduced in the early 1960s as a part of the Department of Defense contracting procedures, known as *work breakdown structure* or *work package management.* Stated simply, it means taking a major block of effort and continually subdividing it until reaching a series of individual tasks that can be performed by individual workers. Whenever possible, the determination of these detail steps should be delegated to those subordinates who will be expected to carry them out. These "how-to's," in general, will be performed more effectively and efficiently by the employee who has had a say in determining them. The superior's prime concern is that the work gets done within agreed-upon cost and schedule limitations. The means of getting it done should be left up to the subordinate, providing that the means are compatible with the rest of the operation.

The action steps identified through this process need not be complex. As with the objectives themselves, the action steps should be worded in terms that are meaningful to those with a critical need to know. They should be as brief and simple as is needed for a clear understanding on the part of those accountable for results. Normally, a written action plan will contain between five and ten major steps. Although there will be exceptions, less than five may indicate that a written action plan is unnecessary; having more than ten is likely to be getting into more detail than is appropriate. A summary of these programming guidelines and their systematic breakdown, plus a list of "Key Questions for Evaluating Action Steps" are included at the end of this chapter, together with some examples of objectives that have been programmed.

## Action Plan Format

Figure 7.3 shows a very simple worksheet that a manager can use in preparing an action plan. I have deliberately called it a "format" rather than a "form" because I think its usefulness will be severely curtailed if it ends up as a standard form, with a number on it, that is issued from a central source. My experience with many organizations, particularly those in the public sector, is that official "forms" are usually completed primarily to satisfy the needs of someone other than the person completing it. That's a necessary requirement in some instances, but not in this one. Establishing this as a standard form, I am afraid, would have the effect of creating one more piece of paper for an already overburdened manager to complete and submit "up the line." That is *not* its purpose. Rather, its value should be seen in helping the accountable manager get a handle on what needs to be done to accomplish his or her objectives. To that end, the manager should feel perfectly free to use as much or as little of the worksheet as will be helpful and to modify, add, or delete any items that will make it a more useful tool.

In using this sheet, we start by entering the objective in the space provided at the top. Next, we list the major action steps, plus those detail steps that are critical to the manager, in the space provided at the left. In Fig. 7.4, we have taken the objective we used earlier in connection with the Alternative Evaluation Chart and have prepared an action to follow. Once again, this plan is for illustration purposes only and will not necessarily be an appropriate one for you to follow in working on a similar objective. (By the way, here is a good example of how a major program step in an objective, "develop audiocassette program and manual," could become an objective in itself for the staff member with that assignment.)

Once the action steps have been identified, we must next establish target dates or time spans within which each step must be completed, followed by an estimate of the cost of accomplishing that particular step in terms of dollars for out-of-pocket expense and hours for the human effort required. The "By Whom" columns fix accountability for that particular step.

ACTION PLAN

What is your objective? To (action or accomplishment verb) (single key result) by (target date) at (cost).

| ACTION STEPS | BY WHEN | COSTS $ | COSTS HOURS | BY WHOM US | BY WHOM THEM |
|---|---|---|---|---|---|
| | | | | | |

**Fig. 7.3** Action Plan format. (Copyright 1973 by George L. Morrisey, MOR Associates, Buena Park, CA 90622)

ACTION PLAN (Sample) (D + # = Today + # working days

What is your objective? To (action or accomplishment verb) (single key result) by (target date) at (cost).
To initiate the effective implementation of the new Affirmative Action policy and
regulations in all offices within 3 months at a maximum cost of $12,000 and 900
work-hours of direct effort.

| ACTION STEPS | BY WHEN | COSTS $ | COSTS HOURS | BY WHOM US | BY WHOM THEM |
|---|---|---|---|---|---|
| 1. Establish method (combination of audiocassette program and manual, EEO administrators training at local level, our staff training EEO administrators and serving as backup) | Done | | | | |
| 2. Gain agreement and support | | | | | |
| a) Our staff | Done | | | | |
| b) Upper management | D + 2 | | 4 | George | Deputy |
| c) Regional management | D + 7 | | 2 | George | Deputy |
| d) EEO administrators | D + 7 | | 12 | Mary | |
| 3. Develop audiocassette program and manual | D +20 | | | George | |
| a) Objectives and outline | D + 1 | | 2 | Carlos | |
| b) Review and agreement | D + 2 | | 2 | George | Deputy |
| c) Script preparation | D + 7 | | 16 | Carlos | |
| d) Manual preparation | D + 7 | | 24 | John | |
| e) Review and agreement | D +10 | | 2 | George | Deputy |
| f) Record audiocassettes | D +10 | 100 | 8 | Geo/Carlos | Contractor |
| g) Duplicate audiocassettes | D +20 | 1000 | 8 | Carlos | Contractor |
| h) Publish manual | D +20 | 600 | 16 | John | Reproductions |
| 4. Develop training plan | D +20 | | 24 | Mary | |
| 5. Train EEO administrators | D +25 | 4000 ↑ travel ↓ 6000 | 240 | Mary/Staff | Deputy & EEO Admin. |
| 6. Establish implementation schedule | D +25 | | 16 | Mary | EEO Admin. |
| -- Start | D +30 | | 350 | Mary | EEO Admin. |
| 7. Followup and evaluation | | | | George & staff | |
| a) After EEO administrators' training program | D +25 | | 30 | " | |
| b) After first 20 offices | D +35 | | 30 | " | |
| c) After program completed | D +55 | 11,700 | 30 816 | " | Deputy |

**Fig. 7.4** Sample Action Plan.

"Us" refers to the accountable manager and anyone from within his or her organizational unit (there will always be a name in this column, even when most of the work will be done elsewhere). "Them" refers to anyone outside the unit — superiors, other organizations, contractors, client/user groups — who will be making a significant contribution to that particular step. (These three elements — scheduling, budgeting, and fixing accountability — will be dealt with in more detail later in this chapter.)

In addition to the obvious value of laying out a logical plan for achieving an objective, the action plan format has another significant value. It enables us to partially validate some of the critical assumptions we made in setting the objective itself — *before* we are firmly committed to action. Entries in the "By When" column may make it clear that the target date for completing the objective is not realistic. The "Costs" columns frequently require an upward revision of the original estimate for the objective. (Most of us tend to make initial cost estimates on the low side, partially because of ego and partially because some critical elements are overlooked.) With a breakdown of costs in an action plan, we can usually do a more realistic job of estimating than can be done with the objective itself. The "By Whom" columns can highlight: (1) a potentially improper balance of workload distribution among staff members; (2) improper accountability for the objective itself (if the responsibility for most of the action plan falls on one key subordinate, it probably should be seen as that individual's objective); and (3) potential problems in coordination with individuals or units that are not under the direct control of the accountable manager.

This kind of visibility is tremendously useful. If we discover these potential problems at this stage, we have three basic options: (1) to modify the objective to accommodate these factors; (2) to modify the action plan to bring it more into line with limitations specified in the objective; or, if necessary, (3) to postpone or abandon the objective entirely. *A decision at this stage not to pursue an objective is just as valid as one to go ahead with it.* The cost of the planning effort to this point is "peanuts" compared with the cost of effort expended on what turns out later to be an unrealistic objective. This further reinforces the statement made in the previous chapter that "a *poor* estimate is still better than *no* estimate." At least a poor estimate provides us with a comparison point. Since in most situations our estimating accuracy increases as pieces of action become smaller and more precise, this visibility provides us with something of a counterbalance to the natural reaction that most of us have to immediately go to work on an objective because its benefits are obviously "good." Remember, an objective has beneficial value only in relation to the cost of achieving it and to the likelihood of its being achieved at all.

## Scheduling, Budgeting, Fixing Accountability, and Reviewing and Reconciling

The remainder of this chapter will go into more detail on the substeps of Scheduling, Budgeting, Fixing Accountability, and Reviewing and Reconciling. The first part of this chapter presented sufficient information to meet the action-planning needs for many, if not most, objectives. My recommendation is that you become generally familiar with the ideas presented in this section, but that you use them only when they will provide you with significant help in your planning efforts. If you attempt to apply them systematically to every objective, you will run the risk of becoming bogged down in excessive detail, which may get in the way of your doing the job.

### What Is Scheduling?

Our definition of scheduling is "establishing time requirements for objectives and action steps." Setting objectives has a time factor built into it. However, the time-phasing of each objective in relation to other objectives may require attention to some of the scheduling factors discussed here. Realistic scheduling is even more critical in programming, since the time-phasing of each action step must be planned in such a way as to ensure the satisfactory completion of the objective.

May we emphasize here, however, that *scheduling is related to calendar time only* — to the number of calendar days required to complete an objective or an action step or the actual date by which it will be completed. It is not related to the number of work hours or workdays of effort required. That is a function of budgeting, which is covered later in this chapter.

## Should Each Action Step Have a Schedule?

The answer in general is yes. Although there may be some action steps to which the actual assignment of a time block is somewhat academic — for example, management review and concurrence — nevertheless we have still gone through the management activity of scheduling if we do no more than designate where in the sequence of events the particular step must take place. For most steps, particularly those requiring a significant amount of effort, the designation of a particular time or time block is highly desirable, if not essential, if the objective is to be satisfactorily accomplished. The discipline of meeting a deadline is an action motivator that should not be taken lightly. Without such milestones, many objectives probably would never be reached.

## How Do We Establish a Realistic Schedule?

Perhaps the easiest way to schedule the action steps in an objective is to start at the end point and work back. Since the completion point of the objective (the end of the forecast period in the case of a continuing objective) has already been determined, this is a logical starting place. Since the action steps have already been placed in priority order, we assign a time period within which we can reasonably expect to complete each step, starting with the last step before completion. The same process can be used in forward motion as well, beginning with a go-ahead date and working forward in sequence, thus in effect withholding a completion date for the objective until all of the action steps have been scheduled.

If the reverse process (from end point backwards) is used, and if each action step is assigned a block of time sequentially, we may be faced with the dramatic realization that we should have started work on this objective six months ago. Since it is somewhat unrealistic to attempt to turn the calendar back, we must then analyze the action steps to determine which can be done concurrently or in an overlap relationship with other steps.

In effect, this process of scheduling follows the basic principles involved in PERT (Program Evaluation Review Technique). Without getting into the technical jargon or some of the many complex factors that can be involved in PERT, we can outline the approach as follows.

1. *Break each action step down into a series of events or milestones* (when necessary or desirable). For example, the action step "train employees in use of ABC system," might require the following events:

   a) Start.

   b) Determine nature and content of training.

   c) Develop training program.

   d) Commence training.

   e) Complete training.

(Each of these events could be further broken down into additional events if the effort is large enough and if there is an operational advantage in doing so. For our purposes here, we will keep it relatively simple.)

2. *Place a time estimate on the activity required to move from one event to the next.* For example:

   a) Start — one-half day.

   b) Determine nature and content of training — three days.

   c) Develop training program — one day.

   d) Commence training — ten days.

   e) Complete training.

3. *Determine which action steps and/or events must be done in sequence and which ones can be in parallel with or independent of one another.*

4. *Determine which sequence of events comprises the longest cumulative length of time and establish that as the "critical path,"* or the sequence on which the entire schedule depends.

For illustration purposes, let's use the following objective, with the numbers representing action steps and the letters the events within each step.

*To install the ABC system throughout the Central Office within 45 days of Go-Ahead at (cost):*

1. Study system and determine its specific applications.
2. Prepare and reproduce the necessary forms for implementing system.
   a) Prepare.
   b) Reproduce.
3. Train employees in use of system.
   a) Determine nature and content of training.
   b) Develop training program.
   c) Commence training.
   d) Complete training.
4. Test system in practice with pilot group.
   a) Determine pilot group.
   b) Train pilot group.
   c) Implement test.
   d) Checkpoint — review and modify.
   e) Checkpoint II — review and modify.
   f) Final checkpoint — review and modify.
5. Implement system.

The establishment of the critical path for this objective is illustrated in Fig. 7.5. The circled numbers represent the events just listed, the numbers over the arrows represent the calendar

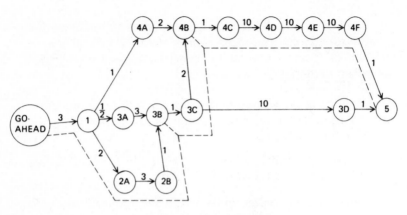

**Fig. 7.5** PERT network.

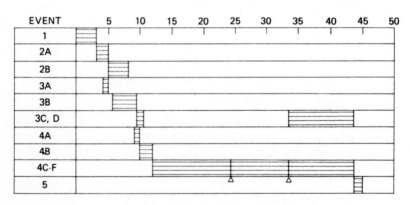

**Fig. 7.6** Milestone chart.

days required to proceed from one event to the next, and the dotted line represents the critical path.

Another method of laying out a schedule is to use a milestone chart. Figure 7.6 shows such a chart as prepared for the same objective as in Fig. 7.5.

There are numerous other methods of laying out a schedule. Two of the simplest are: (1) putting start and completion dates in writing at the conclusion of each identified action step, and (2) marking an ordinary calendar with critical-activity checkpoints. Some of the control methods described in Chapter 8 can be used for scheduling purposes as well. And, of course, the action plan format shown in Fig. 7.3 (p. 119) covers this in the "By When" column.

## What Influences a Schedule?

As you approach the activity of scheduling in relation to objectives and action steps, many factors will have an impact on it. Some of these are within the control of the accountable manager; some are not. Here are a few typical factors that could have a significant impact on the way you do your scheduling:

1. *End point.* This is perhaps the most obvious influencing factor, particularly if that point is firmly established and immovable.

2. *Personnel availability.* Frequently the key to the integrity of the schedule, this can represent many impediments, e.g., epidemics, people out of town, new personnel authorized but not yet hired.

3. *Estimated work hours.* If the estimate is and must remain tight, work may have to be scheduled at the "most favorable" rather than the "most expeditious" time.

4. *Presently assigned work.* There may be conflicts with other equally or more important objectives or with effort that cannot be interrupted.

5. *Key equipment availability.* Open time may not be at most convenient time in terms of the schedule.

6. *Area.* This includes such slow-down factors as extremely close quarters, heavy personnel or equipment concentration or traffic, erratic terrain, etc.

7. *Geographic time zones.* Consideration must frequently be given to coordination or interfacing requirements with people who work in different time zones, such as West Coast versus East Coast.

8. *Workaround points.* Holidays, vacations, key management meetings, VIP visitations, etc., will take their toll.

9. *Weather.* This is particularly important if part of the effort is performed outdoors.

10. *Inputs from others.* Noncontrollable inputs from suppliers, customers/clients/users, legislative groups, other units, etc., may require realignment of the schedule.

Many additional factors have been identified previously. Whether or not any of them are critical in relation to scheduling depends on the individual situation. Although we need to be prepared for schedule contingencies, we need to examine them only in terms of the likelihood of their occurring. In other words, apply your cost-benefit analysis to the situation to determine how much effort you should put into preparing for such contingencies. If the risk to achieving the objective is relatively small, your decision may well be to proceed under the assumption that you will meet the schedule you have established.

## What Is Budgeting?

Budgeting is one of the most misunderstood and misused terms in the management vocabulary. We tend to think of a budget as an assignment of money from "upstairs" that is totally inadequate for what we are expected to do. Therefore, we have a built-in rationalization as to why we cannot get our jobs done. In actuality, budgeting is primarily a function of "us" rather than "them." It means "determining and assigning the resources required to reach objectives." This becomes more a case of "What do we do with what we've got?" than of "What will we get from someone else?" This does not mean, of course, that our approach to management budgeting will not have a significant effect on the latter. What it does mean is that before we can honestly expect additional budgetary support from our superiors, we must demonstrate our ability to get the best mileage out of the resources we already have at our disposal. An assigned budget is an objective, too. It is not an "allotment check" that is ours to spend as we see fit. We have a stewardship obligation to the organization to see that it is used to the best overall organizational advantage.

### What and Why Do We Budget?

Since we have related budgeting to resources, what exactly are we talking about? Normally, resources can be divided into three general categories:

1. *Human effort* — usually the largest and most volatile resource at our disposal; sometimes expressed in work hours, workdays, etc., and sometimes in labor dollars; may include personnel overhead costs.

2. *Materials* — the "things" that become a part of or are expended in support of the objective, usually expressed in terms of dollars; can include human effort provided under a purchase order or contract.

3. *Facilities* — the property, buildings, equipment, durable tools, i.e., things of a more lasting nature, that are generally purchased or constructed for continuing use; usually expressed in dollars charged to either capital or operating expenditures.

Money, of course, is the common denominator in budgeting, and for approval purposes it usually is desirable to express the allocation of resources in terms of dollars. Realistically, however, many jobs are estimated on a headcount or work-hour basis. Although these types of estimates can always be translated into dollars, many times — particularly at the lower levels of supervision — budgeting an objective or action step by work hours provides much more realistic visibility than does budgeting by dollars. Also, the cost of determining dollar costs (by applying a cost-benefit analysis) may be more than the relative value of the information gained.

The management activity of budgeting can and should be a most revealing and useful tool. Many, if not most, managers have little more than a general idea of what it will actually cost to carry out a job. In fact, experience indicates that the average manager has a tendency to underestimate the cost, particularly in human effort, of pursuing an objective. A submitted budget may be "padded" for self-protection against anticipated arbitrary cuts (we'll have more to say about this later), but a manager's own estimate is likely to be low. From an incentive standpoint, this is not necessarily bad, since the tighter the margin, the harder a manager is likely to work to stay within it. However, to proceed with the assignment of work on the basis of this broad, "gut-feel" idea of what it will cost may cause the manager to end up in serious trouble later on. It could result in such unplanned costs as overtime (compensated or uncompensated), delay, modification or abandonment of this or other objectives, or serious impact on the work of other organizations or units.

Since the primary purpose of budgeting as a management activity should be to provide the manager with greater visibility in planning the work of the unit, it should be approached on as analytical and realistic a basis as possible. As was pointed out in both Chapter 1 and the first part of this chapter, a principal advantage in taking a look at costs *before* we are committed to a course of action is that it permits us to determine whether we will get a good return on investment by pursuing what may have initially looked like a good objective. Furthermore, it provides an opportunity to evaluate alternative methods of programming an objective. For example, a careful breakdown of costs involved may indicate that it would be more economical and productive to "farm out" some of the activities (preparing and reproducing manuals, for instance) to outside vendors or to other units than it would be to do the work internally.

### How Do We Budget?

Actually, the process of budgeting is not difficult. If the manager has followed the series of management activities described thus far, the major part of the work has already been done. If the total job has been broken down into a series of objectives which in turn have been divided into action steps with assigned schedules or calendar time blocks, it is simply a matter of logically estimating what it will cost to accomplish the action steps or the events within them. Breaking the action down into digestible pieces — in other words, moving the effort down the funnel until it reaches a size that is tangible and manageable — results in a more realistic and accurate approach to costing out the total effort.

The costing process involves the exercise of judgment in applying historical data and knowledge to future probabilities. In most situations, you know approximately how much effort and other related expenses are required to perform certain activities, either from written records or from your own knowledge and experience plus that of others. The secret, of course, is in having the action steps or events small enough so that they can be predicted with reasonable accuracy, yet large enough to be worth the effort it would take to do an effective job of costing.

Once each of the action steps has been costed out, it becomes simply a matter of adding up all of these costs to produce a budget estimate for the entire objective. Thus it may be best to wait until we have gone through this costing process before making a firm commitment on the cost factor of an objective.

To further support this contention, try an experiment. Identify an objective that you plan to pursue, one that will require a fairly large amount of effort but that you have not yet programmed. Write down your estimate of what it will cost to achieve the total objective. Then break the objective down into action steps and significant events or activities within each step. (You may wish to use the action plan format illustrated in Fig. 7.3 on p. 119.) Estimate a cost as accurately as possible for the accomplishment of each of these steps. Finally, add up these costs and compare the result to your original estimate. The chances are good that the total of the individual estimates will substantially exceed the original estimate. If the two estimates are close, it means one of three things: (1) you were lucky, (2) you have been through identical or similar jobs many times, or (3) you have an exceptionally fine ability to analyze a total job for probable costs. Before you accept the last item as the true reason for your success, however, try the experiment several more times, then compare your estimates with the actual costs incurred by the time you have accomplished the related objectives. If it still looks good, you have developed one of the most useful and saleable skills that a middle- and upper-level manager can have.

As a word of caution at this point, be sure to realize that agreement with or approval of your estimate of the resources required to accomplish a particular objective or action step does not automatically make those resources available. You may have made an exceptionally good estimate of the number of skilled work hours required to do a certain job. You may even have the approval of your superiors to spend the labor dollars you have estimated. This does not, by a long shot, ensure the availability of these resources when you need them. Therefore, recognize that not only must an accurate estimate of costs be made, but also that strong consideration must be given to availability of resources when they are needed.

### What Is Budget Integrity?

Philosophically, the management activity of budgeting is primarily a tool to help the individual manager plan his or her work more effectively. Realistically, it also serves as a valuable communications tool to aid upper management in determining how best to allocate resources within its jurisdiction. Needless to say, the individual manager may be strongly tempted to "pad" the budget to ensure getting as big a "slice of the pie" as possible, to gain protection against unexpected contingencies or poor estimating, or to be prepared for the inevitable across-the-board cut that seems to be an accepted periodic mode of operation in many organizations.

The unfortunate outcome of yielding to this temptation is that in order to justify the action in their own minds, the manager and his or her subordinates tend to rationalize their thinking to the point that they begin to believe that the budget submitted is what is actually needed to get the job done. With that, Parkinson's Law* soon goes into effect. To illustrate this very point, how many instances can you recall when a manager went to the boss part way through the year and indicated that the job could be done with *less* resources than originally allocated, thus suggesting that the excess resources be made available for other uses? Contrast that with the number of instances you can recall when a manager submitted a "padded" budget, but nonetheless came back later during the year to insist that more was needed. Although we would be among the last to condone the practice of across-the-board cuts, it is interesting to note the number of times that productivity in some organizations not only doesn't drop after such a cut, but frequently increases. Is it any wonder that some executives consider such periodic cuts both necessary and desirable?

Budget integrity means, simply, the preparation of a realistic and practical cost estimate for the work to be done and then sticking to it. It also means establishing a method of measurement (see Chapter 8) that will give visibility in time to take proper corrective action. This means allocating additional resources or modifying the program *early* if it appears that an overrun is likely. It also means releasing unneeded resources or assuming additional work *early* if it appears that an underrun is likely.

A well-managed organization is one that has confidence in the budget integrity of its managers. It assumes that the budgetary requirements its managers have agreed to reflect precisely what is needed to get the job done. It further assumes that its managers will take necessary corrective action along the way to ensure that commitments are met. Finally, it assumes that a budgetary cut will result in corresponding reduction in productivity. Therefore, it makes such cuts, when necessary, on a selective basis rather than across the board and evaluates unit objectives on the basis of overall return on investment.

---

* "Work expands so as to fill the time available for its completion." C. Northcote Parkinson, *Parkinson's Law*, Boston: Houghton Mifflin, 1957, p. 2.

## What Is Fixing Accountability?

Defined as "determining who will see to the accomplishment of objectives and action steps," *accountability* is a more precise, results-oriented term than one that is frequently used synonymously with it, *responsibility*. It identifies the individual or unit (which, normally, is headed by an individual) that is the focal point for a specific piece of action. As stated earlier, any action step should be capable of being turned into an objective if it makes sense to do so. Accountability determines whose objective it ought to be; or, if no objective is called for, it at least ensures coverage of that particular action step.

As was specified in our earlier description of the action plan format, a unit manager must either accept personal accountability or fix accountability on some member of the unit for every step identified in the action plan. This is true even when the bulk of the effort will be carried out by someone outside the unit. For example, if a field unit is relying on a data-processing unit to provide some analytical information for use in its action plan, someone within that field unit must be held accountable for: (1) negotiating with the data-processing unit on both the content and delivery date of the information, (2) following up to ensure its delivery, and (3) establishing and maintaining open communications on impacting problems from either end. "We couldn't complete our objective on time because the information we received from Data Processing was wrong (or late)" may be an explanation, but it is not a justifiable *reason*. The individual accountable for that step should have been alert to the situation in sufficient time either to take alternative action or to provide early feedback so that the objective could be renegotiated in line with current reality.

Fixing accountability, when it involves both the ensuring of the step's completion and the direct performance of the actions required (as in the preparation of a document), also provides added visibility to the manager in determining individual workloads. If the plan shows that an excessive amount of the effort is being assigned to one or more individuals, the manager may find it necessary either to reassign some of it or to revise the schedule so that it can be realistically accomplished by those to whom it is assigned.

## What Is "Reviewing and Reconciling?"

Technically, this process goes on continuously throughout the planning function. However, if we define it as "testing and revising a tentative plan, as needed, prior to commitment to action," it logically falls as the final substep under Preparing Action Plans. In effect, we set up a tentative plan on each of the activities as we go along, and we either confirm or modify what we have done as we develop new information or ideas. In addition to this ongoing process, we take one last look at our objectives and action plans before firmly committing ourselves to action, to ensure that we have not overlooked any critical factors.

### Why Do We Review and Reconcile?

Although the approach we have recommended throughout the book thus far is quite systematic and continually stresses the need to look at all significant contingencies, it is almost inevitable that something will "drop through the cracks." Perhaps a critical step was inadvertently left out. Perhaps something totally irrelevant found its way into the operation and needs to be removed. Perhaps there has been a critical change since the planning effort began that will necessitate a reevaluation of some of the steps. Perhaps because of a manager's personal bias, external pressure, or pure oversight, some steps have taken on a disproportionate value and need to be placed in perspective. Whatever the reasons, there is a vital need to regularly step back and take a look at the whole forest to make sure that there aren't any trees out of place.

### How Do We Review and Reconcile?

There are many different ways in which the process of review and reconciliation can take place. Some of the more frequently used methods are listed below.

1. *Individual review.* This is a process the individual manager should go through regardless of which other methods may be

used. It requires the manager's detachment from his or her obvious involvement in the effort, in order to look at the total plan to date objectively, making whatever changes or adjustments appear indicated.

2. *Superior-subordinate review.* The other members of the team who are most concerned with the results should review the plan also, as objectively as possible, to see if anything has been overlooked.

3. *Peer attack.* This is a particularly effective technique, either on an individual basis or as a part of a training program on the subject. Have a few disinterested peers examine the plan and attack it in such a way that the accountable manager must either defend it logically or be prepared to openly consider alternative approaches. So-called Attack and Defense teams can be an effective way to examine and reconcile total organizational objectives as well.

4. *Concerned outsider review.* Have key representatives of other concerned organizations or units (customer/client/user groups, suppliers, support units, interfacing production units, etc.) review the plan in terms of its impact on their operations. A knowledgeable consultant who is familiar with both the process and the organization is another source of helpful feedback at this stage.

5. *Committee review.* A conference can be called of various internal and external key representatives to integrate the best of the ideas into a unified approach to implementing the plan. Needless to say, it's important to see that participants have an opportunity to review the plan before the meeting to ensure the most effective use of their talents.

The astute manager will periodically stop and take a look at his or her planning efforts, using the various sets of "Key Questions" and "Guidelines" included in this book, to make certain that they all tie together. Furthermore, particularly with large-scale efforts, a final review and reconciliation of all critical factors prior to full implementation is in order. To aid in this examination, a list entitled "Key Questions for Review and Reconciliation in Planning," which includes some of the questions from checksheets already used, is given at the end of this chapter.

Lest this whole process of review and reconciliation be viewed as delaying and burdensome, let's make it quite clear that good judgment and common sense must be used in its application. Realistically, many objectives and related action steps are made up of such obvious elements that a formal review and reconciliation would be an empty and unnecessary exercise. Since the process, in itself, is nonproducing and yet has a price tag, it should be used in direct proportion to the criticality of the factors involved, the degree of risk that can be incurred through the use of alternative courses of action, and the amount of impact on other units and individuals. In other words, apply a cost-benefit analysis to this process and use it to the degree that it serves a significant purpose.

## In Summary

Preparing Action Plans helps us determine what plays to call, when to call them, and what resources must be invested in order to ensure the achievement of an objective. Although this step includes five substeps — Programming, Scheduling, Budgeting, Fixing Accountability, and Reviewing and Reconciling — the most critical one, generally, is Programming, the process of breaking objectives down into action steps for effective accomplishment. Some objectives will be simple enough in approach that programming will be unnecessary. However, most objectives, if significant enough to be identified as objectives, can be accomplished much more effectively and efficiently if they are subdivided into workable units of action. These also form "linking pins" in that what may be an action step at one level of management may become an objective for someone else.

The very act of programming an objective is another means of validating it. An objective that initially appears to be extremely important may seem less so once it is laid out in a plan of action. The continuous process of reexamining an objective in light of its programming requirements and applying a more accurate cost-benefit analysis to it may strongly indicate the need for modifying or even dropping an objective that originally looked sound. Should the determination *not* to work toward a particular objective be made as a result of data uncovered during the programming process, the investment of effort in programming has been just as valuable, if not more so, as it would have been in the case of a clear and obvious go-ahead. It may have meant the saving of considerably more wasted time and effort. Considering, however, that most well-prepared objectives will be pursued, the activity of programming them effectively and efficiently becomes the most crucial substep in preparing an action plan.

With varying degrees of importance, depending on the complexity of the effort, the other four substeps — Scheduling, Budgeting, Fixing Accountability, and Reviewing and Reconciling — deserve attention also. In many situations, completing the necessary blocks in the action plan format (Fig. 7.3 on p. 119) will be sufficient; others will require a far more analytical examination.

The key to an effective action plan lies in the visibility it gives to the accountable manager and others who will be participating in it. To help prevent MOR from deteriorating into another massive bureaucratic "paper mill," the action plan must be seen primarily as a tool for the manager preparing it and not as either a detailed procedure or an involved reporting device.

## GUIDELINES FOR PROGRAMMING AN OBJECTIVE

### Six-Step Approach

1. Study the situation and select the method.
2. Gain agreement and support.

3. Develop the plan. (See "Programming Breakdown" below.)
4. Test and review the plan.
5. Implement.
6. Follow up.

## Programming Breakdown

1. What major steps are necessary to achieve the results identified in the objective?
2. What priorities should be assigned to each major step?
3. What are the detail steps necessary to support the major steps that have been identified?

## KEY QUESTIONS FOR EVALUATING ACTION STEPS

1. Will these steps, collectively, lead effectively and efficiently to the accomplishment of the objective?
2. Is each action step well defined and clearly stated? Is the number of words used held to an absolute minimum that is consistent with clear understanding by those required to carry it out?
3. Does it avoid getting into the detailed "how-to's" which should be determined by the person to whom it is assigned?
4. Is it clearly separate from other major steps?
5. Can it be measured and verified? Could it be made into an objective if it were desirable to do so?
6. Have priorities (first things first) been clearly established?
7. Is it consistent with organizational policies and practices?
8. Can the accountability for each action step's completion be clearly fixed to a single individual (possibly the manager himself or herself)?

## KEY QUESTIONS FOR REVIEW AND RECONCILIATION IN PLANNING

1. Are statements of roles and missions consistent with and appropriate to the roles, missions, and objectives of the total organization and other related organizational units and individuals?

2. Are this manager's key results areas consistent with the unit's roles and missions and representative of those requiring high priority use of his or her time, energy, and talent?

3. Are the indicators identified the most appropriate measures of effectiveness for this time period in each of this manager's key results areas?

4. Are the identified objectives consistent with and appropriate to the accountable manager's roles and missions as well as to the roles, missions, and objectives of other related organizational units and individuals?

5. Will these objectives provide the most effective overall use of available resources?

6. Will the specified action plans provide the most effective and efficient available means of accomplishing the stated objective(s)?

7. What new developments have occurred since the initial planning effort began that may have an effect on this effort? What modifications, if any, should be made in consideration of these developments?

8. Can all of the critical commitments be met in light of current knowledge?

## SAMPLE PROGRAMMED OBJECTIVES

Identified here are some examples of typical programmed public-sector objectives. Major steps are identified by letters; detail steps, where included, are identified by numbers in parentheses. The "By When," "Costs," and "By Whom" columns have been deliberately omitted, because they have little relevance except in the context of a particular organization. Also, the program or action steps identified are for illustration purposes only and should not be regarded as a prescribed plan for the objectives given. Such steps, of course, will be determined more by the "real world" circumstances with which the accountable manager is faced.

1. To reduce the number of vehicular accidents on city streets by a minimum of 5% over prior year's level, at no increase in budget.

   a) Determine locations of highest incidence and select those with highest potential for improvement.

   b) Set up ad hoc committee (to include representatives of local citizens, traffic engineering, city planning, and police officers) to analyze and recommend alternative corrective actions including, but not limited to, education, increased surveillance, traffic control equipment, and possible rerouting.

   c) Establish information/motivation plan for police officers.

   d) Inform City Council, City Manager, other related departments, and the media about plans and progress.

   e) Test proposed plans in selected locations.

   f) Implement plans.

   g) Establish monitoring system.

   h) Evaluate and modify implementation plans after three months.

2. To decrease average turnaround time on claims filed from A to B, effective 10/1/76 at an implementation cost of $X and Y work hours and a maintenance cost not to exceed Z work hours per month.

   a) Gain agreement and support for objective and subsequent planned corrective action.

   b) Determine principal causes contributing to delay in filing claims.

c) Determine appropriate courses of corrective action.

d) Establish responsibilities for correcting problems.

e) Determine and assign resources necessary to correct problems.

f) Establish schedule for review of progress.

g) Develop plan of action, obtain approval, and publish for affected groups.

h) Implement plan of action.

i) Follow up — monitor progress.

3. To initiate use of MOR for operational planning in each unit reporting to me, by March 1, at a direct cost not to exceed 240 work hours and $1000.

a) Complete and gain agreement on unit roles and missions.

b) Complete and gain agreement on manager's MOR agreement.

c) Have key subordinates attend MOR seminar.

d) Acquire and use *Self-Teaching Audiocassette Program on Management by Objectives and Results* for review and specific training related to operational planning.

e) Determine and gain agreement on MOR application in specific operational planning areas.

f) Prepare tentative MOR operating plan for next six months.

g) Conduct unit progress review each month.

h) Evaluate and modify MOR application for next planning period.

4. To complete changeover to internal auditing in Agency A by March 31, at a planning cost of 200 work hours and an implementation cost of 300 work hours.

a) Gain agreement and support of objective and proposed plan with

    (1) Unit staff
    (2) Upper management
    (3) Agency A's management.
b) Prepare implementation plan.
c) Develop tools and instructions for internal auditors' use.
d) Train unit staff in role of trainer/coach.
e) Test and review plan and materials.
f) Implement plan as pilot effort.
g) Evaluate and modify
    (1) half way
    (2) conclusion.

5. To develop and implement a plan for slating officers 12 months prior to scheduled assignment, initial effort to be completed by 30 September 1976 at a cost not to exceed $25,000 and one work-year of effort.

a) Gain agreement, approval, and support for objective and proposed plan.
b) Commence preliminary slating efforts.
c) Commence slating process.
d) Develop statistics on subspecialty utilization.
e) Complete FY 77 slate (tentatives).
f) Release initial six-month notification for FY 77.
g) Adjust slate as required.
h) Release first orders for FY 77.
i) Continue slate refinement and modification as required.
j) Evaluate and modify plan for use during FY 77 for FY 78 slating efforts.

# 8

# ESTABLISHING CONTROLS

The management function of Controlling can be described as "ensuring the effective accomplishment of objectives." As such, it is designed to close the loop on the MOR process. The fact that this seems to be missing from many MBO applications I have seen is one of the reasons why I consider the phrase "Management by Objectives. . . ." to be incomplete and have added the phrase". . . . and Results." An objective — or, for that matter, any kind of a plan — has relatively little meaning unless there is some mechanism for making certain it is achieved. Results rarely happen because of management decrees. We have all observed organizations that go through the annual ritual of having every key manager prepare objectives, either individually or at a planning conference, which are then duplicated, distributed to everyone, and promptly shoved in the bottom drawer while everyone gets back to work. At the end of the year the list might be pulled out, dusted off, and scanned to see if there is any resemblance to what actually took place. That sounds more like "Management by Futility." The establishment of realistic controls is designed to make the planning process a viable, ongoing reality and not just a "sometimes" thing.

In approaching this step, please bear in mind that managerial controlling has *only one reason* for its existence — *to alert us when we are about to get into trouble, in sufficient time to take the necessary corrective action.* If we never needed to take corrective action, we would not need controlling as a management function. (By the way, we are referring to "controlling" here as it relates to the individual manager and not to total organization controls or the office of the Controller, both of which serve a broader purpose than we will be describing here.) If we can accept the premise about the reason for managerial controlling, we must also accept "corrective action" as a positive and anticipated part of the management process and not as evidence that someone has "screwed up."

## What Are the Economic Considerations of Control?

While establishing the means by which the controlling function will be performed, the manager must continually keep in mind that controlling is a cost item. Controlling does not produce any unit output. Although it is an essential part of the MOR process, controlling represents time and effort that the manager and his or her subordinates could otherwise be devoting to "producing" activities. Therefore, it must be clearly recognized that *effective controlling provides for adequate visibility in a timely fashion with the least expenditure of time and effort.*

The key words in the statement above are "adequate," "timely," and "least expenditure." By "adequate" we mean the minimum amount of data necessary to inform us of the current status of the critical factors being measured. "Timely" implies the availability of the necessary data in time to take corrective action, should that appear indicated. "Least expenditure" says that the obtaining of data should cause minimal interruption to the ongoing productive effort of the organization or unit.

This point is so obvious that many managers overlook it completely. One of the most frequent comments on the subject of controlling we have heard, from managers and employees alike, goes something like this: "I spend so much time monitoring and reporting on my work that the work itself doesn't get done. When will *they* let me do my job?" It's interesting to note, of course, that the culprit causing this work delay is always one of "them," whoever "they" are. It's never "me"!

The degree of controlling exercised by individual managers tends to be one of extremes. Either there is little or no systematic method of controlling the work, or — at the other other extreme — there is far more control than is necessary to reasonably ensure effective performance. Furthermore, what is even more of a problem is the tendency of many managers to continually vacillate between the two extremes, while rarely stopping at some point in the middle. Consider the following examples:

The head of a support unit (more than 100 employees) insisted that his approval signature appear on every written commitment made to other units requiring service, yet instituted no uniform system for logging verbal commitments made to the same units, even though more than half the services were rendered in this manner.

A local office serving the public maintained records on percentage of time that clerks spend at the counter as compared to their other duties, yet kept no record of *when* that counter time occurred. The result? During the periods from noon to 1:00 P.M. and 4:00 to 5:00 P.M., when the counter traffic was heaviest, the fewest clerks were available for counter duty.

An organization whose employees spent a substantial amount of time in travel required three approval signatures on detailed travel expense vouchers, yet no advance authorization for the trip itself.

Since controlling is a nonproducing cost item, managerial judgment must be exercised to make certain that it is used in a consistent manner and in proportion to the value of the data derived. In other words, a cost-benefit analysis must be applied to the function of controlling. Although there is a risk in this approach, the effective manager *must* take risks — which means that on occasions your judgment will be wrong. However, the cost of being certain that you are always right is prohibitive.

## What Should Be Controlled?

Since we have suggested that it is not economically feasible to place control measures on all factors affecting our objectives, how can we determine where our control emphasis should be placed? First, we need to examine our objectives in terms of their four basic elements — time resources (human and material), quality, and quantity. Anything that will require corrective action will relate to one or more of these basic elements. Next, we take another look at the Principle of the Critical Few (discussed in Chapter 4) and apply it to the function of Controlling. For example, most managers will recognize such things as:

- a small group of employees that can be counted on to produce the greatest amount of acceptable work;

- a small group of employees that can be counted on to produce the largest number of errors;

- a small group of employees that will consistently have the highest rates of accidents, absenteeism, or tardiness;

- a small group of employees that can be counted on to produce the largest number of creative new ideas;

- certain operations or units that will regularly cause the biggest and most frequent bottlenecks;

- certain equipment that will have the heaviest breakdown rate;

- a few products or services that will generate the greatest customer/client/user response;

- a few products or services that will create the most customer/client/user dissatisfaction;

- certain operations that will invite the greatest media reaction, favorable or unfavorable;

- a few legislators who can be counted on to provide the greatest support;

- a few legislators who can be counted on to create the most problems;

- certain times of the day that are most likely to present opportunities or problems;

- certain times of the year that are most likely to present opportunities or problems.

This list could go on indefinitely. The effect, however, should be obvious. In deciding where to place control emphasis, the manager must first identify that relatively small number of critical factors that will have the greatest impact on the achievement or lack of achievement of objectives. Control efforts can then be concentrated in those areas where the risk is greatest.

Another key consideration comes in what Louis Allen calls the *"Principle of Point of Control*. The greatest potential for control tends to exist at the point where action takes place."* This principle drives home the point that control data must be made available to the manager and/or employee directly accountable for the action at least simultaneously with, if not prior to, its availability to higher-level management. This becomes increasingly critical with the use of computers to supply control data. One of the most frustrating and demoralizing things that can happen to a first-line supervisor is to learn about a production problem in his or her unit as a result of a report first issued to upper management and then fed downward. This smacks more of Management by "Gotcha" than of Management by Objectives and Results. Furthermore, consider how much sooner the problem might have been corrected if the supervisor had not had to wait for the data to filter down.

## How Do We Control?

We have divided managerial controlling into three substeps — establishing standards, measuring performance, and taking corrective action. Placing these elements into a practical perspective, we have to ask ourselves three fundamental questions related to the four basic elements we identified earlier: What is likely to go wrong? How and when will you know? What will you do? The matrix shown in Fig. 8.1 identifies the simplest approach to the total function of controlling as used in

---

* Louis A. Allen, *The Management Profession,* New York: McGraw-Hill, 1964, p. 319. Quoted by permission of the publisher.

| BASIC ELEMENTS | WHAT IS LIKELY TO GO WRONG? | HOW AND WHEN WILL YOU KNOW? | WHAT WILL YOU DO? |
|---|---|---|---|
| TIME | | | |
| RESOURCES | | | |
| QUALITY | | | |
| QUANTITY | | | |

**Fig. 8.1** Factors to be weighed in the Controlling function.

MOR. The remainder of this chapter is divided into three sub-sections, each dealing with one of these fundamental questions.

### Establishing Standards — What Is Likely to Go Wrong?

Please note that the question asks, "What is *likely* to go wrong?" rather than "What could *possibly* go wrong?" Bearing in mind the economic considerations mentioned earlier, we have to deal in probabilities here. One of the problems here is the temptation to look at too much, which can be almost as destructive as not looking at enough. In this subsection, we will first take a look at standards in a broad sense. Then we will narrow them down more specifically to the identification of causes of variances, which is the primary application of standards in relation to the achievement of objectives.

### What Are Standards?

A standard can be defined as "a gauge of effective performance in achieving objectives." This implies quantification of performance factors in some manner. In some types of effort this is a relatively simple thing to do. In others, particularly those that rely heavily on creative mental activity, it becomes substantially more difficult. Yet as we discussed earlier in our examination of indicators and objectives, even subjective evaluation can be quantified. The biggest barrier to overcome in this regard is the natural reluctance of many managers to accept an imperfect unit of measurement as a standard against which to evaluate performance. However, since very few "perfect" units of measurement are applicable in today's work environment, we must learn to accept some imperfections and to both establish and use standards that are indicators of successful performance — no more, no less.

### Why Must We Establish Standards?

Since the heart of the controlling function is "measuring performance," there must be something to measure it against. This we have chosen to call a "standard." A person's entire life — not only work life — is built around standards of one sort or another. Relative success or failure in everything we do is determined by accepted standards, whether they be school grades, sports achievement, income level, weight, or gas mileage. Standards in these categories are no more "perfect" than the performance standards we establish in our work. Still, we generally accept them and adjust our living to them until a better method of measurement comes along.

Without performance standards, we have no clear way of knowing whether we are achieving our objectives. Nor do we have any clear way of determining the relative value of the work performed by our subordinates, so that we can reward them commensurately with their contributions.

### What Are Some Advantages of Standards?

The establishment of understood and accepted performance standards has many advantages. Beginning with the two we have already identified, here are some of the more important potential benefits.

1. Yardstick for determining the probability of reaching objectives.
2. Means of measuring individual performance for purposes of:
   a) compensation
   b) employee development

c) work assignments

d) promotions

e) downgrading or disciplinary action.

3. Incentive for individual improvement.

4. Incentive for unit improvement.

5. Incentive for innovative approaches to work performance.

6. Means of *self*-measurement and correction.

7. Means of interpreting the performance of others.

8. Means of making realistic forecasts for:

   a) staff-loading purposes

   b) facility, equipment, and material needs

   c) evaluating and making tradeoffs on objectives

   d) costing purposes (seeking appropriations).

9. Incentive and means for continuous and consistent reevaluation of methods and results.

10. Means of comparison with the performance of other organizations or units.

## How Do We Establish Performance Standards?

To a large degree, many of the factors we have already dealt with in Identifying and Specifying Indicators of Effectiveness and in Selecting and Setting Objectives are equally useful as standards. In the earlier context, they helped us decide what we should be doing. Here, they can serve as a tool for determining if we are actually doing it. Concurrent indicators, in particular, are designed to help us in this step. However, there are many other factors that would not be particularly useful as indicators prior to the setting of objectives that might be extremely critical to watch to make certain we get there.

In determining what is to be measured, we must keep in mind that the prime purpose of a standard in the MOR process is to serve as an indicator of successful performance. In other words, failure to meet a particular standard is nothing more than a "red flag" indicating something is wrong and that some sort of corrective action is indicated. With this prime purpose in mind, perhaps we can learn to look for and accept factors to be measured which we might otherwise resist. The use of student-hours as a means of measuring the effectiveness of a training program, as described at the beginning of Chapter 5, is a good example of this kind of measurable factor.

There are literally thousands of measurable factors that could be used as performance standards. You will have to make your own determination as to which ones will best serve your purposes. A "brainstorming" session with fellow workers may well uncover some useful factors that might otherwise be overlooked — not to mention the motivational value in permitting those concerned to have a say in establishing the standards. The following frequently used measurable factors can serve as thought stimulators in determining your own:

| | |
|---|---|
| People served | Flow time |
| Organizations/units served | Requests for service |
| New customers/clients/users | Degree of acceptance |
| Service complaints | Cost reductions |
| Unit (of production) costs | Accuracy/neatness |
| Number of employees | Units produced |
| Promotions | Errors, rejects |
| Turnover rate | Setup time |
| Lost-time accidents | Turnaround time |
| Percent of savings | Maintenance costs |
| Work hours | Equipment utilization |
| Standard hours | Down time |
| Percent of overtime | Ideas generated |
| Calendar time | Changes initiated |
| Schedule milestones | Problems/opportunities |

Note that some of these examples of measurable performance factors, such as degree of acceptance, ideas generated, problems/opportunities, etc., are quite subjective, whereas others imply varying degrees of objectivity/subjectivity. The fact remains that some form of measurement can be placed on each of them, so that each can serve as an indicator of successful performance. The same applies to the thousands of other factors that can be used as measuring devices. You must decide which factors will be the best indicators of successful performance toward the achievement of your unit's objectives.

Once the measurable factors have been identified, the manager must determine the point of measurement that constitutes effective performance. This is usually expressed as one of the following: (1) *numbers* (hours, units, requests); (2) *dollars* (unit costs, maintenance costs); (3) *percentages* (overtime, errors, equipment utilization); (4) *time lapse* (flow time, setup time, turnaround time); or (5) *completion point* (milestones, acceptance, problems overcome).

The process of determining the specific point of measurement may be influenced by many considerations — past history, the manager's personal capabilities, legislative requirements or limitations, and superior or subordinate recommendations, to mention a few. By whatever means this measurement point is defined, the manager must accept the results as: (1) a reasonable indicator of effective performance, and (2) a point that will provide adequate visibility in a timely fashion with a minimum expenditure of time and effort.

### What About Intangible or Creative Work?

There is no question but that it is much more difficult to establish realistic standards for "think" work. Virtually any factor that might be identified could be refuted quite logically. However, if the standards established are examined in proper perspective and are accepted primarily as indicators or "red flags," they will prove to be extremely valuable management tools. In this regard, anything that can reasonably be quantified could be useful as a performance standard.

In using such standards, of course, there has to be an assumption of reasonable integrity on the part of the employee being measured. The personal pride of most employees would not allow them to do poor work just to beat the system. With these points in mind, here are a few examples of standards that might be used in some typical work of this nature:

*Research and Development*

- Number of new ideas generated
- Number of new applications generated for current products or services

- Approval/implementation of R&D plans
- Anticipated dollar value of new ideas generated
- Anticipated cost savings from innovations
- Cost of R&D investment as related to total organization budget
- Successful testing of prototypes
- Quality of R&D effort — evaluated by accepted professional standards
- Professional recognition of R&D efforts
- Interest/response from legislators
- Interest/response from public/media
- Interest/response from other organizations in similar field

*Purchasing*
- Turnaround time
- Number of vendor contacts
- Unit costs of purchases
- Degree and nature of vendor research
- Complaints/praise from other units
- Complaints/praise from vendors
- Percentage of dollar commitments to disbursements
- Number of purchases versus purchasing expense
- Negotiation time
- Degree of "learning curve" application
- Schedule milestones
- Vendors' performance against requisitions

*Training*
- Number of student-hours
- Student-hour cost ratios
- Number and nature of training completions
- Course content buy-off
- Percentage of participation by classification
- Percentage of training facility usage
- Complaints/praise from customers/clients/users

- Degree and nature of student on-the-job improvement
- Number of students qualified for promotion or new assignments
- Tangible production improvements (rates, errors, service quality, etc.)
- Dropout rates
- Response time

*Analysis*

- Flow time
- Cost-value ratios
- Customers/clients/users buy-off of services
- Number and nature of analyses
- Degree and nature of related research
- Complaints/praise from customers/clients/users
- Number and nature of data sources
- Number and nature of analytical errors
- Average cost per analysis
- Number and nature of resultant operational improvements
- Number and nature of reports published
- Number of requests for service

These particular examples illustrate the types of standards that could be established in measuring work that is primarily of the "think" variety. There are many other possible standards that might serve the specific situations as well or better. The individual manager in this type of operation must apply his or her own knowledge and judgment, together with that of other concerned parties, to the establishment of realistic indicators of successful performance. These indicators will not be perfect, but they can be determined and used effectively by the professional manager.

## Who Must Understand and Accept the Standards?

Standards, to be meaningful, must be both understood and accepted primarily by the three organizational levels most concerned with the objective-related performance — the accountable manager, his or her superior, and his or her subordinates. This is particularly critical as it relates to subordinates. Let's face it! Since our subordinates are the ones who probably will contribute most to the achievement of our objectives, it is neither realistic nor fair to expect them to meet performance standards that they do not understand or are unwilling to accept.

The secret, if we can call it that, to bringing about understanding and acceptance on the part of subordinates is to get their active participation in the determination of the standards against which they will be measured. The degree of this participation will vary substantially, depending on the nature of the work, the knowledge and capabilities of the concerned subordinates, and the degree of sensitivity of the standards to be established. However, it is almost axiomatic that the subordinate's motivation toward meeting performance standards will correlate closely with the amount of involvement that individual has had in their determination. This is especially true of the more subjective measurement factors.

### What Are the Principal Causes of Variances Requiring Corrective Action?

The primary value in applying standards to controlling performance toward objectives comes in the identification of variances. A variance is any significant deviation from planned performance that will require some sort of *overt* action on our part to get it back on target. In making a projection, we generally allow a certain amount of self-adjusting tolerance as we go along. Our concern here is in identifying what that margin is and, more specifically, what is likely to cause actual performance to exceed that margin to the point that we must do something specific to bring it back in line.

Variances fall in one of four general categories. However, the labels assigned to those categories are not important; similarly, we need not agree on which category is appropriate for a particular variance. The only important thing is to *identify the variance*. If my labels help in that identification, then use them; if they get in the way, then don't!

1. *Uncertainties* are reasonable expectations which contain strong possibilities of significant fluctuations. For example, uncertainties in internal operations could include such things as absenteeism, workload, flow time, accidents, errors, or traffic. Typical external factors might be service requests, appropriations, legislative reviews or changes, meetings, and routine correspondence. We can make some reasonable projections on the basis of historical data and our judgment as to the likely outcomes of certain events. However, there is no guarantee that those outcomes will actually occur. What we need is something that will tell us when "actual" is, or is about to be, different enough from "projected" to require some sort of an adjustment.

2. *Unexpected events* are those impacting factors that are *not* reasonable expectations, but whose consequences are of such a magnitude that we need to have contingency plans in order to deal with them. Unexpected events might include acts of nature, an epidemic, an exposé in the media, the death or departure of a key leader, an arbitrary across-the-board budget cut or personnel freeze. Actually, the label "unexpected events" is something of a misnomer, since — with rare exceptions — they should not be really "unexpected." In almost every such situation, there are early warning signs that can alert us to a potential problem, if we know what to look for.

3. *Failures* are stoppages or delays within the normal scope of work that are largely beyond the control of the accountable manager and his or her subordinates. Included here would be such things as machine failures (a computer breakdown, for example), test failures, nonreceipt of critical inputs (parts, outside survey data, legislative rulings), and failure to get anticipated approvals.

4. *Human error* relates to human performance that is largely within the control of the accountable manager. This category can be further subdivided into:

    a) *"Honest" error*, which reflects the performance of basically competent people who for a variety of reasons, some of which may be beyond their control, fail to perform competently. This may come as a result of miscalculation, lack of sufficient knowledge or skill, lack of proper instructions, a too heavy workload, outside distractions, or interferences. It represents conscientious effort that falls short of expectations.

b) *Incompetency*, on the other hand, suggests willful misdoing, gross negligence, or inability to perform the work satisfactorily. Clearly, the kind of corrective action called for here is substantially different from that required under "honest" error.

What we are looking for under the question, "What is likely to go wrong?" is an identification of those critical factors or standards that will alert us to problems before they get beyond the point of no return. Remember, we are dealing with probabilities, not with absolutes. Each of us must determine how much risk we are willing to take to ensure that we have "adequate visibility" without causing a major interference with ongoing productive effort.

### Measuring Performance — How and When Will You Know?

As used in MOR, the management activity of measuring performance is not to be confused with performance appraisal. The latter is concerned with individual employee performance (and is discussed more specifically in my text *Appraisal and Development through Objectives and Results*, Addison-Wesley, 1972); the former deals with progress toward unit objectives. Many of the same factors will be measured, but the approach is quite different. As a management activity, measuring performance is defined as "determining actual versus planned performance." It is the means by which we can observe how work is progressing toward the accomplishment of objectives.

We pointed out earlier that *effective controlling provides for adequate visibility in a timely fashion with the least expenditure of time and effort*. Once we have determined what our standards of performance will be, the management activity of measuring performance against those standards goes into motion. This activity, more than either of the others in the controlling function, is the pivot point around which the *effective controlling* statement revolves. It is concerned with the feedback mechanisms we will use to make that "red flag" pop up at the right time.

### What Methods of Measurement Should Be Selected?

Since controlling is a nonproducing cost item, the selection of methods of measurement should be made with that in mind. In this regard, the individual manager should effectively use data that are already being produced for another purpose, such as unit status reports, weekly timecard summaries, various computer runs, etc., whenever possible. When the data needed for effective measurement are not readily available from an existing source, some other method must be devised to provide the necessary visibility.

Generally speaking, the most effective method of measurement for controlling purposes does not call attention to itself unless there is a significant deviation or variance from the standard. If this statement seems inconsistent with many managerial practices, it is because so-called control data are actually designed to serve other purposes as well — employee motivation, public relations, personal or organizational justification, support data to help influence higher-management decisions (budgets, assignments), etc. Elaborate graphic displays, voluminous reports, dramatic statistical comparisons all fit into this category. Before we raise the ire of the many managers who use such devices, however, let us make it quite clear that we are not condemning this practice. There is no denying the motivational impact on a group of employees of a colorful chart showing productivity improvement. Nor would we minimize the effect on upper management at budget-review time of a display of statistics showing significantly increased workload requirements. Our only concern is that the individual manager does not become convinced that more data or an elaborate display is needed solely in order to perform the controlling function effectively. Unless the proper perspective is kept on such practices, they tend to snowball to the point where subordinates may spend more time in preparing charts and writing reports than they do in performing the work being recorded. That is when the controlling function has passed the "Point of Ridiculosity," that point beyond which it is ridiculous to spend any effort.

## What Types of Measurement Methods Do Managers Use?

As with other techniques identified in this book, there is a virtually limitless supply of measurement methods in use today. The only real limitations are the applicability and availability of certain devices in specific situations, the time and effort required to use them, and the ingenuity of the individual manager in making use of them or in devising new ones. Here are six of the most commonly used feedback mechanisms and my comments on each.

1. *Visual — charts and graphs.* Whenever possible, I favor using simple visual displays of control information. They do not have to be elaborate artistic efforts. In fact, the most effective control displays I have seen are simple line graphs, milestone charts, and problem-oriented charts with color-coded markers; these were hand-prepared by the manager, office secretary, and/or the accountable staff member, and were maintained informally in the manager's office to provide quick visibility for anyone with a need to know. A truly effective chart or graph will: (a) show projections that reflect probable reality rather than a "straight-line averaging," since most factors don't operate on a "straight line," and (b) instantly highlight variances requiring corrective action without a complicated interpretation.

2. *Computer print-outs.* Some of these can be extremely useful, if the manager can easily extract the specific information needed without an interpreter and if the data are available in sufficient time to be usable for corrective action. The pendulum appears to have swung back from early attempts to put everything on the computer to the realization by many mana-

gers that the computer should be used selectively. Often, a manual retrieval system is far more efficient and useful. Incidentally, if you are not receiving the kind of information you need in a usable form, it may be because you have not asked for it specifically enough. The computer has not yet been invented that can read your mind.

3. *Written reports.* Regular written status reports are among the most frequently required, yet least reliable and useful, feedback mechanisms in public-sector organizations. This is particularly true for narrative reports, which seem to earn more "brownie points" for their literary nature than for any useful information they might convey. Furthermore, consider the time cost in both writing and reading voluminous reports. Cost-benefit analysis should apply here also. Written reports, particularly in governmental organizations, are a fact of life, and they are here to stay. Let's make them as effective and efficient as possible. For reports written primarily to convey information for control purposes, I urge that they be: (a) *brief* (one or two pages); (b) in *outline* rather than narrative form (your high school English teacher is not going to grade them); and (c) structured to quickly *highlight* the most critical information. You don't have to wait for "them" to start it, since in all probability you are one of "them" to someone else. If this approach to written reports makes sense to you, try establishing it as your expectation in reports submitted by your subordinates. Next, experiment with it selectively in written reports you must submit. You may discover that "they" will appreciate such simplicity, once "they" get over the initial shock.

4. *Staff meetings.* Periodic staff meetings for reviewing progress toward objectives can be a tremendously useful way of keeping people informed, provided they don't degenerate into ritualistic "show and tell" exercises. To be effective, such meetings should be *brief,* with preestablished (and adhered to) starting and finishing times with *selective reports only* from those with new information to share which is of concern to the majority of those present. Staff meetings are expensive; make them pay off!

5. *"Management by exception."* This is a powerful control concept if applied properly. In accepting accountability for their efforts, subordinates are telling the boss that "no news is good news." They are making a commitment to notify the boss of any significant variances with the accompanying assurance that everything is going according to plan otherwise. For this concept to work, there must be a high level of trust between the boss and the subordinate. The boss must have enough confidence in the subordinate's ability and integrity to believe that performance toward objectives is satisfactory and that there is no need to check up on it. The subordinate must trust the boss not to draw a negative conclusion about ongoing performance because of the predominantly negative data that will be communicated. Furthermore, the boss must resist temptation to react emotionally to negative data if continued openness in feedback is desired. That high level of mutual trust does not appear to exist in most organizations. However, the potential payoff from having an effective "management by exception" understanding is so great that developing that level of trust is a worthwhile self-development objective for many managers to pursue.

6. *Periodic progress reviews.* An essential ongoing control method, regardless of any others employed, is the periodic progress review. As we mentioned earlier when we introduced the MOR Agreement, it is vital that the boss and subordinate agree on a schedule of progress reviews when objectives are negotiated. A progress review is conducted at predetermined times (monthly, bimonthly, quarterly) during the forecast period. It should be seen as an opportunity for the subordinate to bring the boss up to date on performance against *all* objectives — what went well, in addition to problem areas. It is also appropriate for reassessing the priorities established at the time of the original agreement to see if current circumstances might suggest a renegotiation. It places prime emphasis on taking a look at the total job, not just the problems (which are normally dealt with as they occur). The progress review serves as a good start or reinforcement of an approach toward "management by

exception," as it fills in some of the gaps that may exist. We will deal with the progress review again in the next chapter.

*How Can We Evaluate the Control Measures We Have Selected?*

Once we have identified the control measures we plan to use, we need to take one last critical look at them to make certain they are the most appropriate available means of providing us with the visibility we need. The following questions (which are listed again at the end of this chapter as "Key Questions for Evaluating Control Measures") will serve as a valuable aid in this exercise. Whenever possible and practical, ask others — subordinates, superiors, peers — to assist you in this evaluation, to make certain you have not overlooked any critical points.

1.   *What specific variances will this control identify?* We want to be certain that it will accentuate the occurrence of variances that have the greatest impact on the achievement of our objectives. Also, we need to be aware of other variances — less critical to this objective, perhaps — that might appear by this means. This could prove helpful in using the control measure to serve other needs as well or in reducing the size and cost of the measure by eliminating unnecessary data.

2.   *What significant variances may not be effectively identified?* Conversely, of course, we want to be absolutely certain that we have not overlooked any vital points. Taking another look at "What is likely to go wrong?" within the four basic elements of time, resources, quality, and quantity will frequently uncover an important factor that we originally overlooked. If we find that visibility on some significant variance is missing, we must either find another means of gaining this visibility or modify the proposed control measure so as to include it.

3.   *How much lead time is required to take effective corrective action? Does this control measure allow sufficient lead time?* Finding out that something is wrong when it is too late to do

anything about it is as bad as not finding out about it at all. (This is why standard computer runs, for example, often do not serve as effective control measuring devices for the average manager, particularly when there is a lag of two to four weeks between the time the action being reported takes place and the release of the report.) The control measure being used may be nothing more than an understanding with your subordinates to notify you verbally when some action is going off target. If this word reaches you consistently in time for you to recommend or take another course of action, it is an effective control measure. (Incidentally, this is a good opportunity for the application of your managerial judgment in the degree of control. With some employees, instructions to notify you when they are in trouble will be sufficient; with others, you may have to require regular progress reports, whether or not they think they are in trouble.)

4.   *How much time and effort will be required to apply this control measure?* This question has two parts, as we shall see. One of the easiest traps a manager can fall into is to request a certain kind of information from subordinates without giving any serious thought to the amount of time and effort that will be needed to produce that information.

I recall vividly a time when a top executive requested a report, by name and unit, on all supervisors in production operations who had and had not attended a particular supervisory training program. His reasons for wanting the information were quite valid. What was not readily apparent to him, however, was that this information, covering about 1000 individuals, had to be manually retrieved from records of two different programs dating back nearly three years. The task was further complicated by a significantly large number of organizational and personnel changes during the period. The final report, when submitted, represented well over 200 work hours of effort, including two successive Saturdays of clerical overtime. Had this executive realized the ultimate cost, he might well have settled for a less comprehensive report. Unfortunately, as is often the case in such situations, his subordinates (myself included) were reluctant to tell him what the report would or did cost the organization.

So the message here is, before implementing a control measuring method, take a good look at what it will cost to get this information and then ask yourself:

a) *Does the value received justify this cost?*

b) *Is there another, less costly measurement method available?*

5.   *What is the danger of overcontrolling by the manager? How can this be minimized?* Although this question relates to the matter of cost (discussed in Question 4), there is considerably more at stake here. We are referring to the demotivating effect the "checker-upper" has on his or her subordinates. The manager who spends an excessive amount of time looking over subordinates' shoulders and examining their progress is fostering two potentially dangerous reactions — first, the natural resentment on the part of the subordinate for being checked on too frequently, and second, the subordinate's tendency to let the boss catch the errors instead of assuming personal responsibility for catching them. How much controlling is "excessive" must be determined in light of the specific situation. Assuming that your subordinates are competent and will respond to a challenge, particularly if you are in a middle- or upper-management position, it may be better to run the risk of too little control rather than too much. It is a fine line to walk, but it should be examined very carefully as you evaluate the control measures you plan to use.

## Taking Corrective Action — What Will You Do?

This is the moment of truth. As we mentioned earlier, the only reason for having controlling as a management function is to enable us to take necessary corrective action to ensure the achieving of our objectives. If there were never a need for taking corrective action, we would have no need to perform the other controlling activities. Although this statement appears to be almost too elementary, it is an important point to keep in mind. The reason for this is to remove the negative connotation that often is associated with "corrective action." Taking corrective action is, and must be viewed as, a *positive* management activity and a normal part of the manager's job. It does not automatically imply that the manager or someone else in the organization has "screwed up" or done a bad job. Since our performance projections are largely based on estimates, some variance in action performance is almost inevitable. The key lies in knowing what to do and when.

*What Kinds of Corrective Action Are There?*

Assuming that the standards established are realistic and that the method of measurement is reasonably accurate, there are three kinds of corrective action that can take place (sometimes in combination):

1.    *Self-correcting action.* There are certain acceptable tolerances in performance within which deviations tend to balance out over a period of time. For example, an average daily output of 100 units could probably stand a deviation of plus or minus 5% without causing undue concern, provided a trend did not develop.

The other, perhaps more critical, type of self-correcting action is related to the motivation of the individual performing the work. This reinforces the need for availability of control information to those that are closest to the work. Usually, all that the competent individual needs in order to correct his or her own performance is the knowledge of what is expected and of where s/he stands in relation to those expectations. Allowing self-correcting performance without strong direction from above may require considerable restraint on the part of the superior, but should pay off in progressively less need for such direction or correction in the future. This is one important way that employee development can take place through Management by Objectives and Results. Every manager should work toward getting as close to 100% self-correcting action as possible — for economic as well as motivational reasons.

2. *Operating action.* When it becomes evident that corrective action is necessary, the immediate reaction of the average manager is to personally perform or have someone else perform specific operating work. The area manager may step in and handle a disgruntled client. The nursing supervisor may direct a nurse to use a different instrument. The office manager may rewrite a report that is going to top management. A bureau head may direct the firing of an employee who reports to a subordinate. It cannot be denied that such operating action is sometimes the only logical approach. Factors that influence such action are time limitations, emergency situations, technical know-how which the manager alone possesses, policy requirements, and minor corrections that are not likely to recur.

One thing, however, must be kept in mind whenever such specific operating action is used. The manager may be dealing with just the symptoms and overlooking the actual cause of the variance. Sending a special courier out with a late dispatch may satisfy the immediate requirement, but it doesn't determine why the dispatch was late in the first place, so that future such occurrences can be prevented. Also, it is almost axiomatic that the more often we solve our subordinates' problems for them, the more often they will let us.

Remember to resist the natural tendency to "get your hands back in the grease." After all, most of us probably became managers partially as a result of our technical competence and, deep down, we still get our kicks out of solving technical rather than managerial problems. When we do this, though, we should recognize that we are not only performing work that a person in a lesser position (and, presumably, at a lower rate of pay) should be performing, we may also be denying the subordinate a vital learning opportunity.

3. *Management action.* The third kind of corrective action requires the manager to review the management process that led up to the variance. It may have come as a result of poor planning, or an unexpected event may have made the variance

inevitable. The most realistic corrective action under the circumstances may be to change the original objective in some way or to modify the action plan to accommodate or offset the variance. Management action, as such, will require greater discipline on the manager's part but should be designed to both bring the performance back on target toward objectives and prevent the likelihood of similar problems in the future.

## In Summary

Establishing Controls, the final step down the MOR funnel, is designed to close the loop and keep us on the track toward accomplishing what we set out to do as a part of the earlier steps. One of the problems with this step is that the word "controlling" may itself conjure up an interpretation that suggests obedience, keeping in line, and conformity. However, for it to work effectively as a part of the MOR process, controlling must be seen as a human, not a mechanical, tool. As in all of the steps, we are still called on to exercise sound managerial judgment as we ask ourselves the three fundamental questions: What is likely to go wrong? How and when will we know? What will we do? Above all, we must continually remind ourselves that *effective controlling provides for adequate visibility in a timely fashion with the least expenditure of time and effort.*

## KEY QUESTIONS FOR EVALUATING CONTROL MEASURES

1. What specific variances will this control measure identify?
2. What significant variances may not be effectively identified?
3. How much lead time is required to take corrective action? Does this control measure allow sufficient lead time?
4. How much time and effort will be required to apply this control measure?

   a) Does the value justify the cost?

   b) Is there another, less costly measurement method available?

5. What is the danger of overcontrolling by the manager? How can this be minimized?

# 9

# COMMUNICATIONS —
# THE MOR CATALYST

Continually throughout this book, I have been emphasizing the fact that Management by Objectives and Results is a human, not a mechanical, process. Many public-sector organizations have implemented MBO as though it were an administrative procedure or reporting system. In such instances, it is not surprising that most managers in the organization are less than wholeheartedly committed to MBO. It is conceivable, of course, that an arbitrary, mechanical introduction of the steps in this process may produce a higher level of performance on the part of people farther down in the organization, if for no other reason than someone "up there" finally told them specifically what was expected. However, that is not where the real payoff comes from the use of this process.

## Communications Benefits and Applications

The following are some of the basic benefits that come from using the MOR process as a form of participative management — benefits that have economic as well as social aspects.

1. *It encourages commitment rather than compliance.* Compliance implies "doing it because I have to." Commitment means "doing it because I believe in it." The boss can demand compliance, but not commitment; compliance usually results in "doing what has to be done, but not much more." Commit-

ment is a voluntary action and, more often than not, is in direct proportion to the amount of involvement the individual has in the decision-making processes. The more influence I feel I have in determining the things that will affect me, the more likely I am to be committed to their successful accomplishment. Conceptually, the major difference between an objective and an assignment lies in who makes the determination. An objective is something I set for myself, usually with substantial input from my boss, my subordinates, and others. An assignment is something that is given to me by my boss with the expectation that I will carry it out as specified. There is a place for both. Obviously, it is neither practical nor necessary to negotiate an agreement on everything that has to be done. However, if we want real commitment from our people, we've got to give them "a piece of the action." The managerial risk is somewhat higher, of course, when we allow others to exercise their decision-making abilities. When we consider the potential payoff from substantially higher levels of performance, a realistic cost-benefit analysis makes such a risk look like an outstanding investment.

2.   *It encourages innovation balanced by reality.* By challenging those who are significantly affected to make some inputs into proposed courses of action, we can tap the creative potential that lies within everyone. Conversely, highly innovative ideas are of value only when they can be achieved. Getting reactions and suggested modifications from those who have to get the job done can help to keep our planning efforts in a realistic perspective. I am frequently asked if it is more effective to start the MOR process at the top, middle, or bottom of an organization. My semifacetious answer is "Yes!" MOR can be started at any level where there is a responsible manager who wants to make it work. A successful experience at any level can radiate in all directions. More specifically, of course, where there is a high level of personal *and continuing* commitment by members of top management, the chances for successful organization-wide application are substantially higher. (We'll discuss that more as a part of implementation in the next

chapter.) I visualize the formation of organizational objectives, ideally, as following a "yo-yo" pattern. Top management starts by shaping "a big fuzzy ball" that identifies major concerns and a general picture of the direction it wants the organization to follow. This "fuzzy ball" is then "rolled down the string," allowing those with a key responsibility to help shape it. By the time it is "rolled back up the string," the "fuzzy ball" will look somewhat different from when it started. Members of top management now have the benefit of inputs from all those who can make it work or not work and, with this added data, should be able to set a challenging, yet realistic, set of organizational objectives much more effectively than if they had done so in isolation.

3.   *It enables every manager to be President.* Before you start pointing fingers at "them," remember that "top management" is something of a euphemism. "Top management" does not necessarily represent that small, select group that sits on the uppermost point of the total organizational pyramid. You, also, can be "top management," regardless of your level in the organization. This can be approached with what is frequently referred to as the *Unit President Concept.* Consider yourself to be *President* of your "company," i.e., that part of the organization that you head up, whether that be a major bureau with thousands of employees or a small operation of two or three people; your boss represents the *Board of Directors.* Your job is to manage your "company" the best way you know how. All you need from the *Board* is a license to do it your way. Most *Boards* are happy to allow their *Presidents* to manage the "company" in any legal and ethical manner that achieves the results they want. Therefore, if the "fuzzy ball" comes down to you from higher management levels, you can add your inputs together with those from key people in your unit. If you do not have that opportunity to significantly influence higher-level objectives that affect you, you can still create your own "fuzzy ball." Even if most of your "objectives" appear to be "cast in concrete" by the time they reach you, normally there is still a great deal of latitude (more than most managers are willing to

admit) in determining how to achieve them. By defining the outer limits, you can still make it possible for your subordinates to influence what affects them.

4. *It encourages negotiation and mutual agreement.* In most objective-setting discussions, each participant has a somewhat different perspective related to basic information, importance, and approach. This should be seen as healthy. Complete agreement, without some dissenting points of view, could lead to organizational stagnation. Ideally, objectives agreed to will represent the best thinking of all concerned and will be better than what any one person would have come up with individually. Although differences should be aired openly, negotiation must lead to an agreement that all participants understand and accept.

5. *It reduces or eliminates the need for the word "can't."* When a new suggested objective or assignment comes along, there is a natural temptation for the manager with a full workload to say, or at least think, "I can't do it!" By having a realistic set of objectives, particularly if they have been costed out properly, the manager is in a position to make tradeoff decisions or recommendations. Since it is virtually impossible to anticipate all requirements likely to come along, it is almost inevitable that a manager will have to reevaluate priorities at some point during the projected period of time. In fact, it is practically a certainty that actual accomplishments will be somewhat different from what was forecast when objectives were established. That does not invalidate the forecast. The forecast merely provides us with a more valid rationale for shifting directions if later requirements make that necessary. It means, however, that if we do shift, it is with full awareness that we are shifting and that there is a good reason for doing so. Furthermore, a clear change in direction calls for a renegotiation of the original agreement. If a standard pattern is established that new "objectives" or assignments that come along are expected to be accomplished *in addition to* those in the original agreement, it is an open invitation for the assignee

to play games with the original agreement in anticipation of the inevitable. On the other hand, if it is clearly understood at the time of the original agreement that any significant changes are subject to renegotiation, the subordinate manager can say to his or her boss, "I *can* meet the new requirements, and this is what it will cost." The manager may then have to modify, postpone, or cancel some objectives in the original agreement. By once again applying the concept of cost-benefit analysis, we are able to focus more of our attention on what we *can* do rather than on what we *can't* do.

6.    *It provides a rational basis for review and feedback on progress toward objectives.* In many organizations, reviews of progress during the year tend to be ceremonial, "How are things going?" – "Fine!" types of affairs or oriented toward individual problems — usually after the problems have occurred. The recommended MOR practice of agreeing on and adhering to a progress review schedule establishes a built-in mechanism for making sure that both the boss and the subordinate are brought up to date periodically on what is happening related to *total* performance. Furthermore, such a review can be focused on specifics rather than on generalities. The MOR Agreement then becomes an effective tool for ongoing communications.

7.    *It encourages intergroup communication and teamwork.* The various steps in the MOR process tend to reveal areas where open communication and cooperation with other groups or individuals are both necessary and desirable. They also tend to highlight areas where conflict or potential conflict exist, in such a way that they can be more readily dealt with and resolved. There is conflict in every organization. Managed effectively, it can be one of the most powerful tools available for creative growth. Unmanaged, it can be one of the most destructive. A necessary ingredient for managing conflict effectively is the ability to break complex operations down into their component parts and to focus on the specific contributions various individuals or units must make in order to achieve results. That's MOR!

8.   *It provides a common language base.* One of the problems that separates management from most of the other accepted professions is the lack of a common vocabulary. (Louis Allen has done the most comprehensive job of defining management terms that I know of.* Although not identical, the terms used in this text are conceptually consistent with his.) Mention the words "accountability," "responsibility," "authority," "function," "activity," "objective," "control," in a group of a dozen managers, and you are likely to get 12 different interpretations, any of which could be correct. Exposing all managers to MOR and its terminology should reduce the potential for semantic confusion among those who have to communicate with one another about management concerns. The terms used here are certainly not the only ones that could be applied, but they are appropriate to the management processes being described. Their use among people using them in a similar context inevitably facilitates effective communication.

9.   *It provides a tangible rationale for budgeting/funding requests.* It is virtually a universal practice now for organizations that "hold the purse strings" to insist on hard justification for proposed expenditures, even when supporting ongoing efforts. Congressional/legislative committees, approving agencies, foundations, county boards of supervisors, city councils, and school boards, as well as higher-level management in most public-sector organizations, are becoming increasingly concerned about "what we are getting for the money." As the stewards of public funds, they have not only the right but also the obligation to demand such justification. Regardless of the budgeting system used — PPBS or any other — MOR can provide the kind of data needed (measurable results, timing, costs, benefits) to support such budgeting or funding requests.

There are many other communications advantages that can come from applying MOR in an organization, particularly when

---

* See the *Louis A. Allen Common Vocabulary of Professional Management,* Louis A. Allen Associates, Inc., Palo Alto, California.

a participative management approach is used. We have identified some of the more critical ones here. Now, let's see how we can make the communications work.

## Methods for Effective MOR Communications

In examining the various methods of using MOR as a communications medium, we will approach it from five different perspectives: individual (one to one), intraunit (team applications), intergroup (both internal and external to the total organization), organization-wide (particularly top management role), and support or staff units (special concerns). Many of the methods identified here are mentioned elsewhere in this text. This section brings them all together in order to highlight the various options available. Each method will be dealt with briefly, although an entire book could be written about this area alone.

### 1. Individual (One to One)

This is the most frequently used application of the MOR process; an individual manager uses part or all of the steps in the MOR process to communicate on a one-to-one basis with the boss and/or each key subordinate. Place yourself, mentally, in either the boss or subordinate role in studying this application. The same process applies, regardless of which side of the desk you are sitting on.

*Negotiation*

1.   *Roles and Missions* (or their equivalent), if none exist, should be drafted by the subordinate as suggested on pp. 32–33 and agreement reached with the boss as a foundation for all work the subordinate will be held accountable for. Any unresolved questions should have objectives set for dealing with them. Both the boss and the subordinate should have copies of the final agreement for reference.

2.   *MOR Agreement* (key results areas, indicators, objectives), or whatever parts of it are to be applied, should be drafted by

the subordinate, then discussed, modified as appropriate, and final agreement reached with the boss prior to the start of the forecast period which the MOR Agreement is to cover. Both the boss and the subordinate should have copies of the final agreement for reference.

## Problem Discussions

These discussions should be initiated by either the boss or the subordinate as soon as problems — current or potential — related to negotiated agreements become apparent to either party. Discussion should focus on what the problem is and what should be done to take care of it, not on fixing, or trying to escape from, blame.

## Progress Reviews

Reviews are conducted periodically during the forecast period, preferably at predetermined times (monthly, bimonthly, quarterly) as established in the MOR Agreement. These reviews should be seen as an opportunity for the subordinate to bring the boss up to date on everything, good and not so good, affecting the subordinate's area of accountability. The MOR Agreement serves as a logical review document to ensure that the total picture is covered. Discussion of specific problems, when brought up during a progress review, should be seen as secondary to a mutual assessment of the current situation as related to progress toward objectives.

## Renegotiation

Unit roles and missions and/or parts of the MOR Agreement should be renegotiated whenever there is a significant shift in priorities, organizational direction, or uncontrollable circumstances that impact heavily on the subordinate's ability to meet objectives (for example, loss of key personnel, delay in appropriations, etc.). In order to encourage prudent risk-taking on the part of subordinates, there must be an "escape hatch" for dealing with the unanticipated. Otherwise, the subordinate will set only "safe" objectives.

*Performance Reviews*

Conducted at or near the end of the forecast period in the MOR Agreement, performance reviews generally occur once a year, although six-month or quarterly review periods are not uncommon, particularly at lower levels in the organization. A performance *review* is related to, though different from, a performance *appraisal*. Our concern here is with assessing total performance against agreed on objectives, for the purpose of improving our effectiveness in the next forecast period, not for coming up with a "score card" on an individual. Obviously, this performance will be a major factor to be considered when appraisal time comes around, but the two should not be tied together, or the value in future planning is likely to be reduced, if not lost altogether. It is entirely appropriate for a new MOR Agreement to be negotiated at the same time as, or shortly after, completion of the performance review, using that analysis as a partial data base for setting new objectives. Unless there is a clear case of incompetency, the performance review is not a time for recriminations or excuses; rather, it is a learning period for both parties, leading to increasing the managerial effectiveness of both of them.

## 2. Intraunit (Team Applications)

Ironically, the two kinds of groups that seem to function most frequently, and most effectively, as a team in many organizations are the small group of senior managers who comprise the top-management group at one extreme, and small groups of professional and technical specialists reporting to a first-line supervisor at the other. The reasons for the latter are fairly obvious, since most such groups are built around a similar or related set of skills and something of a common purpose. The top-management group, on the other hand, has to be somewhat schizophrenic in that its members are in most cases both heads of major functional units and members of the policy-making, strategic-planning group for the *total* organization. It is in this latter role that the members of this group are more likely to operate as a team. Although the same dynamics can, and frequently do, work at any level in the organization, there tends to be greater diversity of both interest and purpose at middle levels, which makes operating as a team more difficult. My reason for raising that issue, however, is to point out that regardless of the level in the organization, the application of MOR as an intraunit or team-effectiveness process is essentially the same. Differences are primarily ones of scope and magnitude.

## Roles and Missions

Determination of roles and missions frequently serves as an effective initial team effort. Using one of the sets of questions for clarifying roles and missions (see pp. 34, 35), group members can share their perceptions and feelings about key issues affecting the way they operate. Although this may be a time-consuming effort at the outset, it gets at issues that are often taken for granted and rarely discussed. Generally, there are far more differences in points of view among members of a so-called team than most of its members might have predicted. This, perhaps more than any other step in the MOR process, is an example of the fact that the process of getting there is far more critical than the final product. Although the result should be a working statement of roles and missions that all members will subscribe to and support, the "clearing of the air" on controversial or misinterpreted issues is essential for continuing team effectiveness. A retreat or planning conference away from the normal business location, with substantial built-in time flexibility, is usually much more conducive to open discussion and resolution. A third-party facilitator or consultant can be particularly helpful here. Also, although agreement on a final statement might come as a result of an extended meeting, it is more likely to require two or more such meetings before an acceptable draft is developed. The cost, in terms of the time of people, may be moderately high. However, the potential benefit from having all members of the team pulling in essentially the same direction is phenomenal, making it one of the best investments the group could make. One caution: don't allow the group members to get so involved in endless semantic discussions on specific wording to be used that the conceptual value is lost. You are far better off coming out relatively quickly with an imperfect statement that can serve as a working tool, with an agreement to reevaluate and modify it after a given period of time, such as six months.

## Key Results Areas, Indicators, and Objectives

These can be developed for the unit from among team members whose individual contributions form a common thread. These could incorporate only those areas where the group members will be functioning as a team, or they could be expanded to cover the total contributions of the unit. A frequent variation on this occurs when the unit head uses other members of the team as a resource in the determination of his or her own key results areas, indicators, and objectives. In the case of the top-management group, corporate-level objectives are likely to be finalized through such a process.

## Action Plans and Controls

These are logical areas of participation for team members who play partial roles in the achievement of unit objectives. Since, as we mentioned in our discussion of action plans, there are normally several alternative ways of achieving an objective and, in fact, many action steps will become objectives for subordinates, team members' active participation at this stage becomes crucial. Even though the "real world" limits the amount of impact they may have on the objectives, they can and should have some influence on how those objectives are to be achieved. The same thing applies in establishing controls. In addition, since we should be looking for the most economical and effective means, team members can help devise common control methods that will serve all of their needs, reducing or eliminating duplication and wasted effort.

## Intraunit Critique

This is an extremely powerful communications tool — if there is a relatively high level of trust among group members. Here, in addition to developing total unit efforts, each participant uses the other group members as a sounding board for any or all of his or her MOR Agreement. Such a critique process could range from simple feedback and helpful suggestions to including group approval as a requirement. Furthermore, critiquing helps to identify areas where mutual support is needed or where potential conflict exists, in such a way that they can be dealt with positively.

*Intraunit Review*

An extension of the intraunit critique, the intraunit review encourages one or more of each individual's progress reviews to be conducted with the group rather than with only the boss. This serves two purposes: providing a broader feedback base and keeping other group members informed. To be effective, the frequency of this kind of a review should be limited to keep such meetings from turning into ritualistic "show and tell" exercises.

### 3. Intergroup (Both Internal and External to the Total Organization)

Particularly in the public sector, it is a rare organizational unit whose work does not seriously affect, or is not heavily affected by, the work of several other units — peer units in the same organization, support agencies, client/user groups, legislative committees, unions, comparable units in other government branches, etc. The concerned unit should clearly identify those others with which a significant amount of close cooperation and communication is essential. Then, using one or more of the following means, work on improving it. This could be an example of an objective under the key results areas of "Inter-organizational Relationships."

*Roles and Missions, MOR Agreements, and/or Selected Objectives*

These should be shared with other units that are significantly affected. This sharing could range from a detailed discussion, analysis, and negotiation between the unit managers and key members of their staffs to a simple exchange of documents accompanied by whatever clarification may be required. The purpose is to keep both units aware of mutual support needs so that neither is surprised by the other.

*Action Plans and Controls*

These should identify other units affected, what will be done in connection with them, and who will be accountable for seeing that it gets done. In many objectives, a modest amount of advance communication or negotiation with other units could save vast amounts of wasted effort because of inadequate or late support from these other units, not to mention the inevitable recriminations and hard feelings.

*Conflict Resolution*

Interunit conflict can be dealt with much more openly and objectively when the focus is on specific areas of influence, objectives, or action plans. There *will be* conflict between units. The truly effective manager has learned how to turn that conflict into a positive, rather than a destructive, force. Many of the approaches to conflict resolution suggested in the technology of organization development* will work even more effectively when there are clear statements of roles and missions, objectives, and action plans in existence.

### 4. Organization-wide (Particularly Top-Management Role)

As mentioned earlier, members of the top-management group have to be somewhat schizophrenic, since they wear at least two separate "hats" in the organization. When they are filling their roles in organizational policy-making and strategic planning, they must relate more directly to factors that impact on the total organization, even when that action may be at the expense of concerns within the functional units they head up. In the long run, of course, such a posture should increase the value and effectiveness of their functional units as well. Organization-wide implementation of Management by Objectives and Results could be an example of such an application.

---

* See Bibliography for suggested readings in Organization Development.

## Corporate Roles and Missions

Determining and interpreting corporate roles and missions are the responsibility of this group. Using the questions for Clarifying Corporate Roles and Missions (see p. 34), plus any other issues that need to be considered, the top-management group should formulate a tentative statement of roles and missions for the total organization, probably using a retreat or planning conference away from the normal business location, as suggested earlier under team applications. This tentative statement can then be tested with other managers in or out of the organization, modified as appropriate, and put into final form. This statement should then be disseminated throughout the organization, preferably with interpretive discussions conducted by the members of the top-management group who were involved in its formulation. The roles-and-missions statement itself, together with the interpretive discussions with members of top management, can go a long way toward opening up communications throughout the hierarchy, in addition to clarifying organizational direction and the expectations of top management.

## Corporate Objectives

These can be formulated in a similar manner to corporate roles and missions, except that a more organized approach to getting inputs from others is necessary in order to validate the objectives. The "yo-yo" pattern suggested on p. 172 fits such an organized approach conceptually. Practically, such an input process must be facilitated in a short time span, preferably 30 days or less, if it is to work effectively. Corporate objectives should reflect both the short term (usually related to the fiscal year) and the long term (usually beyond the fiscal year — using a rolling five-year plan, for example). Once they are finalized, corporate objectives should be disseminated throughout the organization as quickly as possible, with top-management interpretation as necessary, so that unit managers can prepare their own objectives in support of, or consistent with, those of the total organization.

## Documentation and Reporting Systems

Such systems are necessary ingredients of an organization-wide application of MOR. This does not mean that it has to become another "paper mill." It can, *if managers allow it to,* but that will relegate MOR to another procedural exercise rather than to a dynamic management process. Documentation and reports that go to top management or that are distributed throughout the organization should be limited strictly to those that are of *direct concern* to those receiving them. So-called "information copies" tend to multiply like amoebas, particularly in governmental organizations. By and large, supervisory control must be built on a relationship between a manager and his or her immediate superior. Therefore, most of a given manager's reports should go no farther than one level above and one below. Top management can control the "paper mill" by limiting its documentation and reporting requirements strictly to those things in which the top managers must become directly involved, thereby also communicating a very powerful motivational message — that they trust their managers to manage.

## Periodic Communications from Top Management

Such communications can and should be a regular part of an organization-wide MOR application. These include progress reports on certain corporate objectives and information on new developments affecting corporate roles, missions, and objectives. By building this form of communication around these corporate documents, managers throughout the organization have a common frame of reference and can feel more a part of the total operation.

## 5. Support or Staff Units (Special Concerns)

Obviously, the same factors described above in relation to other organizational units apply equally well to the management of a support or staff unit. However, there are two special concerns related to MOR, one that applies to all such units and one that applies to those with a specific organizational responsibility related to MOR implementation.

## General Support Services

Such services are those provided to other units within the total organization which are, in reality, the unit's customers/clients/users whose needs must be satisfied. Consequently, many support units see themselves largely in a reactive mode of operation — for example, the Personnel unit that responds to requests for filling staff vacancies or the Data-Processing unit that programs and produces a new analytical report when requested. Although a certain amount of reactive service is inevitable, an increasing number of support units are adopting a much stronger anticipatory posture. George Odiorne, in a recent address,* suggested that staff organizations should be setting many of their objectives six months *in advance* of the line organizations they serve, so that their services will be readily available when they are needed, not lagging behind. In order to do that, many support units should have a key results area called something like "Anticipated Needs Assessment." Objectives flowing out of that area would relate to the development of early-warning information systems, involvement in customers' advance planning efforts, and staying ahead of the state-of-the-art. Furthermore, support organizations that set their objectives in anticipation of, rather than in reaction to, their customers' needs are in a much stronger position to influence the direction those needs ultimately take.

## MOR Advisory Services

Informing/training/consulting/reviewing services designed to assist managers in the organization in the implementation and maintenance of MOR fall in this category. These services are frequently provided by organizational units responsible for training, personnel, organizational planning/development, and administrative services, or by special MOR support groups. Such groups can perform an extremely valuable service, *provided* they see their role as primarily advisory or supportive, *not* administrative. Providing information designed to increase understanding of the process as it is being applied, conducting

---

* ASTD Region 8 Conference, Scottsdale, Arizona, October 1, 1975.

or providing training for managers in the necessary skills, assisting individuals or small groups of managers in applying the *process* to their own operations, and providing a sounding board to help managers evaluate and more sharply define their own objectives — all can make a major contribution to the effective implementation of MOR. When such groups have taken on the role of administering, directing, approving, screening, or monitoring the MOR-related efforts of other managers in the total organization, the result has usually been the creation of a new bureaucracy which either usurps the responsibility that managers should accept for themselves or makes the MOR process virtually impotent as a positive managerial tool. Part of the mission of such a support group should be to work itself out of a job. The MBO Adviser concept, as introduced in England and practiced in many other parts of the world, advocates the selection of individuals with line-management experience for a limited-time assignment in that role, following which they will be returned to a line-management position. An appropriate indicator of effectiveness for an MOR advisory group, after initial implementation, might be "number or percentage of managers satisfactorily practicing MOR *without* our assistance." The basic mission of such a group should be to help managers perform their own management work better, not to do it for them.

## In Summary

Management by Objectives and Results (MOR) is a human, not a mechanical, process. Consequently, the six steps in the MOR funnel must be seen as providing a means for increasing the understanding and commitment of the people who must work within that framework. Effective communication at every step along the way provides the catalyst for bringing about that understanding and commitment. We have examined many of the significant benefits that can come to an organization that practices MOR as a form of participative management. We have also looked at several different ways in which MOR can be used to increase the effectiveness of organizational communications. As with each of the other steps we have covered, the ideas presented here are designed more as stimulators than as prescriptions. Only when you have adapted these ideas to your own particular style and situation will they work for you.

# 10

# IMPLEMENTING MOR IN PUBLIC-SECTOR ORGANIZATIONS

This is really the moment of truth. Everything we have covered up to this point has meaning only if it is used. There are many ways in which Management by Objectives and Results can be implemented, ranging from the simple and informal to the comprehensive and formal, with several variations in between. In this chapter, we will approach implementation from two perspectives — that of the individual manager, regardless of position in the organization, and that of the organization itself. The first section, related to the individual manager's perspective, should be studied and analyzed by everyone who plans to do anything at all with MOR, regardless of whether or not the total organization is committed to the MOR approach. It will identify most of the options available to you in such a way that you can develop a plan for implementation that is most appropriate for you. Obviously, if you are a part of an organization that has a formal MBO or MOR process in operation, that will influence your selection of options.

The second section, related to the organizational perspective, addresses itself more to those who will play a planning or implementing role beyond that which affects their own units. If your concern is related primarily to applying MOR within your own area of accountability, you may wish to skip over or merely scan that section. In any case, please don't use the material covered there to "second guess" the implementation efforts of others in your organization unless you are prepared to play an active role in bringing about what you consider to be desirable changes. Specific organizational circumstances may have dictated certain practices which may appear to be contrary to my recommendations. Destructive attack on these practices will serve no useful purpose unless they can realistically be changed and you are able to help with their rebuilding.

## From the Individual Manager's Perspective

1.    *Commitment* is the first key factor you need to consider — primarily your own level of commitment. To what degree are you willing to make an investment of your own time, energy, and talent to make MOR work in your own organizational unit? Do you see yourself adopting it completely as a managerial way of life? Or, do you see it as a major imposition and waste of time to the point that you are unwilling to do any more than you absolutely have to? Or, are you somewhere between those two extremes? Make a subjective judgment as to the degree of current personal commitment you feel, using a scale of 1 (low) to 10 (high), and enter it here _____ if you wish. (This should be an honest personal assessment to guide *you* in the remainder of this effort. If you are concerned about the reactions of others who might see it, I recommend that you leave the space blank rather than enter an inflated or deflated figure.) Obviously, your degree of commitment will have a significant influence on your initial implementation efforts. Furthermore, it is highly likely that your degree of commitment will change after you get into the implementation itself.

Once you have analyzed your own commitment, you should make an assessment of the degree of commitment it is reasonable to expect from others around you who will have an effect on your efforts — your higher-level management, your subordinates, and your colleagues or peer managers with whom you must work regularly. Obviously, if their commitment is likely to be substantially higher or lower than yours, your implementation plan will be affected. Commitment, or lack of it, to a management approach such as MOR is directly related to both knowledge (of the process itself) and inclination. If a lack of knowledge is the primary reason for the fact that their commitment seems somewhat lower than yours, a part of your action plan needs to be pointed at filling that knowledge gap. If you predict that others' commitment will be lower than yours because of their resistance to this kind of a participative approach, the situation is much more sensitive. The degree of mutual trust that exists between you and each of the other groups is a critical element. If that trust is high, it may just be a case of demonstrating the value of the MOR approach and encouraging others to go along with it. If that trust is low, you may wish to set an objective related to improving the level of trust before getting others formally involved in MOR.

2.   *Implementation approaches* can cover a wide range of options. Here are several commonly used ones that you may wish to consider, either separately or in combination with others.

a) *Practicing it yourself first and setting an example.* Clearly, if you plan to implement MOR in your unit in any way, you need to apply it to yourself to avoid being seen as a hypocrite. This particular option, however, carries that a step further. *Before* getting anyone else involved, you may wish to work on MOR strictly as it relates to your own job, becoming comfortable with the process yourself first. You may wish to do that in private — in effect, reaching an MOR Agreement with yourself. Or, you may want to involve your superior, your subordinates, or some of your colleagues or peers either as sounding boards or possibly to the extent of reaching a negotiated agreement as applied to your job.

b) *Informal involvement of others in your objectives and action plans.* This is an extension of option (a), whereby selected individuals, probably subordinates, would actually be involved in helping you prepare your objectives and action plans, rather than merely reacting to them.

c) *Developing roles and missions for your organizational unit.* You may wish to concentrate initially on achieving a common understanding among those around you as to the nature and scope of the work that you are or should be doing. Conceivably, this could also serve as an initial step toward improving mutual trust, if that is one of your concerns.

d) *Determining key results areas.* Clearly establishing what areas you should and should not get involved in could be a major step toward getting your own job under control, particularly if you can also get your boss, subordinates, and others to understand and accept your perception. Or, if your organizational unit consists primarily of a small group of professional or technical specialists performing similar tasks, you may wish to reach agreement on key results areas for the total group.

e) *Starting on a voluntary basis with selected individuals reporting to you.* For a variety of reasons, it may not be practical or desirable to get all of your subordinates involved in MOR. Therefore, it may make sense to invite subordinates to participate on a voluntary basis. The key word there is "voluntary," so that there is no suggestion of possible favor or disfavor associated with a subordinate's decision to participate or not.

f) *Starting on a formal basis with all who report directly to you.* In order to ensure consistency and to avoid some of the problems that may result from purely voluntary participation, you may wish to have each direct subordinate apply all or part of the MOR process to his or her job. Remember, however, that the emphasis here is on those who report *directly* to you. If they also have subordinates, they should be involved in any decision to carry it further down into the organization.

g) *Starting on a project basis.* You may decide that neither you nor any of your key subordinates is ready to apply MOR to the entire job. You may wish to gain some familiarity with the process by applying it to a major project, such as introducing a new service. A project requiring a significant amount of planning can be laid out, using all or part of the MOR funnel as a working model. In that way, you can test MOR out in a relatively narrow framework while continuing to perform the rest of the job as previously. As you achieve success in that application, you can expand it to include other parts of the job as well. To give it a fair test, however, make certain that most of your subordinates *want* the project selected to be successful.

h) *Starting with one unit and developing it there first as a model.* If you are in a middle- or upper-level management position, it may not be practical to introduce MOR throughout your entire operation. Selecting one unit that reports to you and concentrating on making it work there first, with the expectation that it can be expanded to other units later, may be the way to go. The key to the effectiveness of this approach lies in selecting that unit with the highest probability of success. This usually means that the key individuals within that unit are likely to respond favorably to such an approach. Don't try it with your toughest unit, on the assumption that "if it works there, it will work anywhere," unless you are a masochist. A failure there will substantially reduce the likelihood of success elsewhere.

i) *Total implementation, starting with top management.* This option applies only if you are a member of top management or are in a position to significantly influence that group's decision. The second section of this chapter will address itself to this option.

j) *Getting other key managers exposed.* You may wish to get started with MOR, but feel that your chances of success would be much greater if certain other managers (superiors, subordinates, peers) knew more about it. Such exposure could come through:

1) *A public seminar* or training program offered by the Civil Service Commission's General Management Institute, a consulting organization specializing in MOR, a local college or university, or a professional or trade association.

2) *An in-house seminar* or training program conducted exclusively for your organization by you, your own training unit, or an outside contractor.
3) *An in-house motivational presentation* by a recognized expert.
4) *An informal discussion* on the subject conducted by you and/or others in the organization who are familiar with the MOR process.
5) *A self-teaching audiocassette program on MOR,* prepared and presented by George Morrisey, which is available for individual or group orientation or study.
6) *A videotape presentation* on the MOR funnel by George Morrisey.
7) *Other audio- or videotape recordings or films* on the subject.
8) *Reading* this book or selected portions of it and/or some of the many other books and journal articles that have been written on the subject — recognizing that reading, by itself, rarely motivates anybody to do anything.

k) *Organizational survey and analysis,* to determine what may help or hinder MOR implementation in your organization, may be necessary or desirable prior to moving ahead with it. Walt Mahler's book *Diagnostic Studies*\* is a particularly useful resource for this kind of an activity, as are several other publications in the Organization Development field. One caution here: don't use an organizational survey unless you are prepared (1) to hear something you don't want to hear — in other words, to receive feedback from people in your organization or unit that is substantially different from what you might hope for or expect — and (2) to take some positive action based on the feedback you receive. If such feedback causes a visible negative reaction on your part or appears to be ignored, people are likely to perceive problems they didn't know they had before. Such

---

\*  Walter R. Mahler, *Diagnostic Studies,* Reading, Mass.: Addison-Wesley, 1974.

surveys are best conducted by skilled professionals who know what they are doing.

This is by no means an exhaustive list of options. It merely represents ones with which we are familiar. A variation on one of these approaches or even a totally different one might be much more appropriate for you in your circumstances. If so, use it! Our purpose here has been to provide you with as broad a shopping list as possible, highlighting the fact that there is no *right way* to implement MOR in an organization or organizational unit.

3. *Determining who else, specifically, needs to be involved at the outset* is crucial if the process is to work in your unit. Many of the implementation approaches we have identified require *others* to become involved. Now is the time to erase the word *others* and insert the actual names of those you will be approaching. The very act of writing their names down on a piece of paper and indicating how you plan to get each involved will go a long way toward clarifying your own thinking and commitment to action, even if you destroy the piece of paper immediately. The step of getting initial involvement of others (boss, subordinates, peers) is one where many managers tend to procrastinate.

4. *Taking some immediate action* to get the process started is critical. Our experience with managers participating in MOR seminars suggests that unless some specific action related to implementing MOR takes place within the first two weeks after completing the seminar, the likelihood of anything happening is reduced to an anemic level. Such action does not need to be monumental. It could be as simple as completing your own MOR Agreement, discussing various options with other key people, or making a firm decision to proceed with one of the suggested approaches. The secret lies in doing *something* to keep inertia from setting in. It is much easier to sustain a process that is in motion than it is to start it up again after it has stopped. If you are ready to move ahead with MOR in your organizational unit, now is the time to set one or more objec-

tives and lay out action plans, as appropriate, to make certain that you do. A worksheet covering these considerations is included for your convenience and use at the end of this chapter.

## From the Perspective of the Total Organization

As mentioned earlier, the balance of this chapter will be of primary interest to those whose implementation concern goes beyond that of their own organizational units. MOR can and should be implemented at the individual unit level even if the larger organization is not committed to operating in this manner. However, the benefits will be multiplied many times over if a consistent, organization-wide approach is followed. There are many ways in which this can be done, to the point that any organization can design a plan that will meet its unique requirements. Also, although we will be referring to the *total organization*, that term can apply to any major segment of an organization, such as a bureau, region, or area, that is large enough to support the efforts described here.

### Critical Factors

An organization-wide approach requires that some critical factors be recognized if MOR is to become more than just another "fire drill" exercise.

1. *Management commitment.* The key management decision makers must make a total *and continuing* visible commitment to the approach. An attitude of "Let's try it out for a while and see if it works" will almost certainly doom the effort to failure. The key managers must start by defining roles, missions, and objectives for the total organization and for their own specific spheres of influence. Only when subordinate managers see that the boss is willing to practice what s/he preaches is there likely to be a significant incentive to follow through at lower levels. Furthermore, this commitment must be seen as continuing beyond the fanfare of the initial kickoff stages. In too many instances, in both the public and private sectors, key executives have introduced different management approaches, such

as MOR, with the zeal of a spur-of-the-moment religious convert whose prime mission in life is to bring "the word" to the unenlightened. Unfortunately, as frequently happens with such converts, this zeal usually has a relatively short life after the initial euphoria. If, after a few weeks or months, the key individuals who strongly touted MOR at the outset appear to have lost interest or fail to visibly follow through with commitments they have made, the message to the rest of the organization comes through loud and clear. For it to last, the key managers must clearly and visibly maintain their interest in and practice of MOR in the organization.

2. *Time and pace required.* A reasonable expectation of the time required to fully implement MOR in a reasonably large organization (more than 50 members of management) is two to five years. Undoubtedly, some immediate benefits will result from its implementation, and some units will be able to adapt to it faster than others. However, the learning of the specific MOR techniques, the integration of various units into a common approach, and the overcoming of initial skepticism must be accomplished before the real benefit comes for the organization. It would be unrealistic to think that this could be accomplished effectively in less time. The prime payoff from MOR comes in the long range far more than in the short term.

In addition, when the plan is to implement the process formally from the top-management level on down, I recommend a gestation period of about six months before beginning formal implementation at the next major level. There are two reasons for this. First, the time lag provides an opportunity for the boss to demonstrate a personal commitment to the approach. Second, even if someone else is providing the formal skill training in the process, the principal coach or adviser in the process for lower-level managers should be the boss. Therefore, the boss had better become comfortable with the process first. This does not mean that you should wait six months before informing or involving your subordinates at all. Obviously, they can and should participate in various aspects of unit MOR planning. However, six months is a realistic period to wait before requiring a formal commitment to an MOR Agreement.

Finally, MOR requires a fairly substantial amount of managerial time — for training, preparation of plans, negotiations, meetings and consultations, coaching, reviewing, etc. Consequently, attempting to introduce the approach during times of crisis or peak workload periods would be foolhardy; MOR simply will not get the attention it needs. (Of course, if the organization is continually on a "management by crisis" cycle, an executive decision to stop and shift directions may have to be made.) However, recognizing that a significant portion of any manager's time should be devoted to the planning function, effort devoted to the MOR process should be seen as a reallocation of time rather than as time lost. In fact, requiring managers to devote the time needed to get started with MOR may force them to reduce the amount of time and effort they are putting in on things they shouldn't have been doing anyway.

3. *Disenchantment period.* There *will be* a disenchantment period, probably after about six months, during which some managers are likely to wonder if the effort required to implement MOR has been worth it. This is due to several factors, for example:

a) The initial novelty has worn off.

b) Some previously set objectives now appear unlikely to be achieved for a variety of reasons, some of which may be beyond the individual manager's control.

c) Managers are starting to feel the impact of the fact that the results of their efforts toward achieving objectives will figure strongly in their individual performance evaluations. (See later discussion related to the appraisal/reward system.)

d) The problems of integrating efforts with managers not practicing MOR at the same level tend to be magnified.

e) The normal impatience of the manager who hopes for "instant success" but finally realizes that it will require a "long haul" approach gives cause for second thoughts.

This *disenchantment* can be partially offset by including in the implementation plan such things as:

a) A planned renegotiation of objectives or MOR Agreements.

b) Scheduled group progress reviews.

c) An assessment and modification of the implementation plan.

d) Introduction of a new implementation phase.

e) A one-day "refresher" course.

f) An informal "dialogue" session with key executives or an outside expert.

g) Periodic circulation of tapes, brief articles, or new ideas on the subject.

h) Brief "live," recorded, or written executive progress reports.

i) Informal problem-solving clinics conducted by members of the training/coaching staff or by other managers.

There are other techniques for sustaining or revitalizing interest, the substance of which is limited only by the imagination of those desiring to do something about it.

4. *Impact of success.* "Success begets success" is a principle of learning that is as old as learning itself. Therefore, concentrating on the successes achieved through the MOR approach, rather than on the failures, will result in increasing success in its application. There will be failures, some of them substantial. But the effective management decision maker will build on the strengths that come out of the approach without being overly concerned about the initial weaknesses.

5. *Importance of training and coaching.* It would be pure folly to assume that every manager either can or will read this book

and then put the MOR approach into operation. Therefore, a plan for training managers in the use of these principles and techniques must be a part of the introduction of MOR within an organization. A formal training program can be conducted by experienced, forward-thinking managers with an interest in teaching, by competent internal staff specialists, by separate organizations — such as the Civil Service Commission's General Management Institute — that specialize in such efforts, or by outside contractors with a proven track record of assisting public-sector organizations in this approach to management. (An *Instructor's Guide* for use with this text is available separately from the publisher. In addition, *A Self-Teaching Audiocassette Program on Management by Objectives and Results* — six tapes prepared and presented by George Morrisey — and a comprehensive seminar workbook are available from the publisher or from MOR Associates, P.O. Box 5879, Buena Park, CA 90622. This program can be used individually for self-study or review, for small, informal group learning — such as a unit manager with his or her immediate staff — or for inclusion as a part of a formal training program on MOR. The participant workbook is also available separately for use in such a program.)

Irrespective of formal training offered, some provision must be made for ongoing coaching for individual or small groups of managers in specific applications of the MOR process. To the extent that higher-level managers can and will assume that responsibility as a part of their supervisory relationship with subordinates, the impact of the process will be strengthened. This may mean some specialized training for those managers desiring to increase their skill in doing that. If so, such training should be incorporated into the implementation plan. In addition to the coaching role that individual managers will be playing, it may be desirable to identify certain individuals in the organization as MOR advisers.

6. *Internal MOR advisers/administrators.* The "MBO Adviser" is a popular concept in England, as well as in other countries that have been influenced by the work of John Humble, Denis

Ryan, and other strong advocates of that approach. Although some organizations in the United States have formally adopted that practice, most provide such assistance in a more informal manner, usually as a collateral assignment for someone with other responsibilities. Although such assistance is frequently taken on by such support units as training, personnel, organizational planning/development, or administrative services, it is not unusual for certain line managers or, at higher levels, executive staff assistants to assume that responsibility.

Competent individuals respected by the managers they serve can do a great deal to ensure a smooth, sustained, consistent implementation of MOR in an organization. The key to their effectiveness in such a role, however, lies in their seeing it as more advisory or supportive than administrative. Their primary responsibility should be to help managers perform their jobs more effectively through training, coaching, and stimulating. If they take on a more directive role, such as receiving, screening, evaluating, or approving documents for the total organization, MOR is likely to become another "staff program" which line managers see as satisfying some else's needs. Such a role also tends to create a new "paper mill" which will strangle the process. As suggested in Chapter 9, part of the mission of a group performing the MOR adviser/administrator function ought to be to work itself out of a job.

7. *Outside professional assistance.* Many organizations have recognized the value of bringing in someone from outside to assist with parts of the implementation process. Such experts bring two particular strengths not normally available from people on the inside. The first is the experience of working with several different organizations, thus lending greater credibility to the process, together with the ability to draw on that experience to increase the probability of a successful implementation. The second strength is a "third party" objectivity — the lack of a continuing vested interest or potential threat to future security. The internal expert, on the other hand, brings two particular strengths not normally available to people from the outside: specific organizational knowledge and availability

for continuing ongoing assistance. Some of the most effective MOR implementations have come about through the cooperative efforts of an outside/inside team that could capitalize on the strengths of both. Some of the ways an outside expert might be used effectively are:

a) Conducting an organizational survey and analysis.

b) Leading executive planning conferences or consultations.

c) Making motivational presentations.

d) Tailoring the process to specific organizational requirements.

e) Training internal training/consulting staff members.

e) Conducting in-house seminars.

f) Undertaking individual or small-group coaching.

g) Diagnosing or evaluating existing or related efforts.

8. *Relation to appraisal/reward system.* Usually, one of the most controversial issues raised in connection with MOR implementation is how and when it should be tied in to the performance appraisal or compensation system. The fact that most public-sector organizations do not have incentive compensation systems has both advantages and disadvantages. Several private-sector organizations have made the mistake of installing MBO primarily as a vehicle for determining incentive compensation. As a consequence, many managers set and worked to achieve objectives designed to produce maximum compensation recognition, frequently at the expense of managerial effectiveness. It is not unusual in such organizations to see managers working diligently to achieve objectives with short-term revenue-producing results while paying "lip service" to such things as research and development or staff development, the results of which may not show up on the "bottom line" until well into the future.

To a lesser degree, public-sector organizations that attempt to install MOR at the outset as the principal mechanism for individual performance appraisals, fitness reports, salary reviews, or promotional evaluations are openly inviting their managers to "play games." Since I have yet to see a management system that I couldn't "beat" if I set my mind to it, I know that many resourceful managers will put more effort into "getting a good score" than into doing a good job. If they appear devious, it is only because the system encourages that kind of behavior.

Conversely, if superior performance toward agreed-on objectives is not ultimately given greater recognition than is mediocre or marginal performance, MOR will cease to be an effective motivational tool. My observations about these two extremes are not as paradoxical as they may seem. It is primarily a matter of sequence and timing. MOR should be introduced first as a *management* system, designed to help individual managers, as well as the total organization, accomplish more with greater personal satisfaction. Once individual managers, and the organization in general, become reasonably comfortable with MOR as a management system, it is both legitimate and essential that it be expanded to cover other applications as well, including relating it to the appraisal and reward systems. Most organizations that I have observed doing a conscientious job of MOR implementation seem to be ready for this expansion about two or three years after its initial installation as a management system.

Realistically, this is not an either-or situation. Any intelligent manager will make use of whatever relevant information is available, *including* a subordinate's performance against agreed-on objectives, when it comes time for filling out the annual "score card." My recommendation, however, is to *not* change the performance-appraisal system, to incorporate objective-setting, as a part of *initial* MOR implementation. Otherwise, it is likely to encourage managers to set "safe" objectives. Introducing a new *management* system can be anxiety-producing enough in itself. Adding the performance-appraisal dimension to it at the outset will only increase that anxiety level, possibly to a point higher than some managers can handle. In further support of this, the astute senior manager will place far more emphasis on a subordinate's MOR *achievements* during initial implementation, minimizing inadequacies as much as possible. In that way, the subordinate will be encouraged to stretch more in subsequent agreements, rather than backing away from trying new approaches. There is ample time to bring about a more satisfactory balance once the subordinate has developed confidence in the process.

## How to Get MOR Started

Assuming that training and internal consultation will be a vital part of introducing MOR within an organization, there are six general ways in which it can be approached. There are, of course, many variations and combinations of each.

1. *Top down.* Top organization executives prepare a statement of roles and missions and both short- and long-range objectives, for both the total organization and their own organizational units. Their subordinates, in descending order, participate in activities that will result in the preparation of their own statements of roles and missions, MOR Agreements, objectives, and action plans that are consistent with and supportive of those of their superiors.

*Advantages*

a) Improved management support for the program.

b) Greater understanding of the total organization's efforts by all members of management.

c) Easier determination by each individual manager of his or her own roles, missions, and objectives, based on clear definition of those of higher-level management.

*Disadvantages*

a) Danger of a too rigid format that may discourage creative approaches by subordinate managers.

b) Danger of objectives being imposed on individual managers by their superiors rather than coming as a result of individual or joint commitment.

2. *Bottom up.* The process may start at any management level below the top executives; most frequently, it starts at a middle-management level, but in some instances it may even start with first-line supervisors. Guidelines are agreed on, and lower-level managers develop their tentative statements of roles and missions and MOR Agreements for review, modification, and consolidation by their superiors.

*Advantages*

 a) Greater participative impact by lower-level managers.

 b) Critical operational problem areas more readily identified.

*Disadvantages*

 a) Danger of extensive wasted effort because of lack of direction from above.

 b) Tendency of middle and upper managers to avoid doing their own thinking on the subject, letting their subordinates learn by trial and error.

3. *Intraunit.* Each unit head prepares a statement of roles and missions and unit objectives, either as part of a total management program or individually with staff help. The unit head's subordinate managers then participate in a workshop as teams with their own key subordinates. Participants will determine roles and missions and MOR Agreements, individually and collectively within their organizational units. More than one such unit may participate in a learning program at the same time. An advance briefing for the members of management immediately under the unit head is recommended, since they will have to serve as discussion leaders for their own organizational units. (*A Self-Teaching Audiocassette Program on Management by Objectives and Results* can be a particularly useful tool here.)

*Advantages*

 a) Greater likelihood of coordinated team effort.

 b) Generally better evaluations of documents because of participants' greater familiarity with one another's operations.

c) Greater probability of effective follow-through on implementing objectives.

*Disadvantages*

a) Open participation may be inhibited by the presence of one's superiors (or subordinates) and rival peers.

b) Open or hidden resistance to the approach and to the program may be harder to overcome than with a mixed group.

c) Some middle managers may not be capable of performing as discussion leaders effectively with their subordinates. (Overcoming this might be a good objective in itself.)

4. *Open participation program.* The training program is offered to members of management throughout the organization on a voluntary or management-choice basis. Normally, we recommend that participants be from similar levels of management (middle managers with other middle managers, for example), even though they are from different organizational units. Also, whenever practical, participants' bosses should have already gone through a similar program.

*Advantages*

a) Participants are more likely to be self-motivated and thus more receptive to the approach and to the program.

b) Presence of participants from diverse organizational units offers the opportunity for better understanding (and subsequently improved working relationships) among represented functions, in addition to the value of an "outsider's" perspective during workshop evaluation sessions.

*Disadvantages*

a) Workshop-evaluation sessions may be more difficult because of lack of familiarity with terminology and problems of other participants.

b) Effective follow-through may be much more limited because of inconsistency of application within represented organizational units.

c) Some participants may lack purpose or be out to deliberately obstruct the program.

5. *Self-teaching.* Individual manager (or small group of managers) sets own pace for learning the process, following a standard self-teaching program, such as *"A Self-Teaching Audiocassette Program on Management by Objectives and Results*
or an internally developed self-study program.

*Advantages*

a) Participants can work at their own pace, without having
to follow a strict time schedule.

b) Participants can work individually or in small, compatible groups during or after normal working hours.

c) There is consistent input provided to all who follow the
program.

*Disadvantages*

a) This requires a significant amount of self-discipline in
order to stay with it, which some managers do not have;
thus a strong potential for procrastination.

b) Unless it is being done as a group exercise, there is no
opportunity for discussion, evaluation, and feedback
during the training sessions.

c) There is room for misinterpretation of meaning and intent.

6. *Through other training programs.* Participants in other man-
agement-training programs (leadership practices, production
management, problem-solving, for example), are introduced
to the practice of setting and implementing objectives
related to on-the-job application of principles and techniques covered there. They commit themselves to specific
projects, using the objective-setting format, and must re-

port back on their progress as a condition of satisfactory completion of the program.*

### Advantages

a) Participants are introduced to the objective-setting process gradually, so they can gain some moderately successful experience with the approach as well as familiarity with the concept before being exposed to a complete MOR program.

b) It serves as a tremendously effective tool for ensuring practical application of training and for evaluating the effectiveness of the training effort.

### Disadvantages

a) May delay direct involvement in MOR training longer than is desirable.

b) Problem of inconsistency, with some MOR training participants having had this exposure and others not.

## Program Emphasis Based on Management Level

Although the same basic elements of the MOR process are present at all levels of management, the degree of emphasis in both content and approach may be quite different. This is why we recommend participation in the program at similar management levels. Although there will be wide variations within individual organizations, the following breakdowns of content and approach are usually most appropriate to the specific management levels identified. (This assumes a *top-down* approach. Some obvious adjustments need to be made if MOR is introduced in a different manner.)

### Top Management

1. Content

   a) Overview of total MOR process.

   b) Roles and missions for total organization.

---

* See G. L. Morrisey and W. R. Wellstead, "Supervisory Training CAN Be Measured 'Objectively' On the Job," *Training and Development Journal*, June 1971, for a description of this approach.

   c) Short- and long-term objectives for the total organization.

   d) Major units' roles and missions.

   e) Major units' objectives.

   f) MOR Agreements for individual executives.

2. *Approach* (Use any or all of the following, as appropriate.)

   a) Introduce the MOR concept through:
1) Formal presentation by key executive or outside expert.
2) Audio- or videotape recordings.
3) Selected readings, followed by group discussion and clarification.
4) Individual consultation with each executive.

   b) Develop tentative organizational roles, missions, and objectives through:
1) Group brainstorming.
2) Independent development by each executive; sharing and resolution by group.
3) Development of assigned portions by individuals or small groups of executives; sharing and resolution by group.
4) Internal/external consultants available to *assist* executives (not do the job for them).

   c) Determine and agree on organizational roles, missions, and objectives through total group conference, preferably away from normal work location.

   d) Repeat these steps for major organizational units' roles, missions, and objectives.

   e) Consider use of "attack" and "defense" teams in examining tentative plans.

*Middle Management*

1. *Content*

   a) Study of total MOR process.

   b) Examination of organizational roles, missions, and objectives.

c) Roles and missions for own organizational unit.

d) Key results areas, indicators, and objectives for own organizational unit.

e) Examination of action planning and controlling.

f) Middle-management role as adviser to subordinates in MOR.

2. *Approach*  (Use any or all of the following, as appropriate.)

a) Study in depth the MOR concept through:

1) Formal presentation by key executive, outside expert, or competent staff specialist.

2) Advance reading of this text, or portions of it, plus other selected readings, followed by in-depth group discussion and clarification.

3) Audio- or videotape presentation by key executive or outside expert.

b) Examine organizational roles, missions, and objectives through:

1) Presentation made and discussion led by key executive(s) (preferably) or knowledgeable and authoritative staff.

2) Advance review of appropriate organizational documents.

c) Develop statement of roles and missions for own organizational unit in line with those of superior and total organization.

d) Develop one-year MOR Agreement for own operation (include some objectives for longer or shorter periods if desirable, but concentrate on the one-year span at this level). Include firm plan for progress review.

e) Examine remaining MOR activities:

1) Read, discuss, and practice sufficiently to ensure understanding (they must be able to advise their subordinates on the application of these steps).

2) Program those objectives which will enable subordinates to better define their objectives.

f) Study and practice progress review and other communications approaches (see Chapter 9).

g) Define and agree on the middle-management role as
adviser to subordinates in MOR.

*First-line Management*

1. *Content*

a) Overview of total MOR process.

b) Examination of organizational roles, missions, and objectives.

c) Examination of superior's roles, missions, and objectives (where appropriate), including determination of
own roles and missions.

d) Key results areas, indicators, and objectives for own
operation.

e) Study of action planning and controlling.

2. *Approach* (Use any or all of the following, as appropriate.)

a) Introduce the MOR concept through:
   1) Formal presentation by key executive, outside expert, or competent staff specialist (could be "live,"
   on film, or on videotape).
   2) Advance reading of this text, followed by brief and
   pertinent group discussion and clarification.
   3) Advance or in-session listening to *A Self-Teaching
   Audiocassette Program on Management by Objectives and Results.*

b) Examine organization's and superior's roles, missions,
and objectives.

c) Develop own statement of roles and missions if not
adequately identified within that of superior.

d) Develop MOR Agreement for own operation (the measurement period may range from one month to one
year or longer; a quarterly or semiannual target seems
most feasible for the average first-line supervisor, with a

few objectives that may be projected for a full year and beyond).

e) Study in depth the steps involved in action planning and controlling.

f) Study and practice progress reviews and other communications approaches.

g) To ensure comprehension, completely document at least one objective through all steps in the MOR process.

## In Summary

It should appear quite obvious in reviewing this section that the introduction of MOR into an organization is no haphazard event. It requires careful planning. Whether or not all the steps described are followed will be dictated by the specific organization's requirements and capabilities. However, a systematic approach that has been carefully worked out and agreed to by all key people is essential to any attempt to implement MOR in an organization.

## INDIVIDUAL MANAGER'S WORKSHEET FOR IMPLEMENTING MOR

1. On a scale of 1 (low) to 10 (high), how much commitment to MOR implementation is likely from me? ＿＿ my higher level management? ＿＿ my subordinates? ＿＿ my peers? ＿＿

2. What implementation approach (or combination or approaches) makes the most sense for my organizational unit?

＿＿ Practicing it myself first and setting an example — in private ＿＿ with my superior ＿＿ with my subordinates ＿＿ with my peers ＿＿.

_____ Starting on an informal basis with selected individuals assisting me in the development of my objectives and action plans.

_____ Developing roles and missions for my organizational unit.

_____ Determining key results areas — for me personally _____ for my team _____.

_____ Starting on a voluntary basis with selected individuals reporting to me.

_____ Starting on a formal basis with all who report directly to me.

_____ Starting on a project basis.

_____ Starting with one unit (_____) and developing it there first as a model.

_____ Total implementation, starting with top management.

_____ Getting other key managers exposed — through a public seminar _____ an in-house seminar _____ an in-house motivational presentation _____ informal discussion _____ audiocassette _____ videotape _____ film _____ reading _____.

_____ Organizational survey and analysis — by whom? _____

_____ Other _____

3. Who else *specifically* needs to be involved at the outset if the process is to work in our organization or organizational unit? How can I best get them involved?

4. What immediate steps must *I* take to get the process started? By when? (Commit yourself to some action *now* if you intend to do anything with MOR in your unit.)

# 11

# SPECIAL PUBLIC-SECTOR CONCERNS AND HOW TO DEAL WITH THEM

"Our situation is completely different from that in most other organizations" is a comment made regularly in nearly every organization, in both the public and private sectors, that I have visited in my role as a management consultant. Those who say it are absolutely correct. No two organizations are faced with identical circumstances. The nature of their specific business, the individuals who are involved in it, the particular external and internal pressures and other related factors all are unique to that organization. That's why most prescribed "cook book" approaches to management either do not work or are not accepted by most managers within a given organization. MBO (Management By Objectives) often has been introduced into organizations on a "this is the way it's got to be done" basis. Therefore, it should not come as any surprise that its practical effectiveness in most of those organizations usually has a very short life span before it becomes another routine paperwork exercise.

Managers in the public sector frequently state that MBO is really more useful in the private sector, where a clear relationship to the "bottom line" can be shown and where managers don't have to contend with the political scene — legislative bodies, elected or appointed officials, etc. Although no organization remains unaffected by politics, there is no question but that managers in the public sector are faced with some unique influencing factors. In some instances, those differences are more in degree than in kind, but they do require special consideration.

Although the following is certainly not an exhaustive list, it does cite some of the most frequently identified special concerns in the public sector.

1. Leadership — elected officials, political appointees, military turnover, etc.
2. Relation to legislative bodies.
3. Jurisdictional problems — whose "turf" is it?
4. Headquarters versus region/area — who's running the show?
5. Communication within the hierarchy — what's going on?
6. Relation to PPB and other management systems — the "paper mill."
7. Relation of special projects to normal work — what do "they" really want?
8. Setting priorities under austerity conditions — asking for the impossible.
9. Impact of civil service, automatic progression, and other personnel systems.

I will offer some comments and suggestions on each of these special concerns. However, be prepared for a high degree of ambiguity in some of my responses. In most situations, there are no straightforward "how-to-do-it" solutions. That's where management as an art form must come into play. When we are faced with a managerial dilemma or frustration, we usually choose one of three courses of action: (1) we gripe about it; (2) we learn to live with it; or (3) we try to change it. One of those courses is not productive; the other two are, and my suggestions will focus on these two. At the end of this chapter I will suggest a relatively simple approach whereby you can deal with any particular frustration you may have as a manager in the public sector.

## Leadership — Elected Officials, Political Appointees, Military Turnovers, etc.

### The Problem

Governmental departments and agencies, whether at the federal, state, or local level, frequently are headed by people who will have a relatively short tenure in office — much more so than is the case in the private sector. Although most of these individuals are highly competent professionals who make significant contributions while they are in office, relatively few expect to make a permanent career in that organization. "Let's humor this one for awhile; it'll change again the next time around" is a frequent aside heard from long-time permanent employees. What good is MOR if the ground rules are going to change every time there is a new captain at the helm?

### Response

The key to remember here is that MOR has its principal value in enabling each individual to manage his or her operation in a satisfying and productive manner, irrespective of leadership direction from "on high." If MOR is seen in that light rather than as a reporting system, the individual manager can concentrate on the *process* of achieving significant results, even if a change in leadership dictates a change in the kinds of results needed. Application of the six steps in the MOR process (defining roles and missions, determining key results areas, identifying and specifying indicators, setting objectives, preparing action plans, and establishing controls) can be as flexible as is necessary to accommodate the individual manager's particular style and the circumstances of the moment (including new leadership direction). Furthermore, the manager who can demonstrate a well-thought-out planning process with identifiable tangible results is much more likely to get a vote of confidence from a new leader than one who waits "to see which way the wind will blow."

## Relation to Legislative Bodies

### The Problem

Many times, organizational funding, broad-based planning, and approval of specific programs lie in the hands of an elected body of officials, whether that be a local school board or the United States Congress. Some members of that body may be either uninformed or unconcerned about the organization's efforts, whereas others may have their own favorite issues they want to push, occasionally at the expense of issues that managers within the organization feel are more critical. This problem becomes even more sensitive in an election year. Why do a conscientious job of planning when your efforts can get shot down by someone who is more interested in getting reelected than in seeing that something meaningful is accomplished?

### Response

First off, although there have been some notable exceptions, I firmly believe that the vast majority of our elected representatives are well-intentioned, dedicated public servants who do the best job they can with what they have to work with. That they will not always be as concerned and committed to certain courses of action as those who are directly involved is an inevitable fact of life that is a part of the checks and balances in our legislative system. Whether or not that may be the case in a given situation, the manager who uses MOR in planning any effort that requires legislative approval has two positive elements working. (1) Requests for funding or program approval have a much higher probability for favorable action if the results anticipated are clearly spelled out in understandable, measurable terms, including a cost-benefit analysis. (2) A part of a well-laid-out action plan will include one or more steps related to securing legislative approval. In fact, in some cases the engineering of that approval may be a worthwhile objective in itself. A recognition that legislators are "customers" — as much as the recipients of whatever service the organization may render, whose needs and wants must be considered —

will be a critical factor in the portfolio of any successful governmental manager. You may not win them all, but planning your approach with that in mind should increase your batting average.

## Jurisdictional Problems — Whose "Turf" Is It?

### The Problem

Two or more departments, agencies, or work units within them, either get into a direct conflict over which is responsible for a particular kind of effort or are unaware of another organization's interest and involvement. The result often is duplication of effort, counterproductive effort, or — in the case of a standoff — no effort at all. What's the point in planning your work if some other organization is going to undo everything you have done already?

### Response

This problem occurs almost as frequently in the private sector, particularly in large organizations. However, it seems to get more publicity when it happens in government. Although the likelihood of totally eliminating this kind of problem is at best remote, the number of instances can be reduced significantly through three specific kinds of action. (1) A well-prepared statement of roles and missions should identify and help clarify accountability, responsibility, and authority. Where there are clear conflicts (some are inevitable), this action will get them out "on the table" where they can be dealt with and, if necessary, resolved at a higher level. (2) Objectives, prepared in advance, can and should be shared with other organizations that might be affected — *before action is begun.* (3) Part of any action plan should be a step related to coordination with other affected organizations. Jurisdictional disputes, particularly when they affect funding, staffing, or controlling authority, are bound to arise in any operation as complex as most governmental organizations. Such disputes cannot be resolved by ignoring them or by attempting to discredit someone else.

That's a "lose-lose" game! Open discussion between the affected managers is the most productive way to deal with this type of problem. MOR provides a rational basis for such a discussion.

## Headquarters Versus Region/Area — Who's Running the Show?

### The Problem

Many federal agencies have their headquarters in Washington with the bulk of the actual work being done out in the field. A comparable situation exists in many state and local organizations, but the resulting complications are proportionately smaller. Highly decentralized private-sector organizations have similar concerns. Field units tend to resent what they feel are arbitrary decisions and too tight a control from headquarters personnel insensitive to the local situation. People in headquarters are concerned that those in the field may go off on their own track without sufficient consideration for agency policy and the impact their actions may have on other parts of the organization. ("Who gets the flack from Congress when something goes wrong!") How can you plan effectively when you don't have the authority to make decisions that affect your operations?

### Response

As with legislative bodies, both the field unit and the headquarters organization must see each other as one of several "customers" whose needs and wants must be satisfied. Field units may be justified in feeling that the only "customers" that count are those that they are serving locally. However, such field units are being extremely naive if they fail to recognize the positive or negative effect headquarters support can have on that service. Conversely, headquarters personnel may be justified in feeling that they have a stewardship responsibility, particularly as related to funding and organizational policy and direction. However, they are being equally naive if they are not sensitive to the reality that without field support, the need for the headquarters function may soon cease to exist. Therefore, headquarters and field units that have serious problems of this nature must move from a "win-lose" strategy to a "win-win" strategy — by taking positive action and not waiting for the other party to move first.

Every manager, to be effective, first has to identify where the "fences" are — the "givens" within which he or she must operate. One of the roles of a headquarters organization is to help define those "givens." The ability to move freely within those "fences" should be at the discretion of the field manager. Ironically, a clear understanding of where those "fences" are frequently will provide the field manager with a greater sense of freedom than attempting to operate with no clearly defined limits. The same three kinds of action identified under Jurisdictional Problems — clearly stated roles and missions, sharing of objectives, and planning for coordination — are equally applicable here. Both parts of the organization should be in business for the same ultimate reasons. The use of a clear, well-thought-out management process like MOR should increase the probability of cooperative effort in that direction.

## Communication within the Hierachy — What's Going On?

### The Problem

The larger the organization, the greater the likelihood of a breakdown in communications up, down, and across organizational lines. It is not unusual for a unit manager to learn about an action that should have been taken after it was too late to do anything about it, or for an agency director to hear from a legislator about a major control problem somewhere in the organization. How can you establish and monitor objectives when you have "the blind leading the blind"?

### Response

The primary concern here is to determine "what" rather than "who" caused the breakdown. Properly implemented, MOR should help to highlight those points in the chain where communication breakdown is likely to occur. Then appropriate control mechanisms can be set up to guard against it. Effective communication related to objectives has to start, of course, with a negotiation and agreement between subordinate and superior as to what primary accomplishments are to be achieved during the projected measurement period. The next critical step in MOR communication is one that is often neglected — *regularly scheduled progress reviews* between the two during that measurement period. Experience shows that if reviews are not scheduled at the time of the original agreement, they rarely take place until it is too late for them to be of much value. Whether such reviews take place monthly, bimonthly, or quarterly, they provide an opportunity for both parties to bring each other up to date on everything related to their original agreement — including any information that may have "fallen through the cracks" in the normal communication channels.

## Relation to PPB and Other Management Systems — The "Paper Mill"

### The Problem

Many managers in government feel, with some justification, that they have been "systemized" to death. Whether that system be PPBS (Planning-Programming-Budgeting System), PMS (Performance Management System), PARA (Policy Analysis and Resource Allocation), OPS (Operational Planning System), or any of the myriad other "alphabet soup" combinations, it should come as no surprise to hear a chorus of groans when someone suggests that the organization implement MBO, MOR, or any other "new system." Is MOR going to mean one more set of documents and reports in order to cover what I would have done anyway?

### Response

It could, but it doesn't need to. To keep that from happening, we must first recognize that MOR is a "management" system, not a "reporting" system. That's not just a play on words. MOR must be seen as working primarily for the individual manager using it and only secondarily to satisfy an organizational need. Properly implemented, MOR should facilitate the individual's ability to respond effectively to reporting systems that are already in existence (MOR ought to be compatible with any of them). In addition, MOR should allow the manager to exercise greater influence and to maintain better visibility over the use of limited available resources. MOR will become another bureaucratic "paper mill" only if those responsible allow it to. One way to keep that from happening is to establish a ground rule that any new reporting requirement generated because of the implementation of MOR should either eliminate or incorporate one already in existence.

## Relation of Special Projects to Normal Work — What Do "They" Really Want?

### The Problem

"I'm spending so much time working on my 'objectives,' I can't get my job done" is a common complaint. The advent of OMB's (Office of Management and Budget) emphasis on objectives "of Presidential significance" was typical of many initial MBO efforts in that it focused attention on a "critical few" high-priority accomplishments to be achieved by each participating agency. The validity of that approach is certainly sound, since not all performance effort warrants that level of attention. However, in many cases these objectives represented effort that was over and above the normal, ongoing work of units within those agencies. Because of the spotlight directed on those objectives, it was inevitable that a somewhat disproportionate amount of effort was devoted to trying to achieve them, frequently at the expense of other important, but less politically sensitive, work. The old adage that "people do what the boss *inspects*" came through loud and clear in this case. Is MOR designed to cover only those "special projects" that someone "on high" has decreed?

## Response

The answer, obviously, is no. However, I am sure that that answer will not relieve the anxiety of the conscientious manager who is faced with this dilemma. As we discussed earlier, this issue must be resolved between the individual subordinate and his or her superior at the time of the initial negotiation and agreement, and their agreement must be reinforced during the periodic progress reviews. Although it may not be necessary to spend as much time planning and discussing normal ongoing work, failure to give some attention to it will suggest that it is unimportant. The potential result may be an organization that does a great job on the glamour items while it collapses from not meeting its normal obligations. The lead in engineering proper attention to this normal work must, in most cases, come from the superior. (Before you decide that that lets you "off the hook," remember your relationship to those who report to you.)

## Setting Priorities under Austerity Conditions — Asking for the Impossible

### The Problem

The trend in government seems to be to get more and more out of less and less. The days of unlimited budgets and no accountability have virtually disappeared (if they ever really existed). There are countless instances of "bare bones" budgets being slashed still further with the full expectation that there will be more assignments given during the year without additional resources being provided. What's the point of doing a thorough job of planning and budgeting when someone else is going to second-guess you and insist that you do the impossible?

### Response

Any manager who sets objectives that will realistically use up 100% of anticipated resources is courting disaster. I am not advocating that you submit a "padded" budget. I *am* advocating that you prepare a realistic budget flexible enough to take the unknowns into consideration. Within the context of MOR, there are two key assumptions we must make. (1) A manager's list of objectives cannot and will not cover all effort that will be expended within his or her unit. Such a list would be so cumbersome as to have very little meaning. Many routine kinds of activities will continue to be performed effectively, regardless of whether or not they are incorporated into objectives. Some allowance must be made for those in budget preparation. (2) *Priorities will change* while the objectives are in effect. No one can anticipate all of the circumstances that may cause a shift in direction. Once again, the periodic progress review provides an opportunity to reassess the situation and to see what changes, if any, may be indicated. Objectives should never be "set in concrete" (although they should not be so easily changeable as to lack commitment). By applying a realistic cost-benefit analysis in his or her own planning (regardless of whether or not those figures are submitted in a budget), a manager is in a much stronger position to make the necessary tradeoffs, both in internal operations and in negotiations with superiors. Austerity is probably here to stay. Therefore, the use of the MOR process becomes all the more critical in determining where the best payoff will be.

## Impact of Civil Service, Automatic Progression, and Other Personnel Systems

### The Problem

The effectiveness of MOR in an organization is in direct correlation to the performance of its employees. This makes employee motivation a prime concern of the manager. "Just try to fire an incompetent employee under Civil Service!" "Our employees are on 'automatic progression,' which means that they get their annual increase just for being alive and still on the payroll." These and similar statements are familiar laments from managers in government. Pointing out that managers are often able to function in that arena (I have both fired and financially rewarded employees while a government manager) has little impact on the harried manager expressing his or her feelings. Realistically, in many cases it is more difficult in government circles to discharge an unsatisfactory employee and to provide financial rewards based strictly on performance. That's a fact! How, then, can I motivate my employees to work effectively under MOR when my hands are tied?

## Response

There is little point in discussing the fairness of governmental personnel restrictions. I could prepare a logical case for either point of view. The fact is, they exist, and unless they are changed, they are "givens" within which the governmental manager must learn to function. Perhaps we should see the threat of discharge and the promise of financial reward as "crutches" rather than as aids in the matter of employee motivation. At best, those two "incentives" will rarely generate more than compliance ("I'll do it because it's expected of me"). As managers, what we really want from our employees is commitment ("I'll do it because I want to"). The manager who does not have tangible reward or punishment to offer has to look for other motivational options. In MOR, one of the most powerful motivational tools is *involvement*. As people become involved in determining what needs to be done, they become committed to seeing that the goals are achieved. The real power in MOR comes from giving people "a piece of the action." Tangible reward and punishment are critical factors at the survival level. When survival needs are met, self-worth takes on a much greater importance. Although a manager in a government organization may be limited when it comes to meting out reward and punishment, the opportunities for helping employees to achieve self-worth are almost unlimited. Most successful practitioners of MOR have discovered a way to tap in to that gold mine of human potential.

## In Summary

Managers who have read this chapter in the hope of finding some pat "cook book" answers to some of the special concerns facing them as a result of their positions in the public sector no doubt feel cheated by now. In several instances, the responses given were a reiteration of points made earlier in the book, although in a somewhat more precise context. There *are* some significant differences in managing in the public sector, as compared to the private sector. The beauty of MOR as a conceptual approach to management lies in its tremendous flexibility. It can and must be adapted to the individual manager and the local situation.

Knowing *what* management tools to use, whether related to MOR or any other approach, is knowledge that any intelligent person can acquire. Knowing *when* and *how* to use them is where the "art" of management comes in. That requires the exercise of sound managerial judgment and a remarkable tolerance for ambiguity. One of the basic premises in Management by Objectives and Results is that something that is large and complex is unmanageable in its totality. It can be managed only when it is reduced to a digestible size. If you want to overcome some of the frustration you may feel about managing in the public sector, *pick one problem* that you find particularly irritating, break it down until you can identify *something specific* that you can do (one alternative may be to learn to accept it), then *do it*. Your move!

# 12

# SUMMARY:
# THE MOR PROCESS
# IN BRIEF

So, here it is! That magic formula called Management by Objectives and Results (MOR) that will solve all of your problems as a manager in the public sector! Despite the absurdity of that claim, there is no doubt in my mind that systematically following the approach to management discussed in this text, tempered by good judgment and the practice of effective leadership principles, will result in increased productive output and job satisfaction for the individual manager and greater overall results for the total organization.

The basic process described here is applicable to any manager at any level (and, for that matter, to many individual employees) in any kind of an organization. Although there are some significant differences between the job of a manager in a public sector organization and one in the private sector, there are far more similarities. Management in either situation is still "the effective use of limited resources to achieve desired results."

For summary purposes, we will recap the entire process here in brief, outline form and without explanation. As such, this review will provide:

1. A brief "how-to-do-it" for those readers who are already familiar with the philosophy and principles of Management by Objectives and Results;

2. A quick overview of the total process which can be read prior to studying each of the critical steps (thus providing

the reader with the opportunity for selective reading, if desired);

3. A concentrated review of the process for later reference.

In brief, Management by Objectives and Results (MOR) is a common-sense, systematic approach to getting things done and is based on principles and techniques that many good managers have been practicing for decades. It requires the manager to focus on *results* rather than on activities, building on the strengths that have been developed over the years, with modifications and additions as good judgment dictates.

The MOR process is simple — deceptively simple. It can be illustrated graphically as a horizontal funnel, as shown in Fig. 12.1. As a process, it moves from the general to the specific. Its purpose is to subdivide a large, complex effort until it reaches a manageable unit size. Then it is integrated, through a human process that promotes understanding, involvement, and commitment.

1. *Defining roles and missions* (determining the nature and scope of work to be performed).

   a) Identify total organization's roles and missions (either from its formal statement or by your own analysis).

   b) Identify roles and missions of the major functional unit of which you are a part, including those of your immediate superior.

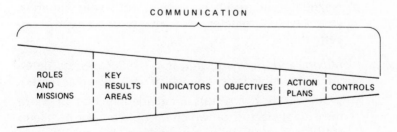

**Fig. 12.1** The MOR funnel.

c) Prepare your statement of roles and missions, including the economic, functional, and other commitments you should make for your unit together with the major work elements that describe the work to be performed. Use the "think" questions on "Clarifying Organizational Unit Roles and Missions" on p. 35 as stimulators. Involve others as appropriate.

d) Review against "Key Questions for Evaluating Statements of Roles and Missions" (see p. 36) as well as with your superior, your key subordinates, and other knowledgeable and concerned individuals.

e) Get approval by your superior and understanding by others directly concerned.

2. *Determining key results areas* (determining where to invest time, energy, and talent).

a) Determine the five to ten major areas or categories within which you (or the members of your group) should be investing time, energy, and talent for the immediate future (quarter, half-year, year).

b) Evaluate these areas according to the "Guidelines for Determining Key Results Areas" on pp. 52–53. Involve others as appropriate.

c) Set priorities on each by determining the "critical few" and placing them in rank order or by calculating the percentage of time/attention being given to each — as it is "now" and as you believe it "should be."

d) Negotiate and reach agreement with your superior, your key subordinates, and anyone else directly concerned.

3. *Identifying and specifying indicators of effectiveness* (determining measurable factors on which objectives may be set).

a) Within each key results area, identify one or more measurable factors on which it would be worthwhile to set objectives. Identify more factors than may be currently needed.

b) Evaluate these factors according to the "Guidelines for Identifying and Specifying Indicators" on pp. 63–64, with the help of your superior, key subordinates, and/or others directly concerned.

c) Select those indicators on which you plan to set objectives at this time.

4. *Selecting and setting objectives* (determining results to be achieved).

a) Using the key results areas and indicators developed, or using the three routes of analysis identified on p. 71, decide on the objectives, including the specific measurable results, target dates or time spans, and related costs you wish to set for the projected measurement period.

b) Establish priorities for identified objectives (see Figs. 6.2 and 6.3 on pp. 77 and 79 for ideas on setting priorities).

c) Write each objective so as to ensure its use as an effective working tool (See "Guidelines for Writing Objectives" on pp. 97–98).

d) Review your objectives against "Key Questions for Evaluating Objectives" on p. 98 as well as with your superior, key subordinates, and other knowledgeable and concerned individuals.

e) Prepare an MOR Agreement (see Fig. 6.5 on p. 102), including your key results areas, indicators, and objectives for the projected measurement period.

f) Negotiate with and get approval by your superior and understanding by your key subordinates and others directly concerned.

5. *Preparing action plans* (determining how to achieve specific objectives).

a) For each objective requiring further breakdown, follow these steps, as appropriate.
   1) Study situation and select method.
   2) Gain agreement and support.

3) Develop plan.
4) Test and review plan.
5) Implement.
6) Follow up.

b) For large-scale objectives and action plans:
1) Determine the major steps necessary to achieve the results identified.
2) Determine the priorities to be assigned to each major step.
3) Determine the detail steps necessary to support the steps.

c) Delegate, whenever possible, the actual determination of program steps to those subordinates who will be expected to carry them out. (These program steps, in turn, may become objectives for each related subordinate.)

d) Review against "Key Questions for Evaluating Action Steps" on p. 139 and with other concerned individuals as appropriate.

e) Establish a time framework within which each critical action step is to be completed.

f) Confirm or modify (as needed) target dates established for your objectives.

g) Estimate the cost (dollars for out-of-pocket, work-hours for time of people) of accomplishing each action step.

h) Confirm or modify (as needed) target costs established for your objectives.

i) Fix accountability for each action step on an individual in your unit, yourself in some instances. Identify other units or individuals outside your unit with heavy input to a given action step, as appropriate.

j) Complete the action plan format (see Fig. 7.3 on p. 119) for objectives requiring a written action plan.

k) Review total MOR plan to date, as appropriate, using "Key Questions for Review and Reconciliation in Planning" on p. 140.

6. *Establishing controls* (ensuring the effective accomplishment of objectives).

   a) Determine what is to be measured. (See Fig. 8.1 on p. 149 plus list of frequently used measurable factors on p. 152 for ideas on what to measure.)

   b) Determine what point of measurement (expressed in numbers, dollars, percentages, time lapse, or completion points) constitutes effective performance.

   c) Determine probable causes of variances likely to require corrective action.

   d) Select the method(s) of measurement that will provide you with the necessary performance visibility with the least expenditure of time and effort. (See suggested approaches beginning on p. 160.)

   e) Review selected methods against "Key Questions for Evaluating Control Measures" on pp. 168–169.

   f) Institute measures as determined.

   g) Determine appropriate type of corrective action (self-correcting, operating, or management) and apply it accordingly.

7. *Communication* (the catalyst that ties it together).

   a) Determine the communications methods you will use in applying MOR in your organizational unit (see methods described, starting on p. 176).

   b) Give particular attention to the use of the progress review (see pp. 162 and 177).

8. *Implementing MOR.*

   a) Determine which approach, or combination of approaches, you should use in implementing MOR in your unit, using the worksheet on pp. 211–212 for guidance.

   b) Commit yourself to some specific implementing action *now.*

## In Summary

The manager who is able to work in an organization that is practicing this approach to management throughout will find it a tremendously satisfying experience, once having overcome the problems of adjustment. The manager who is working in an organization that is not yet practicing this approach will still find personal satisfaction in applying the process to his or her own operation, even though the job of following this method will be somewhat more difficult. However, it may provide the added incentive to educate others, including the boss, to the benefits that can be achieved through *Management by Objectives and Results*.

# BIBLIOGRAPHY

Many of the books written in recent years have made significant contributions to results-oriented management. I will comment on some that are particularly relevant and will also list several others that are worth investigation.

Allen, Louis A., *The Management Profession*, New York: McGraw-Hill, 1964.

This particular book had more influence on my management practices and early writings than did any other single work. Allen deals with management as a unified concept, breaking it down systematically into its component parts. His "Common Vocabulary of Professional Management" (since updated) and "Principles of Professional Management" make a major contribution to the literature of the profession.

Drucker, Peter F., *Management Tasks: Responsibilities, Practices*, New York: Harper & Row, 1974.

Drucker's contributions to the study of management are legendary. This book incorporates much of the philosophy and many of the processes covered in his previous works — without replacing them. It's "the compleat Drucker" — 'nuff said!

Humble, John W., ed., *Management by Objectives in Action*, London: McGraw-Hill, 1970.

By perhaps the best-known MBO advocate outside the United States, this is a book of readings which Humble has gathered and tied together in a working sequence. The section "Training MBO Advisers" by D. H. Frean has particular value for those wishing to investigate that option.

Lyden, Fremont J., and Ernest G. Miller, eds., *Planning-Programming-Budgeting; A Systems Approach to Management,* 2d ed., Chicago: Markham, 1972.

This is a collection of writings on the subject by several authors from various government organizations as well as from academia. Particularly relevant to MOR applications are: "Strategic Planning" by Charles M. Mottley, "Establishing a Program Structure" by Paul L. Brown, "Criteria for Evaluation in Planning State and Local Programs" by Harry P. Hatry, "PPB in HEW: Some Management Issues" by David R. Seidmen, and "The Use of PPBS in a Public System of Higher Education: Is It Cost Effective?" by James S. Dyer. This is a worthwhile reference book to have.

Mackenzie, R. Alec, *The Time Trap,* New York: AMACOM, 1972.

This is the best of several books on time management I have seen. It is chock full of techniques for more effective and efficient management of that most elusive of all resources — our own time.

Mager, Robert F., *Goal Analysis* (1972), and (with Peter Pipe), *Analyzing Performance Problems* (1970), Belmont, Calif.: Fearon.

Bob Mager's books are fun to read, but more important, they pack a powerful message in easy-to-understand language. *Goal Analysis* is designed to help you take a broad statement of intent and remove it from "the land of Fuzz" so that "you will know one when you see one." *Analyzing Performance Problems,* subtitled "You Really Oughta Wanna," takes you through a series of basic questions to consider when someone is not performing satisfactorily. When the questions are answered, the solution is obvious — and it may not be the one that was obvious at the beginning. Read both of these books!

McConkey, Dale D., *Management by Objectives for Staff Managers,* Chicago: Vantage Press, 1972.

This book addresses itself specifically to the role of a staff manager and the particularly ambiguous status that it entails. The book faces head-on the traditional conflict problems and provides both a rationale and the tools for making the staff manager as much a part of the mainstream of MBO application as any other manager is.

Morrisey, George L., *Appraisal and Development through Objectives and Results,* Reading, Mass.: Addison-Wesley, 1972.

This book was written as a sequel to *Management by Objectives and Results* (the original version of this text) and places particular attention on the human element. It takes a fresh look at the appraisal and development roles of the manager, using the principles of MOR, with primary emphasis on *development*. It includes working models for professional, technical, and clerical, as well as managerial employees, plus tools and techniques for effective coaching and counseling and bringing about favorable behavior change.

———— , *Management by Objectives and Results with George Morrisey*, A Self-Teaching Audiocassette Program, Buena Park, Calif.: MOR Associates, 1975.

This miniversion of my complete seminar on MOR comes on six cassettes, with a comprehensive workbook. I *guarantee* that anyone completing this program and its practice exercises will know *how* to manage by objectives and results.

Myers, M. Scott, *Every Employee A Manager*, New York: McGraw-Hill, 1970.

Based largely on his experience at Texas Instruments, Myers' book is one of the pioneer works on Job Enrichment. Through a simple "meaningful work model" (Plan-Do-Control), he shows how the basic principles of management can be applied to *any job* in an organization, regardless of level.

Odiorne, George S., is a name that is virtually synonymous with MBO. He has written extensively on the subject. The two books that have been most helpful to me are:

———— , *Management Decisions by Objectives*, Englewood Cliffs, N.J.: Prentice-Hall, 1969.

Although his earlier book, *Management by Objectives*, is more widely known, this one organizes the basic Odiorne philosophy into a series of practical, usable tools for the individual manager, particularly as related to decision-making and problem-solving responsibilities.

———— , *Management and the Activity Trap*, New York: Harper & Row, 1974.

"The major task of this book is to point up a common root cause of errors in the management of change: the Activity Trap — how to avoid it, and how to get out if once in." (p. ix). Here, Odiorne points out shortcomings that most of us can identify with. But rather than just attacking, he offers practical ways to deal with these shortcomings. It's *Up the Organization* with "real world," goal-oriented solutions.

Raia, Anthony P., *Managing by Objectives*, Glenview, Ill.: Scott, Foresman, 1974.

This book presents MBO as an integrated system. Particularly strong are: Chapter 8, in which he shows the relationship with manager training and self-development, compensation, and career and manpower planning; Chapter 9, which deals with installing MBO; and Chapter 10, which contains the most comprehensive annotated bibliography I have ever seen.

Reddin, W.J., *Effective Management by Objectives*, New York: McGraw-Hill, 1971.

Bill Reddin's section on "Effectiveness Areas" alone is worth many times the price of this book. In that section, he states that "all managerial positions are best seen in terms of the outputs associated with them" and then goes on to provide a sound basis for analysis. His whole process is a bit more complex than many managers care to study, but used selectively, it is an immensely valuable resource.

Sayles, Leonard R., and Margaret K. Chandler, *Managing Large Systems: Organizations for the Future*, New York: Harper & Row, 1971.

Primarily a research study of the largest organizational operation ever undertaken — the NASA space effort of the 1960s — this book makes fascinating reading because it is written in English, not Researchese. It makes a good case for the contention that the greatest contribution to come from that massive effort may well have been in *management*, rather than scientific, technology.

Schleh, Edward C., *The Management Tactician*, New York: McGraw-Hill, 1974.

An immensely practical book by one of the pioneers in results-oriented management; Schleh's emphasis on first-level problems as the key determinant in organizational approach, joint versus unique accountability, and refocusing of staff units make extremely thought-provoking reading. Although oriented primarily to the private sector, this book provides superb guidance to any forward-thinking manager.

Toffler, Alvin, *Future Shock*, New York: Random House, 1970.

So much has been written about this book that anything I might add would be redundant. It is enough to say that it should be required reading for anyone wishing to play an influential role in the present as well as in the future.

Cleveland, Harlan, *The Future Executive,* New York: Harper & Row, 1972.

I have listed this book out of alphabetical sequence because it is the manager's guide to "Future Shock." It addresses the changing role of the "public executive" in a changing world, with emphasis on the need for new perspectives on management. It's a mind-stretcher.

## Organization Development

*Addison-Wesley Organization Development Series*

This is the most comprehensive series of short treatises currently available in the technology of Organization Development, with new titles being added periodically as appropriate. Each book contributes to current OD theory and practice. Titles available as of this writing:

*Organization Development: Strategies and Models,* Richard Beckhard, 1969.

*Organization Development: Its Nature, Origins, and Prospects,* Warren G. Bennis, 1969.

*Building a Dynamic Corporation through Grid Organization Development,* Robert R. Blake and Jane S. Mouton, 1969.

*Designing Complex Organizations,* Jay Galbraith, 1973.

*Developing Organizations: Diagnosis and Action,* Paul R. Lawrence and Jay W. Lorsch, 1969.

*Organization in a Changing Environment,* Richard J. C. Roeber, 1973.

*Process Consultation: Its Role in Organization Development,* Edgar H. Schein, 1969.

*Physical Settings and Organization Development,* Fred I. Steele, 1973.

*Interpersonal Peacemaking: Confrontations and Third Party Consultation,* Richard E. Walton, 1969.

Fordyce, Jack K., and Raymond Weil, *Managing with People,* Reading, Mass.: Addison-Wesley, 1971.

This is one of the few "how to" books on OD that deals with practical methodologies that a manager can understand and relate to without an interpreter. It is the resource book I use most often when I am designing special-purpose interventions for clients.

Mahler, Walter R., *Diagnostic Studies,* Reading, Mass.: Addison-Wesley, 1974.

This is far and away the most realistic and practical book I have seen on organizational diagnosis. It is a *must* for the professional who wants to do a thorough job of assessing where an organization is prior to installing any comprehensive management system or planning a major intervention.

Marrow, Alfred J., *Making Waves in Foggy Bottom,* Washington, D.C.: NTL Institute, 1974.

Written by one of the most respected behavioral scientists, this "no holds barred" analysis of extended efforts to bring about organizational change in the United States is a fascinating study of some of the colossal failures as well as the significant successes of a major attempt to institute "participative" management.

Partin, J. Jennings, ed., *Current Perspectives in Organization Development,* Reading, Mass.: Addison-Wesley, 1973.

This is a series of "grass roots" OD experiences, including five from public-sector organizations (federal, state mental health, city government, public school, student organization). The appendix to the city-government paper by Joel M. Cohen contains some particularly useful assessment tools, as does the paper on public schools by A. Walden Ends and David J. Mullen.

## Recommended, But Not Annotated

Argyris, Chris, *Intervention Theory and Method,* Reading, Mass.: Addison-Wesley, 1970.

Beck, Arthur C., Jr., and Ellis D. Hillmar, eds., *A Practical Approach to Organization Development through MBO — Selected Readings,* Reading, Mass.: Addison-Wesley, 1972.

Bittel, Lester R., *Management by Exception,* New York: McGraw-Hill, 1964.

———— , *The Nine Master Keys of Management,* New York: McGraw-Hill, 1972.

Carroll, Stephen J., Jr., and Henry L. Tosi, Jr., *Management by Objectives, Applications and Research,* New York: Macmillan, 1973.

Coffee, Donn T., *Managing by Objectives* (audiocassette program), New York: AMR International, 1975.

Drucker, Peter F., *The Practice of Management,* New York: Harper & Row, 1954.

_____ , *Managing for Results,* New York: Harper & Row, 1964.

_____ , *The Effective Executive,* New York: Harper & Row, 1966.

Emery, David A., *The Compleat Manager,* New York: McGraw-Hill, 1970.

Ford, Robert N., *Motivation through the Work Itself,* New York: AMACOM, 1969.

Herzberg, Frederick, *Work and the Nature of Man,* Cleveland: World, 1966.

Hughes, Charles L., *Goal-Setting: Key to Individual and Organizational Effectiveness,* New York: AMACOM, 1965.

Humble, John W., *Improving Business Results,* London: McGraw-Hill, 1967.

Kellogg, Marion S., What to Do about Performance Appraisal, rev. ed., New York: AMACOM, 1975.

Kepner, Charles, and Benjamin B. Tregoe, *The Rational Manager,* New York: McGraw-Hill, 1965.

Kuriloff, Arthur H., *Organization Development for Survival,* New York: AMACOM, 1972.

Levin, Richard I., and Charles A. Kirkpatrick, *Planning and Control with PERT/CPM,* New York: McGraw-Hill, 1966.

Marrow, Alfred J., *The Failure of Success,* New York: AMACOM, 1972.

_____ , D. G. Bowers, and S. E. Seashore, *Management by Participation,* New York: Harper & Row, 1967.

McConkey, Dale D., *How to Manage by Results,* New York: AMACOM, 1965.

_____ , *No-Nonsense Delegation,* New York: AMACOM, 1974.

_____ , *Management by Objectives for Non-Profit Organizations,* New York: AMACOM, 1975.

McGregor, Douglas, *The Human Side of Enterprise,* New York: McGraw-Hill, 1960.

_____ , *The Professional Manager,* New York: McGraw-Hill, 1967.

Morrisey, George L., *Management by Objectives and Results,* Reading, Mass.: Addison-Wesley, 1970.

———— , *Management by Objectives and Results* (videocassette), Reading, Mass.: Addison-Wesley, 1975.

———— , *Management by Objectives and Results Overview* (audiocassette), Reading, Mass.: Addison-Wesley, 1973.

Odiorne, George S., *Management by Objectives,* New York: Pitman, 1965.

———— , *Training by Objectives,* New York: Macmillan, 1970.

———— , *Executive Skills* (audiocassette program), Westfield, Mass.: MBO, Inc., 1972.

Pyhrr, Peter A., *Zero-Base Budgeting,* New York: Wiley, 1973.

Ross, Joel E., and Robert G. Murdick, *Management Update: The Answer to Obsolescence,* New York: AMACOM, 1973.

Schleh, Edward C., *Management by Results,* New York: McGraw-Hill, 1961.

Steiner, George A., *Top Management Planning,* New York: Macmillan, 1969.

Tagliere, Daniel A., *People, Power, and Organization,* New York: AMACOM, 1973.

Varney, Glenn H., *Management by Objectives,* Chicago: The Dartnell Corporation, 1971.

Walters, Roy W. *et al., Job Enrichment for Results,* Reading, Mass.: Addison-Wesley, 1975.

Warren, Malcolm W., *Training for Results: A Systems Approach to the Development of Human Resources in Industry,* Reading, Mass.: Addison-Wesley, 1969.

Weisselberg, Robert C., and Joseph G. Cowley, *The Executive Strategist,* New York: McGraw-Hill, 1969.

*Work in America — Report of a Special Task Force to the Secretary of Health, Education, and Welfare,* Cambridge, Mass.: M.I.T. Press, 1973.

## Other Resources

There are many excellent articles, far too numerous to mention, on MBO and related subjects, in and out of the public sector, in the various management journals. A watchful eye will reveal several every month. For those who are particularly interested in following the latest happenings in MBO, I recommend the following publications.

(The first two listed are available through MBO, Inc., 157 Pontoosic Road, Westfield, Massachusetts 01085.)

*Management by Objectives Newsletter,* a six-page treatise written monthly by George Odiorne which includes many brief highlights of various organizational experiences, as well as surveys of current literature.

*Management by Objectives,* a quarterly journal published in England, with contributions from experts throughout the world (including George Morrisey).

*Annual International Conference on Management by Objectives: State of the Art,* sponsored annually in late summer by Management Center, Bowling Green State University, Bowling Green, Ohio. Copies of the proceedings of past conferences are available from the sponsors.

# APPENDIX: "EXPERIENCE" ARTICLES

In order to lend credibility to the application of Management by Objectives and Results (MOR) in public-sector organizations, I invited four professionals, from organizations with which I have worked as a consultant, to write brief articles describing their experiences with this process. The nature of my request to all of them was the same. I asked them to write it from the point of view of the organizer, stressing: (1) how the approach was set up in the first place; (2) what went well; (3) what did not go well; (4) what modifications in the approach were made as they went along; and (5) what they would have done differently if they could repeat the process. The only editing in the articles has been "cosmetic." The basic content is as they wrote it.

By design, each of the writers represents a different level of government — federal, state, provincial (Canadian), and county. What was not designed was the radically different treatment that each has given the subject.

1. *Doug Rabel,* of the *Bureau of Indian Affairs,* describes a highly decentralized federal government operation with many unique management concerns. He talks about MOR as the last of four phases in a total management development program. He and a small, central staff recruited and trained line managers as trainers in the total effort, which included work with tribal representatives.

2. *Dennis Butler,* from the *Pennsylvania Department of En-*

*vironmental Resources,* describes the application of MOR from an individual manager's point of view in making it work in his own operation. Taking an Organization Development approach, he and his staff completely reorganized their bureau from a traditional activity-oriented operation to one that was built around the outputs to come from the bureau's key results areas.

3.   The *Alberta Highways and Transport* story, as told by *Jim Bussard,* concentrates particularly on the role of the MBO coordinators — line managers recruited originally as consultants to help with the implementation of a performance-appraisal system. After working through the problems of relationship to performance pay and the lack of ownership of the process by managers within the organization, they have adapted MOR to the point that it is now seen and accepted by managers throughout the department as a working management process that is improving steadily as they become more comfortable with it.

4.   *Doris Seward's* description of the MOR implementation effort in the *Los Angeles County Assessor's Office* covers a span of three years. In her article, she places heavy emphasis on the assessment and analysis processes that took place along the way. The results of these processes had significant influence on phases that followed. Top management's continued involvement in the implementation process is one of the important factors there.

Other "experiences" could have been included here as well. However, these four illustrate beautifully the flexibility in the process and the recognition that it works only when it is shaped to the local situation. None of these efforts has been an unqualified success. Each has had its own problems, as you will in your efforts. The ability to adapt to the circumstances being faced has been the key to the progress being described here. Allow your imagination to work as you read each of these articles, and then develop the approach that must be uniquely yours.

# MANAGEMENT BY OBJECTIVES AND RESULTS IN THE BUREAU OF INDIAN AFFAIRS

**Douglas E. Rabel**
*Director, Management Training Institute*

During the 1960s, American Indians became increasingly aware of both their own identities and their place in American society. Part of this awareness included a growing appreciation of their resources — both human and natural — and an increasing understanding of the importance of wisely managing their resources for the future. The challenge of management is great to American Indians, who number 827,000, occupy nearly two percent of the land area of the United States, and control significant agricultural, mineral, and financial resources. With the growing complexity of the United States economy, American Indians need modern management techniques.

Recognizing this need, the Bureau of Indian Affairs (BIA) established the Management Training Institute in the spring of 1970. The Institute's primary task was to train BIA field personnel and Indian tribal leaders in the techniques of Management by Objectives and Results (MOR); its secondary task was to open new lines of communication between BIA and tribal managers by providing a common management language for setting mutual goals.

The Institute's three-man staff set out to train all levels of BIA's field organization in the methods of Management by Objectives. The central office in Washington had set broad mission statements and objectives under its mandate from Congress; at the second level of organization, each of BIA's 11 area offices would set more specific objectives; further down the line, these objectives would be refined by each agency in an area; finally, operational objectives were to be set by the smallest organizational units, and in some cases, by individuals. It was at this final, or operational, level that BIA managers would attempt to work out mutual mission and objectives with tribal leaders and to reach a consensus on how objectives should be achieved.

In order to train BIA's 2000 field managers in MOR techniques, the Institute's staff — in cooperation with BIA's Director of Training — designed a four-phase curriculum. The first three phases ("Managerial Styles," "Communication Problems," and "Problem Solving") were preparation for the fourth, which consisted of the actual MOR training. During the first three phases, a few selected personnel from each area (about 40 people in all) traveled to Denver, where the Institute's staff taught them a phase of the curriculum. After completing the phase as students, the group learned how to be instructors — how to teach the phase themselves back in their home areas. In order to ensure the quality of instruction, each instructor's first attempt to teach a phase was monitored by one of the Institute's staff, who then certified the instructor for that phase. After certification, this group of instructors taught the phase throughout their home areas until all BIA field managers had completed it.

It took nearly two years to complete the first three phases of the curriculum. During this time, the instructors, who also had their own jobs to do, were hard-pressed to meet both teaching and operational assignments. In order to help ease this pressure during Phase IV, BIA's central office in Washington allowed each area office to bring in additional help from the outside. Six of the 11 area offices elected to have the Institute's staff carry out Phase IV in their area, and the remainder found help from universities or private consulting firms.

For the six areas which requested help from the Institute, Phase IV instruction became a joint effort of Institute's staff and the area's instructors who had taught the first three phases. Phase IV typically began with an orientation session for the staff of the area office. At this session, the Institute's staff explained how to implement an MOR system. George Morrisey's *Management by Objectives and Results* was used as a textbook in conjunction with a special study guide prepared by the Institute. At the end of the orientation session, each participant was asked to prepare a mission statement and objectives, which were to be submitted to his or her immediate supervisor within two weeks. Following completion of the orientation at the Area Office, a similar session was held at each Agency in the Area. Both Agency personnel and Tribal managers were invited to participate and to develop mission statements and objectives. Once orientations were completed and reviewed at the Agency level, mission statements and objectives developed at all levels — Area Office, Agency, and Tribal management — were reviewed by "third-party facilitators" (Institute staff and Area instructors). Once this review was completed, the facilitators asked for action plans to implement objectives, which they also reviewed.

Although the action plans have only just begun to operate, some strengths and weaknesses are already noticeable. First, the strengths:

- By encouraging BIA and Tribal managers to develop mutual objectives, the MOR system created stronger commitments from both groups. The technique of reaching a consensus on goals could well be MOR's most important tool for helping the federal government relate to other levels of government and other nongovernment groups.

- By clearly stating the mission and goals of each Agency's operating units, the MOR system helped to show where organizational overlaps occurred and thus to correct any duplication of effort.

- By developing long-range objectives, MOR developed a continuity of tribal management which survives through tribal elections. In the past, management objectives were sometimes discarded when the Tribal Chairman left office.

The problems of implementing MOR usually centered on individuals who for various reasons were either indifferent to or lacked motivation to adopt this new management technique. For example:

- Supervisors were sometimes reluctant to follow up on the accomplishment of objectives unless they were prodded by the "third party" facilitator.
- BIA and Tribal managers hammering out objectives at the Agency level sometimes received little feedback from managers further up in the chain of command.
- Managers usually found it difficult to set standards for objectives for which results could not be readily quantified.

In looking back over the Institute's experience in implementing an MOR system at BIA, perhaps the most significant lesson to be learned was the importance of communication on all levels — between the central office, area offices, agencies, and tribal managers. In retrospect, some channels of communication which would have proved valuable include:

- A feedback system, which would allow Tribal managers to get a response to their objective planning from BIA managers at the Area or National level.
- An annual meeting of third-party facilitators, at which experience and problems could be discussed and evaluated.
- A newsletter, which would keep each Area Office and Agency abreast of the BIA's progress in implementing the MOR system.

In a larger sense, good communications are essential in the total development of an MOR system. Only through good communications can people at all organizational levels reach a consensus on objectives, which in turn creates a common commitment to reaching those objectives.

To sum up our experience: (1) the MOR system allows BIA and Tribal managers to reach an accord on their common mission and objectives; (2) it provides a common management language; (3) it gives everyone in the organization a chance to measure his or her performance against an agreed idea of accomplishment; (4) and most important, MOR is working to help solve the day-to-day problems of management.

The future success of MOR depends on how well people at BIA learn to use it. MOR is, after all, only the skeleton of a management system. To extend the metaphor, the muscle and sinew which animate the system are the people who carry out the mission. Communication is the lifeblood of the system which motivates people to act. And finally, a common commitment is the heart of the system which makes it vital and alive.

# THE EVOLUTION OF MBO IN A STATE GOVERNMENTAL AGENCY

**Dennis E. Butler**
*Director, Bureau of Human Resource Management,
Department of Environmental Resources*

Our first efforts at installing an MBO system in a state governmental agency began about five and a half years ago, when the Department of Environmental Resources (DER) was created by the Pennsylvania state legislature. The major impetus for installing an MBO system came from the Chief Administrative Officer of the former Forests and Waters Department. DER was created by merging the Departments of Forests and Waters, Mines and Minerals Industries, and several organizational elements of other state agencies, such as the Air Pollution Control, Water Quality Management, and Sanitation programs from the Department of Health.

The most likely candidate for heading up this new agency was the former Secretary of Forests and Waters, Dr. Maurice K. Goddard. He is one of the few appointed officials in the Commonwealth of Pennsylvania to have been successively appointed by five different governors representing both major political parties. Dr. Goddard is well known for his long history of accomplishments in the area of conservation and natural resource management.

In Forests and Waters, Dr. Goddard's Chief Administrative Officer, Edward M. Seladones, enjoyed the reputation of being one of the Commonwealth's most successful and knowledgeable managers. In addition to his general belief that MBO is the best way to manage any program, Ed was keenly interested in seeing that the managerial accomplishments of Forests and Waters not be lost in the merger and creation of DER.

Consequently, about mid-1969, Ed developed what he called a "management system." This "management system" was used to guide the operations of the Bureau of Fiscal Management, Bureau of Personnel Services, Bureau of Systems Management, and the Bureau of Office Services.

As was expected, when DER was actually created in January 1971, Dr. Goddard was appointed as the Acting Secretary, later to be confirmed as the actual Secretary. Consequently, Ed Seladones became the Deputy Secretary for Administration, and I became the Personnel Director. At that point, I saw my major responsibility as acquiring, organizing, developing, and ultimately managing a competent and respected human resource management staff.

I feel that the assimilation, reorganization, and development of the personnel staff was unusually complicated because: (1) DER was granted agency-wide civil service coverage, whereas most of the former organizations were non–civil service (this added to the scope and complexity of our paperwork processing); (2) during that year a gubernatorial candidate of the opposing party replaced the incumbent; and (3) the Pennsylvania State legislature had just passed a bill legalizing collective bargaining and public employes' right to strike. All three of these factors placed considerable strain on the newly formed personnel staff's ability to function effectively.

Looking back on those difficult days, I feel that it was Ed's management system that helped pull us through. Although the management system once served an essential role, today it has been greatly modified and, we believe, greatly improved. The rest of this article relates how our management system grew into the organic MBO process that we use today.

Section #6 of our management system dealt with objectives. Neither Ed nor I had had any formal training in MBO. What little we knew was the result of having read such authors as Drucker, Odiorne, and Morrisey. From looking back on our early experience with MBO, I feel that we got quite skilled at writing what I like to refer to as textbook objectives. However, we did not seem to have too much success in having them carried out. Our hindsight analysis has revealed that we made the following errors in our initial MBO efforts:

1. Objectives were given as assignments. There was little real give-and-take participation on the part of the receivers.

2. Objectives were formulated predominantly from the viewpoint of the "good of the organization." Little effort was made to accommodate the personal needs and goals of the receivers.

3. Little time or energy was devoted to developing strategies for accomplishing the objectives.

4. Control points (milestones) were inconsistent and often overlooked until the final deadline was due.

5. There was no actual tie-in with our performance appraisal and reward systems.

6. I had the sole responsibility for ensuring that there were no duplicate, competing, and conflicting objectives among the various work groups in the Bureau of Human Resource Management. I felt overworked and pretty much alone.

7. We had too many objectives. Each manager might have 30 or 40 annually.

After reading the above, I'm sure you're probably wondering how we could think that we were operating according to MBO principles. I guess that's one of the virtues of ignorance.

Although we weren't enjoying much success with our MBO efforts, we were still persuaded that it was the best process available, if we could only learn to master it. In the summer of 1973, we decided to invite an outside consultant to help us with our problem. After surveying the field, we finally contracted with George Morrisey to provide us with nine days of professional services. George came in and listened to our problems, conducted several seminars for us, and offered many helpful suggestions concerning how we might improve our MBO results. Some of the most valuable things I feel we learned from George were: (1) to really take the time necessary to define and clarify our roles and missions; (2) to clearly differentiate our key results areas from our activities; and (3) to spend the time needed to develop workable operational strategies for attaining our objectives.

By its very nature, government tends to be activity-oriented. The fact that any citizen can, and many do, ask for an accounting of how we're spending their tax dollars and that each citizen feels that his or her needs should be the primary target of our activities leads government to be overcontrolled, overdirected, and extremely activity-oriented. In my opinion, most governments generally do not have efficient priority setting/managerial decision-making processes. I feel that this is generally a result of constituents' plurality of interests and the sometimes awkward relationships that develop between the Executive and Legislative branches. Consequently, this leads to a crisis-to-crisis and CYA (cover your anatomy) method of operation. We were no exception to the management-by-activity-and-reaction (MAR) syndrome.

As I see it, it was through George Morrisey's encouragement and Ed Seladones' willingness to accept the risks of not operating in the more or less typical crisis-to-crisis manner that we were able to really clarify our roles and missions and to combine our more than 200 activities into fewer than a dozen key results areas (KRA's). This was our first big step away from MAR and toward Management by Objectives and Results (MOR).

It took us about a year to get our role and mission statements and KRA's refined and defined to a point where we felt comfortable with them. Naturally, we were not able to devote our full or even most of our energies toward this task. I wish we could have, but our main responsibility was to perform our basic activities and services. Our sessions on role and mission clarification served as very effective team-building sessions for our staff. By having our staff meet together as a group to discuss in a frank and open manner why we are in business and who our customers are, everyone gained a greater appreciation of the need for synthesis and integration of each person's activities. We finally arrived at role and mission statements for each of our key results areas, as well as an overall mission statement for our Bureau.

The following is our overall mission statement as we see it for the Bureau of Human Resource Management.

"Through the use of consultative services and some regulatory activities, to assist DER management to effectively and efficiently acquire, develop, maintain, and utilize an optimally productive and satisfied workforce."

After we developed this mission statement, we realized that for us to more efficiently and effectively manage our key results areas, we would need to reorganize our operations. Up to this point, we had been organized according to the traditional model of most other Commonwealth personnel offices (see Fig. A.). The underlying rationale for that traditional organization is one of functional (process) alignment. In other words, people performing similar activities, regardless of final results or outputs, were organized into common groups. Another fundamental premise of organizational ideology which influenced our original structure was that a personnel office (or any governmental office) should be managed according to military chain-of-command, multilevel-hierarchy concepts.

In spite of some opposition, we reorganized our office according to key results areas and outputs. We also flattened our organizational levels and began to use a matrix/team management approach to managing our more conceptual activities, such as Job Analysis, Labor Relations, Organization Development, and Training (see Fig. A2). We also changed our name to more clearly describe our roles and mission.

Instead of being called the Bureau of Personnel Services and having five divisions and eleven sections, each with a supervisor, we are now called the Bureau of Human Resource Management, and we now have four divisions, only two of which have full-time managers — Manpower Management and Employe Relations. Both our OD and Training Divisions are or-

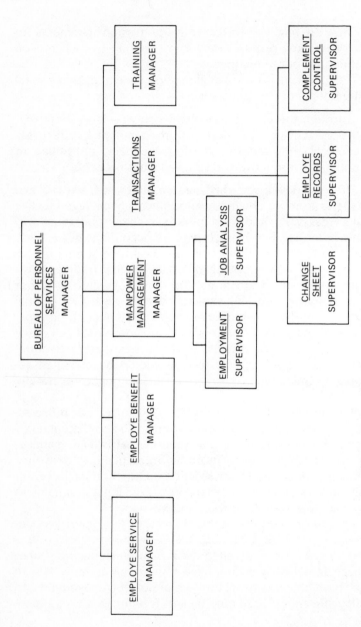

**Fig. A.1** Traditional model of organizational alignment.

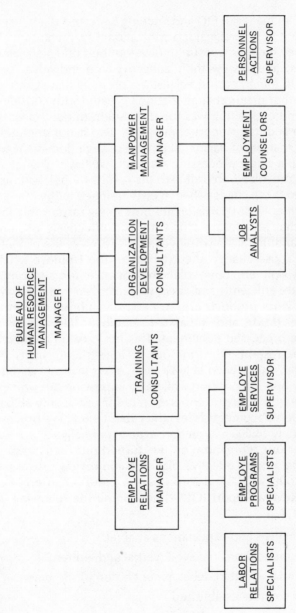

**Fig. A.2** Matrix/team management model of organizational alignment.

ganized so that each OD and Training Specialist is a full-service consultant to several major organizational segments (clients) of DER. They meet as a group to develop their budget, plan their activities, and review their collective and individual performance. In effect, each specialist is a program manager.

Another major change that was greeted with considerable doubt and opposition was the dissolution of our Transactions Division and its reapportionment into two major operation divisions. Instead of having all payroll change document typists report to a single processing manager, we have "change sheet typists" organized according to the results of their actions. For example, those change sheet typists assigned to the Manpower Management (MM) Division are now solely responsible for ensuring that people are efficiently and effectively *put on* the payroll and that each employe in DER receives the proper rate of pay. Those change sheet typists in the Employe Relations (ER) Division are now solely responsible for ensuring that people are efficiently and effectively *removed from* the payroll.

The work products are, respectively, a hired or promoted employe (MM) and separated employe (ER) rather than merely a processed document. This has created an increased sense of responsibility for our change sheet typists. Consequently, we've been able to reduce our manpower requirement by one full position while also improving our processing effectiveness. Our current error rate for processing all payroll transaction documents is less than about 1.6%. We process approximately 18,000 payroll transactions annually.

After our reorganization, we turned our focus toward establishing a more effective planning and review process. Each work group was asked to prepare a group Quarterly Performance Review Report (QPRR) containing the following information:

1. Objectives and expectations attained
2. Commendations received (verbal and written)
3. Personal and staff development accomplishments
4. New services established

5. Services improved — in terms of quality, quantity, and/or timeliness
6. Cost savings
7. Other significant accomplishments
8. Unattained objectives and expectations; off schedule.

The Quarterly Performance Review Report is prepared and submitted to me by each work group by the tenth of the month of each new quarter. When we first embarked on the quarterly review system, most of our work groups were rather reluctant to do more than a token job on preparing the QPRR because: (1) there wasn't much trust and cooperation among the members in most of the work groups; and (2) there was a belief that if the QPRR system wasn't quashed, it would be used to control and harass employes.

It took considerable time and energy to overcome these feelings. First, five key staff members and I went to an NTL Basic Management Work Conference (a T-group experience). Second, we began some intensive team-building work within each work group to help increase the level of trust and cooperation among team members and between the various work groups. Third, we went off-site to a remote "live-in" training and conference center so that one representative from each work group could observe a live quarterly review in progress.

Our most productive and self-confident work group was asked to undertake its quarterly review in front of observers from the other groups. The group agreed to do so, and we did it. As a result, the other work groups were able to see first-hand how helpful and stimulating quarterly reviews could be. Most important, they saw how turned-on a work group can get when the members work together in identifying and solving work problems.

For the past two years, we've been using the QPRR system. Presently, we go off-site to our training and conference center to participate in an annual planning and review session. We also hold a midyear review session off-site. Each session lasts about a week. One representative from each work group is expected to be present for the entire week. Each work group generally spends about 1½ days at the review session. We usually have two complete work groups present during any one group's review. The purpose of this is to strengthen intergroup teamwork by sharing information about common problems and common successes.

During the actual review process, each work group member discusses his or her proposed objectives, past achievements, and any existing or anticipated problems. Any supportive resources needed from fellow team members or other work groups are identified and arranged. We generally run three or four evening problem-solving sessions at which key issues affecting the entire bureau are discussed and usually resolved.

All in all, we feel that the review process allows us enough time to assess the progress, provide feedback, and modify our plans if necessary for each of our eight work groups. We feel that our MBO/QPRR system has produced far more benefits in terms of increased productivity and job satisfaction than it costs to install and operate the system. I'd like to share with you the following successes that we're rather proud of:

1.    Perhaps our most notable achievement has happened in our Training Division. Here, productivity more than doubled, from 2214 student hours taught per instructor annually to 5481 student hours taught. This increase was achieved mainly because our training consultants improved their ability to define training needs and custom tailor our courses to the individual needs of various managers throughout DER. Attendance at all of our courses is strictly voluntary.

2.    Another achievement we feel proud about is that we were able to organize and staff the first Organization Development team in any Commonwealth agency. We were able to do this without any increase in our staffing complement by making internal reassignments, using prior job performance and employe career-development goals as reassignment criteria.

3.    Also, the Governor has recently enlisted the services of a group of businessmen to review the operations of Pennsyl-

vania state government to seek ways of improving its efficiency and effectiveness. We've received several commendations from them about the effectiveness of our MBO efforts.

4.  We are actively trying to share the benefits of our experience with interested managers throughout DER. Our training group is presently teaching basic MBO concepts to interested managers on a self-nomination basis. However, our objective is to have all managerial personnel and their work groups participate in our basic MBO concepts course by June 30, 1977, at the latest.

5.  Presently, we follow up our basic concepts course with a workshop in rewriting job descriptions using KRA's and Key Indicators rather than emphasizing activities. We also provide hands-on instruction in how to write objectives and MBO contracts.

6.  So far, we have encountered the most success with managers who are fairly well skilled in participative management techniques and who manage work groups that have healthy internal relationships. We find that not much effective learning takes place for work groups that have serious internal conflicts and/or are managed from a predominantly authoritarian point of view.

In addition to the effects of managerial style and workgroup climate, I feel that there are at least three other serious obstacles to implementing MBO in a government organization. Not being able to significantly tie MBO into a viable reward program is one major obstacle. Another is the resistance of many political officials and governmental managers to clearly fix accountability for results. The third obstacle is the unwillingness or inability of elected or appointed political officials to take a clear stand on funding priorities. Too often, too many people are promised more than can possibly be delivered within existing funding. Consequently, the shifting sands of governmental fiscal management make it difficult to set realistic and attainable long-range objectives.

We have made some slight progress in resolving the obstacle of the reward system. However, we've made practically no headway in resolving this fiscal uncertainty or the multiplicity of priorities. Although we are presently unable to tie MBO accomplishments into direct cash rewards, we are able to allot scarce self-development resources (training funds) on the basis of MBO results.

In summary, I feel that the implementation of MBO concepts is a long-range process which requires a certain amount of optimism and a lot of energy and faith to help surmount the obstacles which invariably arise. However, we feel it's the "only way to run a railroad." At least it's far ahead of whatever is in second place. I wish you all the success in the world with your MBO endeavors. Good luck!

# MBO IN ALBERTA HIGHWAYS AND TRANSPORT

**D. J. Bussard,**
*MBO Coordinator*

In the summer of 1973, the Government of Alberta introduced a new Management Classification and Pay Plan. The intent of this plan was to allow each department greater freedom and responsibility in managerial development as well as to provide individual recognition and incentive through performance pay. Each department, in order to qualify, was required to develop an objective, results-oriented performance appraisal system.

The Organization Development Division of the government's Central Personnel Office was assigned the responsibility for developing a satisfactory method of measuring performance as well as assisting departments with implementation. Through the efforts of this division, many senior managers had attended seminars and workshops directed toward individual improvement. Their decision was to adopt a management-process model as a standard base for evaluation of performance. This would also provide opportunity for organization development.

The process model, titled the Performance Appraisal System (PAS), and the Management Classification and Pay Plan were presented to the Deputy Ministers (Chiet Executive Officers) of all departments, and support in development of an implementation program was obtained.

Each department was required to provide line managers as in-house coordinators responsible for implementation of the PAS process. The project team for Alberta Highways and

Transport was made up of four middle managers. None of us had had previous experience with management systems. However, our managerial work experience varied between 14 and 19 years.

Coordinator training consisted of a two-week seminar in September, 1973, during which the steps of the PAS process were defined and consultative/communication skills were workshopped. The new-born PAS coordinators were turned loose on their respective departments to first negotiate implementation plans with their Chief Executive Officers and then work through the PAS process steps with managers. In Alberta Highways, which has 3000 permanent staff, approximately 120 managers had been designated under the Management Classification and Pay Plan.

## The PAS Process

The PAS process, which was initially proposed, was represented as a yearly cycle (see Fig. A.3). "Role definition," the first phase of the process, was completed with all managers by April 1974.

"Purpose" statements, "Key Result Areas," and "Indicators" were arrived at individually in consultation with a coordinator. The role definitions were then presented by each individual at a team meeting. These meetings proved of very definite value from an organizational development and awareness point of view, with managers establishing their organizational makeup (teams), in some cases for the first time. The end result or reason for each position was critically looked at and did much to move thinking away from activity orientation. Overlaps were uncovered, and in many cases responsibility areas were reassigned in a more precise and unique manner. Managers, in general, arrived at better understanding of their roles, and communication improved.

"Planning Analysis" was presented as the logical step to lead into "Goal" setting. It involved formal analysis of performance gaps in Key Result Areas, followed by weighing the pros

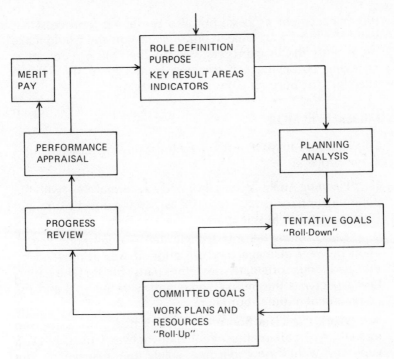

**Fig. A.3** The PAS process.

and cons of various alternative actions, including determining the resource requirements for each tentative goal. A very uneasy feeling resulted with regard to the time and paper commitment, and our managers bogged down at this stage of the process.

We coordinators became increasingly concerned due to inactivity with the process, and we called on coordinating resources in other departments for assistance. We were steered onto a Management by Objectives and Results (MOR) seminar presented by George Morrisey and Gus Matzorkis in May 1974. Two of us attended and brought back thinking that not only gave us greater understanding of the basic concepts behind the management process, but also presented a process that would be more adaptable to our organization and would make more sense to our managers. We saw the "MOR" concept as changing our managers' thinking from "going through an exercise" to "becoming my way of managing."

## Influences of MOR

This exposure to MOR influenced the following basic changes in our process:

1.  "Planning Analysis" was dropped as a formal step, with the determination of "Goals" (objectives) flowing directly from the Indicators in Key Result areas.

2.  "Goal" setting became a single step — one-to-one negotiation between manager and superior. It was acknowledged that goals could originate with either party, but that the important aspect was the mutual agreement with the goal and the commitment of the subordinate.

3.  "Work Plans" (action plans), which had previously been looked at as part of the negotiation between manager and superior, would now become solely the manager's. The superior's interest shoud relate to the manager's results, not his or her methods or activities. This concept brought out "how to delegate," as well as developed specific and unique responsibility for each goal or action step in a work plan.

4.  "Monitoring Systems" or "Controls" were introduced as an integral part of our process. It was recognized that a basic reason our managers were not delegating responsibility for results and were far too involved in the day-to-day activities of subordinates was a need for information about what was going on in the organization.

5.  "Progress Reviews," held regularly (preferably once a month), also became recognized as essential for continuance of the process. Previously, we had suggested that these be held only when the subordinate felt a need. However, this haphazard approach resulted in no formal progress reviews, a

falling back to the old style of getting together a few times a week, and the manager's becoming too involved in the subordinate's activities.

6.   "Performance Appraisal" tied with "Merit Pay" was deemphasized.

Our PAS process had now taken on a genuine MOR flavor, as represented in the funnel concept shown in Fig. A.4.

In general terms, the revisions to the process which MOR influenced were:

1. Less paper work;
2. Reduced manager involvement (time) in subordinate's activities;
3. Improved delegation by managers;
4. Increased accountability of subordinates;
5. A process more acceptable to our managers (more structured, specific, and not requiring complex evaluation and analysis steps);
6. A process which could be patterned to our organization, rather than a rigid, superimposed system.

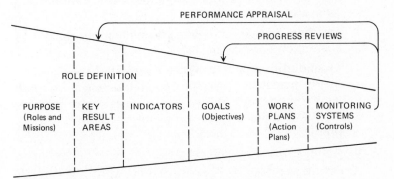

**Fig. A.4** The PAS process within the funnel concept.

## Further Progress and Problems

We enjoyed marked success in the following months, working through the goal-setting and work-planning stages with those branches whose "Heads" acknowledged the benefits to their organizations. The process, however, stalled in a number of branches due to the failure of the Branch Heads to hand goals and work plans for the branch down to their subordinates.

We were again faced with inactivity; however, this time the problem was not seen as relating to imperfections in the process, but rather as resulting from a combination of external pressures and attitudes about the process. The most obvious were:

1. *Summer months* — holidays and the middle of our "Work" season; was the wrong time to set goals and determine work plans. Planning naturally takes place in winter.

2. *Departmental Reorganization* — two new high-executive positions created. Reluctance to make any changes with existing work patterns until the Assistant Deputy Ministers were established in positions.

3. *Branch Head reluctance* to carry through goal-setting process with subordinates, due to:

   a) Lack of direction and on-the-job working with process from above.

   b) Difficulty in establishing responsibility for goals, due to shared, one-on-one positions.

   c) Expanded programs combined with staff shortages. A major increase in program requirements was coupled with a shortage of manpower, materials, and industry capacity. Once-a-week problems became everyday problems.

   d) Conflict with management style.

   e) Failure to recognize benefits of using MBO.

4. *Minimal involvement of the Chief Executive Officer*

*(D.M.)* — absence of departmental roles and missions and long-term goals.

5. *Identification as the coordinator's process* rather than as moving toward the manager's way of work. Viewed by those not using it as an additional exercise which increased an already heavy work load. (Those using the process communicated that improvements had occurred in working conditions.)

## Commitment Through Involvement

Our feeling was that to get the managers moving once more, it was necessary that they receive first-hand the type of message which was given by George Morrisey and Gus Matzorkis. This, we hoped, would accomplish the following:

1. Ownership of the process by the managers (rather than getting it second-hand from coordinators);
2. Management understanding of the MBO process (MOR) and recognition of benefits from management skill development.
3. Visible involvement of the Deputy Minister and his three assistants (including two new A.D.M.'s) in using the process.

Our Deputy Minister attended a Morrisey-Matzorkis seminar in August 1974, arrangements were made to bring in this team in November to expose 90 of our managers to MOR. An intense, two-day "learn-and-work" experience was provided, with the opportunity for the new A.D.M.'s to meet their people and learn about the Department's operation.

With the workshop seminar as the starting point, the Deputy and three A.D.M.'s have been using the MOR process in developing the roles and missions of the Department and Divisions. The top-executive team has assumed responsibility for developing the department's managers in the use of MBO. Most important, they have begun working with MBO in their own management activity.

Implementation has, therefore, changed somewhat from an overall concept to a top-down approach. It is recognized that working with the process is required and that in many cases, this will happen only when the process is brought to the individual by his or her manager. Patience must be exercised, and implementation may require up to five years rather than the initially proposed one year. The role of the coordinators can be looked back on as basically introductory, with their service fading out in the next few months and real implementation being done by the managers at an ever-increasing rate as the process works down through the organization structure.

## Looking Back

In examining what might have been done differently in bringing MBO into the department, one is faced with contradictory values. The initial relation to performance pay was undesirable from a management-process point of view, but we may never have become involved except for that incentive.

The use of in-house coordinators with no academic MBO background rather than outside experts can be questioned from the knowledge standpoint; however, the acceptance by managers and adaptation of the process to the organization are pluses. (Note that other departments with only one coordinator had problems getting the process off the ground. Four coordinators permitted a healthy interaction of ideas and keeping on course, although decisions were often delayed unreasonably due to the desire for consensus.)

Initial use of the MOR concept by the coordinators would have minimized process modifications and introduction time; however, the preexperience of working with bringing a management process into the Department allowed the correlation of the MOR message with real-life experience. This learning experience might not have been nearly as illuminating and lasting without the earlier involvement in the problems and uncertainties of a much less practical approach.

Earlier exposure of our managers to an intensive MOR workshop-seminar may have been premature without prior familiarization with the basic process steps and recognition of the need to improve the process.

## Conclusion

One finds it difficult to suggest mechanical alterations to the implementation plans and to state the advantages. I can only express the feeling that of utmost importance is the level of trust and joint participation developed between coordinators and managers in undertaking this project. We have often fallen from the easy path to MBO implementation, but in no case has there been a lack of honest effort to keep going. Even beating around in the bush has often led to our managers' learning something of value about either themselves or the organization. The journey has been well worth it, even though the destination is not yet in sight.

Our MBO process is no longer considered just an exercise and a tool by which the department could qualify for performance pay. It is a way of managing which is becoming more and more recognized as assisting the development of our organization and the personal development of our managers.

# MOR IN LOCAL GOVERNMENT — A CASE HISTORY

**Doris K. Seward, D.P.A.**
*Los Angeles County Assessor's Office*

Los Angeles County government is unique in size, variety of functions, and structure. Serving a population of over seven million people dispersed throughout 77 cities, it consists of some 50 departments who view a five-member Board of Supervisors as "top management" and look to a Chief Administrative Officer and Director of Personnel for central staff advice. Three departments are headed by elected officials. One of these three — the Assessor's Department — is the subject of this case history.

This department is headed by the Assessor, Assistant Assessor, Chief Field Deputy, and five Directors of "subdepartments." These eight people comprise the Executive Staff of the department. Reporting to them are Division Heads and a complex hierarchy of middle managers and first-line supervisors. Production activities related to valuation of property for property-tax purposes are decentralized, with authority and responsibility delegated to area or regional managers. Prior to the initiation of Management by Objectives and Results, these geographically dispersed managers and the divisions to which they reported tended to work somewhat independently toward an overall production goal which was understood rather than enunciated. Interdependency of divisions existed but was seldom discussed.

## The Beginnings of MOR

In late 1972 the Assessor's Department implementation of Management by Objectives and Results began at the top, with a half-day Executive Staff conference conducted by George Morrisey. This session was designed to explore MOR concepts, results, and problems to be expected, and time and cost requirements for implementation. The objective of the conference was a "go/no go" decision for the department concerning MOR. Had the decision been negative, the implementation project would have gone no further; as it happened, the Executive Staff decided to proceed with MOR on a top-down basis and by levels of management.

During further sessions with Morrisey, departmental executives defined roles and missions and overall goals of the department and the functional directorates they term "sub-departments." Discussions of specific roles of each directorate were particularly valuable in moving toward interdependency of these functional structures and in clarifying problems of overlap.

Post-workshop activity for the Executive Staff required regularly scheduled shared examinations of progress toward objectives and one-to-one consultations with each direct subordinate (Division Head) following attendance of managers at the Division Head level at an MOR orientation session. Dialogue with subordinates was planned at periodic intervals. Also, roles, missions, objectives, and the MOR implementation plan were reexamined and modified as necessary after the initial six months of the implementation process.

## Division Head Activity

After evaluation of the executive-level effort and a decision that understandings at that level were well established, the MOR system was extended to the Division Head level in early 1973. Prior to a preparatory educational workshop, roles, missions, and objectives established by the Executive Staff were distributed to Division Heads, along with the Morrisey text *Management by Objectives and Results*.

For the first half-day, the workshop covered topics similar to those included in executive-level conferences. Then, the practical work began — defining roles and missions for divisions, drafting objectives for this level so that they contributed to higher-level goals and objectives, developing a tentative action plan for an equally tentative objective, and creating performance indicators, or standards, through which to measure results.

At the conclusion of the second day of the preparatory workshop, Division Heads completed a force-field analysis designed to indicate present and potential forces within the organization perceived by managers as favorable or unfavorable to successful MOR implementation. A compilation of results indicates that 88% of the sample ranked departmental top-management commitment as a favorable factor, with the preparatory training provided to managers only slightly behind, with 77% of the group perceiving this as a helping force. Potential favorable forces were more diverse; slightly less than half of the managers listed training for the next lower level of management (regional managers) as potentially favorable, with an equal percentage indicating recognition of achievement as a significant helping factor. Top-management followup and success experiences with MOR were also listed on the plus side. Among existing unfavorable factors, resistance to change was listed by two-thirds of the group, with interdivisional conflict noted by slightly more than half of the managers who completed the force-field analysis. Apathy and lack of total middle-management commitment were also listed. Potential unfavorable forces included loss of interest by the Executive Staff, lack of training for the next level of management, lack of followup, and continuing interdivisional conflicts.

Following the preparatory workshop, Division Heads and their Directors conferred informally to finalize and agree on divisional roles, missions, and objectives. At a series of implementing workshops, the consultant worked with superior-subordinate teams and groups of divisions to facilitate problem solving. Post-workshop activity for this middle-management level required dissemination of agreed on mission statements and objectives to subordinates and others with a need to know. Again, continuing conferences to share progress, consult with superiors on a one-to-one basis, and finally review objectives and action plans were built into the implementation project.

## Regional Manager Activity

In late 1973, a series of preparatory workshops and implementing workshops was conducted for regional managers by a member of the MOR Associates staff and the departmental Training Officer. Educational sessions were structured so that members of various functional groups met together; implementing workshops conducted by Division Heads and including Subdepartment Heads were structured on a team basis (generally by division except for small staff divisions, which were grouped together).

Regional managers were given an opportunity at the beginning of the preparatory workshop to define the objectives they wanted to achieve during the session and to express concerns about the MOR process. Their "wants" included an understanding of MOR, defining the expectations of the regional manager in implementing the system, discussing methods of measuring progress, and clarifying why MOR was initiated by the department. Also, development of a departmental plan for integrating objectives between units and resolution of line-staff conflicts were listed as desired outcomes of the session. The last two "wants" were beyond the scope of the workshop, but provided insight as to some existing organizational problems. A concern was expressed as to the legitimacy of Management by Objectives and Results as a departmental system; this concern was based primarily on a false MBO start several years prior to 1972.

Implementing workshops for the regional manager level were varied in format and results. Some of the purely organizational problems were resolved during these meetings of regional and divisional managers.

## The Progress of MOR — Some Observations

In early 1974, slightly more than one year after the Assessor's Management by Objectives and Results system was launched, some observations as to its reception and progress were gained through structured interviews with Division Heads selected equally from line and staff units. Responses to a question as to the purposes of MOR differed markedly. Some related the system to increased productivity, accomplishment through goal setting, and establishment of a process of identifying and accomplishing goals. Others tied MOR to movement away from MAR and away from win-lose competition between organizational elements. Potential benefits were identified as increased effectiveness through resolution of quality/quantity conflicts, improvement of communication, clarification of department's direction, and participation in planning and decison making at all levels of management. Managers also saw in MOR an opportunity to find better ways of doing their jobs within their existing budgets and to promote coordination between divisions.

Because MOR implementation encourages problem solving, managers were asked about potential problems of this system. Some potential benefits were also seen as problems to be solved, particularly participation in planning and coordination of functions. The role of top management was perceived as crucial to implementation of the MOR system, not only in terms of support, but also in relation to delegation of responsibility for achievement of objectives with commensurate authority. Feedback concerning progress toward expected results and understanding of MOR at all levels of management were also noted as potential problems.

Managers interviewed to "feel the pulse" of the Assessor's MOR system recommended that emphasis be placed on the development of action plans for each objective rather than solely on the writing of objectives. They proposed a departmental report of MOR progress so that success experiences could be shared. An additional suggestion was the integration of MOR with budgeting. Most of the interviewees perceived a need for eventual integration of the MOR system with managerial performance evaluation, production and project planning, and an incentive/reward system. They generally saw little change in effectiveness of managerial communication, encouragement of manager development, and motivation of managers as the result of MOR; however, they agreed that helpful changes could be effected as the system matured. The consensus opinion of the managers interviewed was that processes, such as decision making and communication, were destined to change with an improved management system; structural change was not perceived as essential to the success of this system.

## MOR — Advanced Phase

In 1975 MOR Associates was reemployed by the Assessor's Department as consultants to the Executive Staff in continuing the MOR implementation. Included in this advanced phase were:

1. Design, administration, and interpretation of an analytical instrument or methodology to assess current progress in MOR implementation and to help determine future developmental needs.

2. Design and conduct of an educational workshop based on identified and mutually agreed on developmental needs of middle-level managers.

3. Follow-up evaluation of the educational workshop and other developmental efforts to assess progress and to help plan for future requirements.

MOR Associates stressed commitment by the Executive Staff to a fully effective system and participation of top managers in all elements of the advanced phase.

A beginning step was construction of an MOR Evaluation Questionnaire by MOR Associates, with input from the Executive Staff. Methodology for administration was designed to maximize involvement of all managerial levels and anonymity of respondents. Results were to be discussed with respondents so as to give them an opportunity to interpret results and to recommend system changes where responses indicated some change might be beneficial.

The first two categories of questions on the questionnaire related to higher-level management and to the manager's job. Responses indicated that Assessor's Department managers were generally familiar with departmental roles and missions and objectives and were, in most cases, completely familiar with the objectives of their immediate superiors. Most respondents perceived satisfactory success in achieving agreed on objectives. Recommendations as to possible departmental objectives for the next two years ranged from an ongoing need to produce the assessment roll on schedule to wider use of computer technology. Career development was stressed in the personnel area; improved cooperation between subdepartments was noted as an important organizational issue.

In response to a question asking managers to assign positive, neutral, or negative values to each of a list of factors likely to influence performance in achieving objectives, commitment of top management and of individual managers was strongly on the plus side. Also seen as positive factors were coaching of subordinates by managers, clear directions from superiors to subordinates, and feedback concerning progress toward accomplishment of objectives. On the neutral or negative side were current workload, changing priorities, and support from other units. Principal benefits of MOR were reported to be systems analysis, focusing of effort, and awareness of the interdependency of units within the department. Time and paperwork requirements were indicated to be major drawbacks of the system.

A primary purpose of the questionnaire was to identify training needs on which an educational activity would be based. Questionnaire results particularly pinpointed the need for additional training in establishing priorities, preparing action plans, monitoring objectives achievement, and improving unit productivity. Also emphasized were skill in coaching and developing subordinates, team development, conducting progress reviews, and measuring performance results against objectives. Skill in team development was also indicated to be a training need.

To provide some of these skills and to complete the second component of the advanced MOR phase, MOR Associates designed a workshop, "Updating Management Skills," to be tested first on Executive Staff members and, after modification, presented to Division Head-level managers. General content of the workshop, conducted informally in the participative mode, included definition of the systems approach to management, basic values of people, and development of a basic definition of management. The MOR funnel model was analyzed so as to stress the process of communication as applied to MOR. Participants learned through dyadic encounters and small-group exercises how to obtain voluntary active support of people with whom they worked. Communication skill as related to initial agreement on objectives and progress reviews was practiced through structured simulations of typical work situations. The final assignment for each participant in the workshop was to prepare objectives for discussion, review, and followup with the next higher-level manager.

Evaluation of results of this advanced phase will be accomplished on an ongoing basis. As the MOR system increasingly becomes a "way of life" in the Assessor's Department, evaluation will provide clues as to future directions for the department and for its management system.

## Conclusion

In its 1972 letter to the County Board of Supervisors recommending approval of the initial workshop for the Executive Staff, the Civil Service Commission stated, "This workshop is designed to provide training for top level executives as the cornerstone of a management by objectives system. It is essen-

tial that the training begin with top level management to establish overall departmental objectives as the point of focus for all
later and continuing MBO activities."

In 1975 a five-year long-range plan was developed by the
Executive Staff, with participation of middle managers, as a
major product of the Management by Objectives and Results
system. The focus of the plan is on new and still developing
programs. Thus the Assessor's Department, whose traditional
role has been to assess property in Los Angeles County for the
purpose of providing a value base for next year's local government revenue-raising efforts, is now itself living in the future.